Multipolar Globalization

Like a giant oil tanker, the world is slowly turning. The rapid growth of economies in Asia and the global South leads to momentous shifts in the world order, leaving much of the traditional literature on globalization behind. *Multipolar Globalization* is the perfect guide to the ongoing 21st-century transformations, combining engaging and wide-ranging coverage with cutting-edge analysis.

The rise of China and other emerging economies has led to a new geography of trade, new economic and political combinations, new financial actors, investors and donors, and weaker American hegemony. This interdisciplinary volume combines development studies, global political economy, sociology, and cultural studies to examine the role of multipolarity in reshaping globalization and to probe what this means for inequality and emancipation.

Renowned globalization scholar Jan Nederveen Pieterse deftly guides readers through the development of globalization in the West and the East, explaining key topics such as the 2008 crash, trends in inequality, the changing fortunes of the BRICs, and the role of governance, institutions and democracy. Accessible and insightful, this book is an essential guide for both students in social sciences and for professionals and scholars seeking a fresh perspective.

Jan Nederveen Pieterse is Duncan and Suzanne Mellichamp Distinguished Professor of Global Studies and Sociology at the University of California Santa Barbara, US. He specializes in globalization, development studies, and cultural studies with a focus on 21st-century trends. He held the Pok Rafeah Distinguished Chair at Malaysia National University, 2014–2015.

Rethinking Development

Rethinking Development offers accessible and thought-provoking overviews of contemporary topics in international development and aid. Providing original empirical and analytical insights, the books in this series push thinking in new directions by challenging current conceptualizations and developing new ones.

This is a dynamic and inspiring series for all those engaged with today's debates surrounding development issues, whether they be students, scholars, policy makers and practitioners internationally. These interdisciplinary books provide an invaluable resource for discussion in advanced undergraduate and postgraduate courses in development studies as well as in anthropology, economics, politics, geography, media studies and sociology.

New Media and International Development
Representation and affect in microfinance
Anke Schwittay

Art, Culture and International Development
Humanizing social transformation
John Clammer

Celebrity Humanitarianism and North–South Relations
Politics, place and power
Edited by Lisa-Ann Richey

Education, Learning and the Transformation of Development
Edited by Amy Skinner, Matt Baillie Smith, Eleanor Brown and Tobias Troll

Learning and Volunteering Abroad for Development
Unpacking host organisation and volunteer rationales
Rebecca Tiessen

Communicating Development with Communities
Linje Manyozo

Multipolar Globalization
Emerging economies and development
Jan Nederveen Pieterse

Multipolar Globalization
Emerging Economies and Development

Jan Nederveen Pieterse

LONDON AND NEW YORK

First published 2018
by Routledge
2 Park Square, Milton Park, Abingdon, Oxon OX14 4RN

and by Routledge
711 Third Avenue, New York, NY 10017

Routledge is an imprint of the Taylor & Francis Group, an informa business

© 2018 Jan Nederveen Pieterse

British Library Cataloguing-in-Publication Data

A catalogue record for this book is available from the British Library

Library of Congress Cataloging-in-Publication Data
Names: Nederveen Pieterse, Jan, author.
Title: Multipolar globalization : emerging economies and development /
    authored by Jan Nederveen Pieterse.
Description: Abingdon, Oxon ; New York, NY : Routledge is an imprint
    of the Taylor & Francis Group, an Informa Business, [2017] |
Series: Rethinking development | Includes bibliographical references.
Identifiers: LCCN 2017003340| ISBN 9781138228375 (hbk) | ISBN
    9781138232280 (pbk) | ISBN 9781138400290 (ebk)
Subjects: LCSH: Developing countries—Economic aspects. |
    Globalization. | Economic history—21st century
Classification: LCC HC59.7 .N3345 2017 | DDC 337—dc23
LC record available at https://lccn.loc.gov/2017003340

ISBN: 978-1-138-22837-5 (hbk)
ISBN: 978-1-138-23228-0 (pbk)
ISBN: 978-1-138-40029-0 (ebk)

Typeset in Bembo
by Swales & Willis, Exeter, Devon, UK

Contents

Figures

Tables

Acknowledgments

To several chapters in this book there is a history of a conference, a workshop, a response to questions. Some chapters draw on work that has been published before in quite different versions. Also in new chapters, some sections derive from earlier discussions or publications. An overview is in the table below. I thank the journals, editors, and publishers for their kind permission to reuse the material.

An early version of Chapter 3 was presented at Seoul National University (and Open University, Milton Keynes; Humboldt University, Berlin), of Chapter 6 at the Institute of Social Studies, The Hague (and Maastricht University, Pusan National University, Xiamen University), of Chapter 8.2 at Chulalongkorn University, Bangkok. Chapter 7 was originally a keynote at an International Association for Media and Communication Research conference (Media and global divides, Stockholm, 2008) and a talk at Punjab University, Lahore. The cartoon in Chapter 6 is reprinted with permission.

I am indebted to the insights of many more colleagues than I can acknowledge here. They include Abdul Rahman Embong, Benjamin Cohen, Sérgio Costa, Veronica Davidov, Hans-Dieter Evers, Barry Gills, Terence Gomez, Min Gong, Changgang Guo, Jeffrey Henderson, Björn Hettne, Nubar Hovsepian, Jin-Ho Jang, Nick Jepson, Andrew Kam, Jongtae Kim, Habib Khondker, Don Lehman, Hyun-Chin Lim, George Lipsitz, Aashish Mehta, Manoranjan Mohanty, Desiderio Navarro, Henk Overbeek, Bhikhu Parekh, Tim Racket, Jack Rasmus, Elisa Reis, Fazal Rizvi, Ashwani Saith, Marc Saxer, Markus Schulz, Tim Shaw, Peter de Souza, Mark Swilling, Florian Stoll, Dan Vukovich, Robert Wade, Wing Woo, Surichai Wungaeo, and many more. I recall with fondness late friends and colleagues Giovanni Arrighi, Ulrich Beck, Jan Ekecrantz, and David Slater.

Colleagues in many countries hosted me for seminars, conferences, or visiting professorships (in Bangkok, Berlin, Freiburg, Kuala Lumpur, Paris, Maastricht, New Delhi, Stockholm, Shanghai, Xiamen) for which I am grateful. I am greatly indebted to colleagues at IKMAS, National University of Malaysia for their insights. Fruitful learning experiences were Global Studies conferences I co-organized with Bill Cope of Common Ground Publications and local hosts (in Chicago, Dubai, Busan, Rio de Janeiro,

Moscow, New Delhi, Shanghai). I also thank many colleagues and cohorts of students, graduate and undergraduate, at University of California Santa Barbara who shared their views and enabled me to clarify mine. For invaluable research assistance over the years I thank Andrew Michael Lee, Allison McManus, Clayton Caroon, Andrew Kam Jia Yi, and Lan Xuan Le. I claim credit for the many mistakes and omissions in this work.

Chapters	Earlier publication
2	*Theory Culture & Society* 23, 2–3, 2006: 391–4
	In G. Delanty, ed. *Europe and Asia beyond East and West.* London, Routledge, 2006, 61–73
3	In H.-C. Lim, W. Schäfer, S.-M. Hwang, eds. *Global challenges in Asia.* Seoul National University Press, 2014, 31–62
6	*Development and Change* 42, 1, 2011: 22–48
	In A. B. Güven and R. Sandbrook, eds. *Civilizing globalization.* Albany, NY, SUNY Press, 2nd ed., 2014, 33–48
6.4	An X-ray of economic stagnation, *Perspectives Libres*, 2016 (French trans.)
7	*Global Media and Communication* 5, 2, 2009
	In I. Volkmer, ed. *The handbook of global media research.* London, Wiley-Blackwell, 2012, 57–73
8.2	Democracy is coming, in C. Wungaeo, B. Rehbein and S. Wungaeo, eds. *Globalization and democracy in Southeast Asia.* London, Palgrave Macmillan, 2016, 17–41

Introduction

Like a giant oil tanker, the world is slowly turning. New growth poles of the world economy have emerged in Asia and the global South. Multipolarity is no longer in question. The rise of emerging economies marks momentous shifts. North-South relations have been dominant for 200 years and now an East-South turn is taking shape. Most literature on globalization, however, has a 20th-century feel and outlook. This book seeks to chart major 21st-century transformations and reset the cutting edge of globalization research.

How do emerging trends differ from 20th-century globalization? They involve a new geography of trade, new economic and political combinations, new financial actors, investors and donors, and weaker American hegemony, which poses many questions. Is it just markets and states that are emerging, or also societies? Is the rise of Asia, China, and other emerging economies just another episode in the rise and decline of nations, a reshuffling of accumulation centers that doesn't affect the overall logics of accumulation? Does it add franchises of Anglo-American capitalism or does it involve different kinds of capitalism? Does it bypass, halt, sustain, or extend neoliberalization? In many respects the rise of emerging economies unfolds outside the neoliberal mold. Are BRICS and EM just investment asset classes or are they gaining wider significance? What is the quality of growth in emerging economies, what does growth bode for domestic and global inequality? How does multipolarity reshape globalization?

With emerging economies growing faster than advanced economies, can they catch up with living standards in advanced countries? During the noughties, the growth advantage of emerging economies was such that for several countries convergence could take place almost in the timespan of a generation. The growth advantage of emerging economies and developing countries peaked in 2008 and has tapered off ever since (Chapter 1).

What kind of approach can hold the diverse variables, dynamics, and zones together? The book takes an interdisciplinary approach and combines development studies, global political economy, sociology, and cultural studies. The book builds on my earlier work in global studies, development studies, global political economy, and cultural studies.[1]

The outline of the book is as follows. Chapter 1 provides a genealogy of the rise of the rest going back to the late 19th century and identifies pattern changes by contrasting late 20th- and 21st-century globalization. Chapter 2 takes up the historical backdrop of oriental globalization and the trade links, past and present, between the Middle East and Asia. Chapter 3 on the rise of Asia resumes oriental globalization in present times. Chapter 4 on the BRICS widens the lens to different geographies and political economies. Chapter 5 widens the angle further with patterns of inequality in emerging economies, developing countries, and developed countries. Chapter 6 on the 2007–2009 crisis discusses ramifications of crisis and diverse policy responses. Chapter 7 examines how western media represent the rise of the rest. Chapter 8 considers the role of the middle classes, democracy, social protest, and governance with an emphasis on emerging economies. Chapter 9 asks what it takes to rethink globalization in a multipolar world and focuses on analytical and methodological debugging. Brief synopses of the chapters follow.

The rise of the rest goes back to the anti-colonial movements of the late 19th century and the Meiji revolution in Japan. Most salient has been the rise of Asia, beginning with the Tiger economies and taking on further momentum with the rise of China. North-South relations—which have been dominant for 200 years—gradually give way to East-South relations. Patterns during 1980–2000 and 2000–present are markedly different in trade, finance, international institutions, and hegemony, with a new geography of trade, the rise of new institutions and sovereign wealth funds, the G20, and adjustments in international institutions. The rise of the rest is a rollercoaster with several phases—a surge during the noughties, slowdown in the wake of the 2008 crisis which exposed weaknesses of governance in several countries, and an uneven uptick in the second decade of the 21st century (Chapter 1).

For 18 out of the past 20 centuries, Asia has been a driving force in the world economy. Oriental globalization long preceded occidental globalization in the caravan trade from the Middle East to Asia, the Silk Roads from China to the Mediterranean, and the spice trade that linked Southeast Asia to the Indian Ocean and the Levant trade. In the 21st century, oriental globalization makes a comeback in various guises. Oil and gas, pipelines, fiber optic cables, satellite links, trade and infrastructure, information, investments, and finance are the 'new silk'. A 'Chime' (China, India, Middle East) economic field is emerging. Sovereign wealth funds from Asia and the Gulf play a growing role in investments. China's One Belt, One Road projects of roads, high-speed rail and Maritime Silk Road ports add to this momentum (Chapter 2).

Chapter 3 views the rise of Asia as a comeback and examines the significance and quality of growth in rising Asia with a focus on Japan, Northeast Asia, and the Tiger economies.

Among emerging economies, the BRICS are the largest and most prominent. While they are leading emerging economies they are also developing countries with poor majorities, which together comprise almost half of the world's poor (Chapter 4). The BRICS seek to participate in the existing order as responsible stakeholders; seek reform of international institutions to ensure better representation of developing countries; initiate new institutions and develop cooperation frameworks that are outside or not dependent on the old networks, so they can operate at multiple fronts simultaneously and engage in omni-channel politics. The chapter examines BRICS' boosterism and skepticism and inequality within the BRICS.

Chapter 5 concerns patterns and institutions of inequality in countries at different levels of development. In advanced economies globalization and tech change are blamed for rising inequality, while in emerging economies globalization and tech change are credited with lifting millions out of poverty. In the US and UK inequality has grown steeply over past decades, while in Nordic European countries inequality has also increased but relatively marginally. The same variables, tech change and globalization, yield widely different patterns of inequality. The disparities reflect different initial conditions and different institutions, so it follows (a) goldilocks globalization has changed place and (b) it's the institutions, stupid! In China, poverty is acceptable (it's still a developing country), but inequality is not (it undercuts the legitimacy of the party). In India, inequality is accepted but poverty is not (it is a blight on national pride). Instead of a generalizing macro approach that focuses on global trends and global perspectives, we need multicentric approaches that are attuned to diverse initial conditions, different institutions, and cultures of inequality, which means a fundamental shift in the conversation. General trends (such as the decreasing profitability of assembly industry and labor flowing into nontradable services) affect different conditions in different ways.

Chapter 6 considers the 2008 crash as part of global realignment. Current developments can be read in two ways: towards refurbishing the old order or as the emergence of new logics. One scenario is global plutocracy with Anglo-American capitalism and financial markets in the west back in the lead and emerging markets joining the club. A scenario at the other extreme of the continuum is global restructuring, considering that developing countries that represent the majority of the world's population have joined the global head table (G20) and initiate new international institutions. In the middle is multipolarity as a wobbly in-between. Financialization is a major hurdle in advanced economies, particularly in liberal market economies, as well as after the crisis. The chapter closes with China's One Belt, One Road, a major new initiative that shows a fundamentally different approach and represents a trend break with far-reaching implications.

Western media and representations have celebrated the rise of the west for 200 years; how then do they represent the rise of the rest? Major trends are that the rise of the rest is ignored because it doesn't fit national narratives in the west, is represented as a threat because it fits existing enemy images, is blamed for the stagnation and decline of the West, or is celebrated in business media as triumphs of market forces (Chapter 7). The theme of this chapter is representations of emerging economies.

The big three in social science are the state, market, and society. The varieties of capitalism—liberal, coordinated, and state-led market economies—each refer to a different balance of the big three. In liberal market economies markets come first; in state-led economies the state leads; and in coordinated market economies all three are represented. Global rebalancing after the 2008 crisis concerned economic policies and financial trends; the protests and the political and governance crises that followed are concerned with rebalancing the big three.

Stock answers to governance in emerging economies and developing countries—democracy, the middle class, good governance—are generic and outdated. Is the issue democracy, or rather *what kind* of democracy and with what institutions? The role of democracy is overstated and the role of institutions is understated—institutions act as a check on state power and elite power. Democracy is mostly understood as liberal democracy, while for developing countries social democracy is more relevant in view of its in-built institutions. Middle classes are plural and diverse. Contemporary waves of protests show that it isn't just markets and economies that are emerging but societies as well (Chapter 8).

Chapter 9 discusses debugging theory to come to grips with contemporary multipolarity. Among the hurdles are Eurocentric conceptual generalizations and miscasting the units of analysis, conceptual shortcuts, and generalizing categories. Because developments are layered and diverse trends intermingle, sweeping generalizations don't work. Convergence (to transnational standards), divergence (national and local), and hybridity (new combinations) unfold at the same time. The discussion examines notions of emergence (emerging markets, economies, powers, societies) and their premises. Are 'Southern theories' such as postcolonial studies relevant in the contemporary multipolar world, or are they late-dependency approaches that remain wedded to North-South polarity in an increasingly East-South world?

The conclusion asks which 21st-century changes are structural, in the sense of long term, and which are temporary; which fluctuations are fluctuations within a general trend and which represent trend breaks. Ongoing dynamics point towards global restructuring and a fork in the road for emerging economies and advanced economies as well, and in some respects widening differences between liberal (US, UK) and coordinated market economies (Nordic Europe, Northeast Asia).

The 14th-century scholar of society Ibn Khaldun distinguished between history that deals with surface *appearances* (*zahir*) and history that is concerned with the *meanings* of historical processes (*batin*), which include sociological patterns that explain processes.[2] The French historian Fernand Braudel drew a distinction between events—such as whether a statesman won a battle, or fell off a horse—which he called the 'dust' of history and structural transformations in social and economic conditions that unfold over a long time, the *longue durée*, and that should be the actual subject matter for historians.[3]

This book unfolds in-between events and structural transformations. The perspective of the *longue durée*, the hindsight of hundreds of years in which social and economic transformations crystallize and debates settle isn't available in the history of the present. The book seeks to detect patterns and trends, short of structures.

This book has been long in the making and difficult to write. Not because it is global and multidimensional (which I have done in other books) but because it is a history of a turbulent present in which major dynamics are changing in diverse directions. The book aims to provide an understanding of the rise of emerging economies and the multipolar world in the making. To achieve this, the book must evoke what is going on, analyze what is going on, and reflect critically on analytical perspectives. This cannot be a standard textbook with a neat overview of issues and literatures because the processes it refers to are not standard; a standard literature doesn't exist, there is flux and uncertainty and analytical perspectives are outdated, elementary, or partial and uneven. Key actors are keenly aware of contingency. Yet there is a need for overview and synthesis of current dynamics.

For a history of the present to detect patterns, it must also be a theory of the present. What kind of theory would that be? Sociology distinguishes grand, middle-range, and micro theories. Micro theories or hypotheses seek to explain a limited set of phenomena; grand theories seek to formulate all-encompassing perspectives on social and historical formations, theories of everything such as Hegel's philosophy of history, Marx's historical materialism, Parsons' structural functionalism, and Wallerstein's world-system theory. One-size-fits-all macro theories that identify grand patterns and underlying structures have become old fashioned because they underplay contingency and non-linearity. In later work, Wallerstein disavows this status and opts instead for world-system thinking as an open-ended analytic.[4] Arguably, the best format for a history and theory of the present is middle-range theory, a combination of theories, some familiar, some not (Chapter 9).

Twentieth-century narratives of globalization are frameworks that typify an epoch. Analyzing 21st-century dynamics through these lenses is looking at contemporary trends through the rearview mirror, through the lens of a stagnant and declining hegemony. This involves several problems: the lenses are ideological and not research based; they uphold the matrix of Anglo-American capitalism as the gold standard; they don't take into account threshold conditions under which liberalization works and pays off. Because of the idée fixe of market forces, they downplay the role of the state in advanced economies as well as developing countries. I will not spell out the arguments here, but chapters that follow draw attention to different dynamics—historical depth (Chapter 2), developmental states (Chapters 3, 4, and 8), institutions and governance (Chapters 5 and 8), which intertwine with questions of comparative capitalisms, and liberal, coordinated, and state-led market economies (Chapters 3, 5, and 9). Inequality is an organizing theme throughout, also as an indicator of the quality of growth (Chapters 3, 4, and 5). Growth models and industrialization are a recurrent theme (Chapters 1 and 8). The reorganization of globalization gradually emerges on the foreground (Chapters 6 and 10).

Abbreviations used in the text include EM for emerging markets/ emerging economies (also EME, emerging market economies), AE for advanced economies, and EMDC for emerging economies and developing countries. BRIC refers to Brazil, Russia, India, China; and BRICS includes South Africa (after 2010). See also the Glossary.

Notes

1 Nederveen Pieterse 1989, 1992a, 2004, 2007, 2010a, 2015a.
2 Alatas 2013.
3 Braudel 1980.
4 Wallerstein 2013.

1   Into the multipolar world

Lenovo bought IBM's PC division, Geely bought Volvo, Tata Motors bought Jaguar and Land Rover, Mittal bought Corus and other steel industries, Brazilian companies bought Burger King and Anheuser Busch (brewer of the all-American Budweiser beer; in 2004 Belgian Interbrew merged with Brazilian AmBev and created the world's largest brewer, InBev), Qatar Holdings bought Harrods, Qatar and Dubai investment companies bought 48 percent of the London Stock Exchange, emerging economies' sovereign wealth funds made major investments in Western financial houses. In the luxury market, Asian fashion houses bought Western companies such as S C Fang in Hong Kong that bought Pringle of Scotland. China acquired a 69 percent share in the Greek port Piraeus. ChemChina bought Pirelli and seeks to buy the Swiss firm Syngenta. A Chinese company seeks to buy the German semiconductor company Aixtron.

Bollywood's Sahara India Pariwar made a bid for the MGM movie studio. Tencent in China bought IM Global, a Hollywood film financier, and a majority stake in Supercell, a Finnish mobile gaming company; China's Dalian Wanda acquired controlling stakes in Legendary and AMC Entertainment and Dick Clark Productions. Brazil joins the Paris Club of donor countries; South Korea is already among OECD donors, and so forth.

The share of emerging markets in global GDP rose from 21 percent in 1999 to 36 percent in 2010 and 50.4 percent in 2013, when it peaked.[1] Emerging economies are rising in trade, multinational firms, finance, international influence, and cultural presence.[2] This unfolds under headings such as the rise of the second world, the rise of the South, the rise of the rest and the BRICs (Brazil, Russia, India, China). These trends represent the next big thing in globalization and development. Consider a sample of recent headlines as writing on the wall:

Why brands now rise in the east
Consumption starts to shift to China, India and Brazil
Developing economies lead the way in 2010 [IMF] forecast, while rich nations lag
Developing countries underpin boom in advertising spending
Architecture firms go east for work
Bankers sense shift in capital flows
Emerging market debt is the new safe haven
Emerging economies set to play leading investment role
Benchmark expert watches market weight shift eastwards
U.S. cities seek to woo Chinese investment
Chinese investment keeps Greece, Iccland and others afloat
The deal makers who matter are rising in the East.[3]

Fukuyama's triumphalist account of the 'end of history' to mark the end of the Cold War seems long past. In a case of political economy outflanking ideology and geopolitics, the rise of new industrializing economies has gradually overtaken this narrative. Accounts of the new emerging configuration range widely. It is described as a flat world and a 'spiked world', a post-American world and a condition of 'globality' in which everyone competes with everyone.[4] The US National Intelligence Council anticipates the end of American superpower by 2025.[5]

Not too long ago, it may have been sufficient for many purposes to view the world as split between North and South, core and periphery, developed and developing, industrial and agro-mineral economies. This is the classic international division of labor that goes back to colonial times. In the 1970s, this began to change with multinational corporations investing in low-wage countries in Latin America, the Caribbean, and Asia, which was then termed the 'new international division of labor'.

Dependency thinkers argued this trend was a fad, a fata morgana; dependent capitalist development brings only underdevelopment and foreign investors will flee again when labor costs rise. A new branch of studies began to critically examine the *semiperiphery* as a formation in-between the core and the periphery, which acts as a periphery in relation to the core (export raw materials, adopt its cultural styles) and as a core in relation to the periphery (export finished products, set cultural standards, act as regional gendarme). Immanuel Wallerstein argued that the emergence of the semiperiphery gives the world-system a more stable structure; rather than the polarized North-South field, balancing forces in-between give the overall global field greater resilience.[6] Table 1.1 summarizes the schema of the three-way division.

In the 21st century, the semiperiphery has come of age and global dynamics are radically changing. 'The noughties of the 21st century', observes Martin Wolf, 'now have the same fin-de-regime feeling as those of a century ago'

Table 1.1 Three worlds revisited

North	East and South	South
Core	Semiperiphery	Periphery
Developed	Developed and developing	Developing, least developed
Industrial and post-industrial	Industrial and agro-mineral	Agro-mineral

(when the British Empire went down).[7] According to Robert Zoellick, then president of the World Bank:

> [t]he developing world is becoming a driver of the global economy. Even though developing world imports are about half of the imports of high-income countries, they are growing at a much faster rate. As a result, they accounted for more than half of the increase in world import demand since 2000.

He adds:

> The world economy is rebalancing. Some of this is new. Some represents a restoration. According to Angus Maddison, Asia accounted for over half of world output for 18 of the last 20 centuries. We are witnessing a move towards multiple poles of growth as middle classes grow in developing countries, billions of people join the world economy, and new patterns of integration combine regional intensification with global openness.[8]

Emerging markets are developing countries with growth of over 5 percent and number 23. Advanced economies number 23 and developing countries 60 (2010).[9] EM and developing countries represent 45 percent of world GDP in 2011 (anticipated to rise to 60 percent by 2030). The developing world's share of global GDP in PPP terms increased from 33.7 percent in 1980, 43.4 percent in 2010 and 50 percent in 2013. Figure 1.1 is a graph of economic trends in advanced economies relative to emerging markets based on an optimistic estimate of 2012.

According to McKinsey:

> The developing world's rapidly growing middle class, which includes about two billion people in a dozen emerging economies, spends $6.9 trillion a year. McKinsey research suggests that, during the next decade, their annual spending will rise to $20 trillion, a very big market indeed—twice current US consumption, in fact.[10]

What is at stake in these changes? First is 'the rising influence of rising affluence'.[11] This is where the big new growth markets are, so in business, finance, commodities,

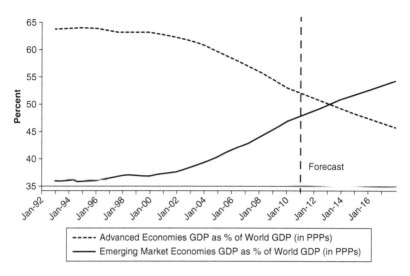

Figure 1.1 Advanced economies and EM as a percentage of world GDP
Source: McKinsey Quarterly, 2010.

transport, advertising, technology, architecture, this is the big story, the next great frontier that inspires enthusiasm in business schools. New iconic buildings arise in Kuala Lumpur, Taipei, Seoul, Shanghai, Beijing, Dubai, Qatar, along with new museums, new biennales, new art markets, and record sales of luxury goods. Shanghai chic sets a new tone. Major retailers, global brands, diamond traders, wine merchants, architects, advertising agencies, universities, bankers, all head east. Major international cultural events—the Olympic Games, the World Cup, the World Expo—have been drawn to emerging economies, beginning with the 1988 Olympic Games in Seoul. Perhaps the refrain is simply 'follow the money', but in the meantime, our global horizons are changing.

According to a Londoner, 'Spend two days in Seoul and London starts to look and feel like a sleepy, stagnant backwater'[12] (which some deem exaggerated). The avant-garde architect Jacques Herzog who designed Beijing's Bird's Nest Stadium observes, 'I think we may be able to learn from China, Brazil and India, to see how society is able to transform'.[13] Thus, what is also happening is a revitalization of modernity and the staging of new modernities.[14] This comes with new spheres of cultural influence such as Mandarin pop, K pop, and the 'Korean wave',[15] the popularity of Thai soaps in China, Turkish soaps in Saudi Arabia, and Brazilian TV in Lusophone Africa.

Third, it is a reconfiguration of the world economy. A 'new geography of trade' has taken shape in relations between Asia, Latin America, the Middle East, and Africa. In development studies, the talk is of 'Asian drivers' of growth in developing countries.[16] Emerging economies are increasingly fulfilling core functions on the world stage—acting as development role models, providing markets, loans, aid, and security, with China as the leading force. Emerging economies don't just play this role in relation to developing countries; some of their model, creditor, and stabilizing functions unfold at a global level.

Fourth, the role of emerging economies in finance has been growing as well. Sovereign wealth funds from Asia and energy exporting countries provide credit on a world scale and to international financial institutions.[17] 'It was the emerging markets, most notably China, that pulled the world back from the brink of financial meltdown'.[18] In the noughties there was a remarkable reversal of creditor-debtor relations between the US and Asia and Mid-East oil exporters, remarkable because it unfolded in international finance, the powerhouse of Western influence through which the US has sought to shape emerging economies.

Fifth, there has been a reversal, too, of perspectives on globalization and classic economic postures. EM are now the world's leading protagonists of free trade, while the US and advanced economies opt for protectionism.

Sixth, it portends a reconfiguration of world order, which so far is only dimly visible on the horizon. The unipolar world is no more, neither is the world of the big powers, as indicated in the shift from the G8 to the G20 in the wake of the 2008 crisis.[19] Yet, even as hegemonic capacity isn't what it used to be, the habits of hegemony and following hegemony linger on. Global governance is 'still lost in the old Bretton Woods'.[20] The G20 may actually be a step back for it expands the rule of big countries over small[21] and has transformed into an arena of contention over trade and currencies. Political transformations are more salient at regional levels, as in the Shanghai Cooperation Organization, the Association of Southeast Asian Nations (ASEAN) Economic Community, China's free trade agreements (FTAs) with ASEAN, ASEAN plus Three, and cross-regional cooperation such as IBSA (India, Brazil, South Africa), and between Persian Gulf and Asian countries.

Taken together, these trends signal a tipping point in history. North-South relations have been dominant for about 200 years (1800–2000), and current trends see the onset of an East-South turn. Hence, there are now three sets of relations to consider. First, between the *core* and *semiperiphery*, or between incumbents and new forces; second, relations between *the semiperiphery* and *periphery*, East-South or South-South relations, such as between China and Africa and Latin America, which is the theme of a fast-growing literature; and third, relations *within* semiperipheral countries, between industrial and agro-mineral sectors, between rich and poor, and between urban and rural populations. All are important. This chapter focuses mostly on the first theme. Chapters 3 and 4 address the second theme. Chapters 5 and 8 address the third set (which is also the theme of a recent volume).[22]

We can view contemporary transformations through various lenses—the rise of emerging economies, 21st-century globalization, the rise of the rest, and oriental globalization. Each perspective involves different dynamics, emphases, and time series.

The *rise of emerging economies* is the most obvious and widely discussed pattern change. This shows a steep upward curve during the first decade of the 21st century, a downturn after 2009 and rollercoaster trends since then.

The rise of emerging economies overlaps with a pattern of differences between 20th- and 21st-century globalization. The keynote of 21st-century globalization as a lens is a comparison of the 1980–2000 era of neoliberalism and the Washington consensus, and the 21st-century rise of emerging economies. While this involves large pattern changes, they are understood and gauged in short-term changes. The degree to which these are trends or blips, time will tell. As a theme, 21st-century globalization is episodic, with an argument structure in the order of 40 years (1980–2020). Thus, the risk of a perspective centered on 21st-century globalization is that it is short term.

If our task is to look behind immediate changes in graphs and statistics, and to situate ongoing transformations in the *longue durée* of structural change, we must look further. The *rise of the rest* is a larger and wider angle than 21st-century globalization. Then, the rise of emerging economies is part of long time series. This perspective enables us to view ongoing developments in the context of long-term dynamics that unfold over a hundred years or more. Alice Amsden used the notion of the rise of the rest in her book about the new industrializing economies of Northeast Asia, in particular South Korea.[23] It was a spoof, of course, on the rise of the West, a theme well established in economics and as a civilizational trope. Yet a subtext of the rise of the rest is that it implicitly accepts the narrative of the rise of the West—the West rose and now it's the turn of the rest—and thus implicitly recycles a Eurocentric account of global history. Besides, is the rest rising? The category is rhetorical and too wide; not *all* the rest is rising. Least developed countries, landlocked low-income countries such as Niger and Burundi have not been rising.

Table 1.2 Perspectives on global transformation

Oriental globalization	
500 CE–1800	Oriental globalization
The rise of the rest	
1800s	Decolonization of the Americas
Late 19C	Anti-colonial movements in Asia, Middle East, Africa
1868	Meiji Restoration Japan (1906 Japan victory in Russian-Japanese war)
20C	Decolonization of Asia, Middle East, Africa
1970s	New international division of labor
The rise of emerging economies	
1980s–90s	Rise of Asian tigers and NIEs
21st-century globalization	
2001	China joins WTO
2003–2009	High growth of EMDC; commodities supercycle; BRICS
2011	Stagnation in AE, mixed trends in EMDC
2015	New institutions, New Development Bank, CRA; AIIB, Silk Road Fund

A perspective with a still longer time frame is *oriental globalization*, which involves two arguments. First, the focus is on the rise of Asia, which led the rise of emerging economies. Second, the rise of Asia is a return of the East and part of a much longer time series. Table 1.2 gives an overview of major narratives of ongoing transformations.

This chapter provides an initial overview of trends and pattern changes with a focus on the rise of the rest and 21st-century globalization. The next sections address the rise of the rest (with only highlights of major episodes, or else this chapter would become a world encyclopedia). The rise of emerging economies is, likewise, an overview discussion. Subsequent chapters spell out these dynamics further. Chapter 2 takes up oriental globalization.

1 Genealogies

The anti-colonial and decolonization movements have unfolded over a long period, intertwined with the unraveling of empires and the reshuffling of hegemony. They go back to the ripple effects of the French Revolution, from the Haitian Revolution of Toussaint Louverture to the decolonization of the Americas. The independence of the American Republic and the decolonization of Latin America in the early 19th century signaled the unraveling of empires—the Spanish-Habsburg, Portuguese, and British Empires. They intertwined with slave rebellions and maroon movements in the Caribbean and the Americas. They coincided with the abolitionist movement that was inspired by religious movements (notably the Quakers), the Enlightenment, and the romantic movement, alongside other emancipation movements and class struggles—the emancipation of women, Catholics, Jews, serfs, and minorities in Europe. The national question and the social question (which over time became nationalism and socialism) interacted in this equation, as in the social upheavals in Europe that came to a head in 1848—the 'springtime of peoples' and the spread of the idea of national and popular sovereignty.

These movements overlapped with developments across the world. In the Arab world, the Nahda (reawakening) gave rise to movements seeking national self-determination and cultural revival. When the Berlin Congress (1885) divided Africa among European powers, it was soon followed by the emergence of independence movements in several African countries. In India, the Congress party vied for self-determination. Young Turks and Young Persians clamored for political reforms. The Russian Revolution of 1917 ousted the Tsar. In the Baku conference of 1920, Lenin ushered in a major policy shift and made cooperation between communist parties and anti-colonial movements across the world a major priority for socialist revolution, on a par with the cooperation of the Soviet communist party and socialist parties in advanced industrial countries, which had been the earlier priority. Communist parties in India, Indonesia, and China established cooperation with the Bolsheviks.

Among historical accounts of this period are Stavrianos' books. My *Empire and Emancipation* discusses the dialectics of empire and emancipation: liberation and emancipation movements learn from empires and hegemons (technically, organizationally, normatively), while empires learn from and adjust to liberation movements; liberation movements adapt their tactics and strategies to changing metropolitan maneuvers, and so forth in an ascending spiral.[24] Sun Yat Sen studied in Tokyo, Sukarno obtained an engineering degree in the Netherlands, Léopold Senghor was a member of the French Assemblée, Ho-Chi Minh studied in Paris, Pol Pot worked in France, Nkrumah studied in London, W.E.B. Dubois in the US joined the World Anti-imperialist League, etc. As Basil Davidson noted, virtually all the leaders of African independence were educated in mission schools in Africa and many studied in England, France, Belgium, etc.[25]

Thus, the rise of the rest intertwined with divisions and rivalries among Western powers and with the breakup of European imperialism. Balance of power conflicts shaped colonial expansion all along, as in the 'new imperialism' of the late 19th century when European balance of power conflicts were superimposed on the world map. The rise of the rest, then, occurred at the confluence of several historical currents:

- Oriental globalization—building on the older lead of Asia and the orient in the world economy (Chapter 2).
- Divisions in the West and the breakup of European empires (which includes British support for the US and for Japan as counterweights against German and Russian expansion, which over time contributed to Japan's rise and the rise of American hegemony).
- Soviet support for anti-colonial movements (after the Baku conference of 1920).
- The rise of American hegemony, which includes expansionist and colonial episodes (Westward continental expansion, the Spanish-American war, the Monroe doctrine, colonization of the Philippines) and an anti-colonial stance in relation to European colonies.
- Learning curves of development and industrialization.

2 The rise of the rest

When during the First World War 'the lights went out all over Europe', the beginnings of industrialization and catch-up took shape in Argentina and Brazil. With the great powers occupied by war and rivalry, supply links and supplies were interrupted and import-substitution industrialization in dependent zones became viable.

One of the reasons why in Latin America this was not sustained to the degree of a takeoff to growth is the influence of entrenched landholding oligarchies. A major difference between Northeast Asia and Latin America is land reform and redistribution, not just because of its effects on agricultural productivity but also in view of its political and social ramifications. Landlordism remained a major hurdle in Latin America and came with caudillismo, dictatorships, misguided economic policies, and long-lasting social and political struggles.

Northeast Asia in broad strokes followed Meiji Japan, which, in turn, followed the model of Friedrich List and Bismarck Germany. In Japan, land reform was implemented under American influence as part of the demobilization settlement after the Second World War. South Korea undertook land reform after the Korean war as did Taiwan, again under American auspices as part of Cold War contestation. What ensued over time is Germany's postwar 'Wirtschaftswunder' and Japan's 'economic miracle', in which Japan emerged as the world's second largest economy challenging the American lead in automobiles and other sectors (discussed in Chapter 3).

Japan, South Korea, and Taiwan share developmental states, but while Japan's industrialization involved a military-industrial complex, industrialization in Korea and Taiwan did not. In Korea, as in Japan, heavy industries, steel, and chemicals played a major part, but the emphasis was on shipbuilding, not a war navy. Of course, the Cold War setting and the American military umbrella in the region made a difference. Industrialization in Northeast Asia was further propelled by geographical proximity to Japan and the Korean and Vietnam wars, which required supplies within the region. The Washington connection, domino theory, and counterinsurgency were part of regional equations.

The rise of the Tiger economies, dubbed the 'East Asian miracle', was followed by the Southeast Asian 'tiger cubs' and China's reform and opening up in 1978–81. However, over time, major differences between Southeast Asia and Northeast Asia became apparent. In Southeast Asia, there was no land reform; industrialization was led by FDI, rather than nationally organized; industry was mainly light industry and offshore assembly industry; and while in Northeast Asia the Japanese model led the way, American influence dominated in much of Southeast Asia. Singapore acted as a beachhead of American influence. Thus, the rise of the Pacific Rim, the 'Pacific century' and the 'Asian century' came to an Asia and a Pacific that were deeply divided and diverse, with Northeast Asia following the example of Japan and Southeast Asia following the lead of the US and the 'Singapore model' (Chapter 3).

In the 1990s, culturalist claims took the foreground such as 'Asian values', the new Confucian ethic, and in the Middle East, Islamic values, Islamic science, and Islamic finance. In Latin America, the rise of 'Latin Americanidad' ushered in a new sense of self-confidence. While culturalist accounts of emergence led the way, in the US Samuel Huntington proclaimed a 'clash of civilizations' along culturalist lines as the successor to ideological East-West divides.[26] With the Asian crisis of 1997 and IMF intervention, the flourish of 'Asian values' subsided. The crisis exposed structural weaknesses of crony capitalism in the region, particularly in Southeast Asia.

3 The rise of emerging economies

The factor that sets the 21st century apart from 20th-century globalization and from which many other changes follow is the rise of emerging economies. Growth in emerging economies in the 21st century outstripped growth in developed economies to the point that they became drivers of the world economy. Like any major story, this comes in many flavors. Key themes are convergence, the middle class, decoupling, and the middle-income trap.

Until fairly recently, this was a straightforward account of convergence: developing countries are growing faster than developed countries, hence in the not too distant future, for some countries even within a generation or so, they will converge with developed countries in per capita GDP and living standards.

Part of this is the growth of the middle class and urbanization in developing countries, hence their growing importance as markets of goods and services across a wide spectrum, including luxury goods and investment markets. This involves long- and short-term dynamics. The growth of the middle class and urbanization in developing countries is a long-term trend and consumption patterns, life-styles, and ideological leanings are trend-sensitive and subject to fluctuations in purchasing power and volatility.

A strong version of these dynamics was the idea of decoupling. During the noughties, the growth of EM was so momentous that they no longer seemed to depend on developments in advanced economies. The 2008 crash belied this notion that was controversial all along. When downturn in the EU followed slowdown in the US, lagging demand for exports caused a slowdown in emerging economies, notably China. China responded with momentous stimulus spending, which kept up growth but also set a precarious course of investment-led growth and growing debt.

The idea that per capita GDP in developing and developed nations is converging has fallen by the wayside, or it is occurring but much more slowly than was thought earlier.[27] What has come in its stead is the idea of the *middle-income trap*. Long time series of developing countries show that as they rise to a level of around 30 percent of the living standards of the US, they often remain stuck at this level.[28]

Nevertheless, we are at a major turning point in historical curves. Emerging economies are the world's leading economies in the 21st century. This is a profoundly significant turnaround of a 200-year pattern of North-South domination and its familiar expressions of colonialism, imperialism, and American hegemony. It poses major questions. Is the lead of emerging economies a temporary deviation or does it reflect structural transformations? How sustainable is this lead? Across which dimensions does it unfold? The lead of the North (or the West) involved a technological lead, usually summed up as the industrial revolution (and second, third, and fourth waves of industrialization). Is the rise of emerging economies merely a matter of growth numbers (GDP-ism as they say in China), or does it involve more profound transformations, including technological and sociopolitical changes?

The rise of EM is an expression of several curves. One is the demand for commodities—as an expression of industrialization and urbanization notably in Asia and Latin America. In a structural sense, this matches the postwar decades when industrialization in the US, Europe, and Japan drove worldwide demand for commodities. It finds expression in the commodities supercycle of 2003–2009, which tapered off after the crash of 2008. In the years ahead, will demand for commodities climb back up in view of ongoing urbanization and infrastructure investment, particularly in Asia? The second curve is high growth in emerging economies, relative to slow growth or stagnation in advanced economies. Is above-average growth sustainable over time? The third curve is industrialization. With more and more EM entering industrial export-led growth, industry becoming more globalized and dynamic and manufactured goods becoming cheaper, is industrialization a sustainable growth path? Industrialization as growth path requires climbing higher on the productivity ladder, or else it leads to 'premature deindustrialization'.[29] Leading growth economies such as South Korea and Taiwan—which have emerged already—are able to continue doing this, but are others? The fourth curve is ecological sustainability, which is of global significance. Are EMDC able to marshal resources in sustainable ways in energy use, urban design, industrial technology, and agricultural transformation? Thus, the brave new world of multipolarity led by emerging economies is a world of promise that is fraught with peril.

The 21st-century momentum of globalization is markedly different from 20th-century globalization and involves a new geography of trade, weaker hegemony, and growing multipolarity, which presents major questions. Is the rise of East Asia, China, and India just another episode in the rise and decline of nations, another reshuffling of capitalism, a relocation of accumulation centers without affecting the logics of accumulation? Does it advance, sustain, deviate from or halt neoliberalism? The rise of Asia has been interdependent with neoliberal globalization and yet unfolds outside the neoliberal mold. What is the relationship between zones of accumulation and modes of regulation? What are the ramifications for social inequality? The next section discusses trends in trade, finance, international institutions, and hegemony.

According to IMF estimates, China and India will overtake the GDP of the world's leading economies in the coming decades. China passed the GDP of Japan in 2015 and will pass that of the US by 2025. In 2005, China surpassed the US as Japan's biggest trading partner, surpassed Canada as the biggest trading partner of the US and surpassed the US as the world's top choice of foreign direct investment. If these trends continue, China will become the biggest trading partner of practically every nation. By 2025, the combined GDP of the BRIC would grow to one-half the combined GDP of the G6 (US, Japan, Germany, France, Italy, Britain). By 2050, according to a Goldman Sachs paper, the combined BRIC will surpass that group and 'China, India, Brazil and Russia will be the first-, third-, fifth- and sixth-biggest economies by 2050, with the United States and Japan in second and fourth place, respectively'.[30]

The US, Europe, and Japan rode the previous wave of globalization during 1970–2000, but in recent years their lead in manufacturing, trade, finance, and international politics has been slipping. The US set macroeconomic rules through the Washington consensus, in trade, through the WTO, in finance, through the IMF and the dollar standard, and in security, through its hegemony and formidable military. Each of these dimensions has been out of whack for some time. The old winners are still winning, but the terms on which they are winning cedes more and more to emerging forces. In production and services, education and demography, the advantages are no longer squarely with the old winners. In several respects, in the maelstrom of globalization, the incumbents have become conservative forces.

Examining this poses methodological problems. Extrapolating trends is risky. The units of analysis are not what they used to be, or seem to be. Statistics measure countries, but economies are part of crossborder production and value networks. The story is not merely one of change but also continuity, although in some respects, seeming continuity.

There is a certain stickiness and stodginess to social change. Power plays continue for as long as they can. Policies continue old style until a policy paradigm change is inevitable, not unlike Thomas Kuhn's revolutions in science. There is a sleepwalking choreography to collective existence, never quite in sync with actual trends; or rather, trends are only trends when they enter discourse. (In a similar way, what we teach in universities is often years behind what we know or what we are thinking about because there is no convenient structure or heading yet under which to communicate it.) Changes manifest after time lags—a discursive lag, an institutional lag, a policy lag; yet changes are underway even if the language to signal them is not quite there yet. Some changes we can name, some we can surmise, some escape detection and will catch up with us. So at times, it feels much like business as usual. Thus, we should identify pattern shifts, discursive changes, and tipping points that may tilt the pattern.

According to Kemal Dervis, then director of the UN Development Program, globalization in the past was a profoundly 'unequalising process', yet:

> [t]oday, the process is rapidly turning on its head. The south is grow-
> ing faster than the north. Southern companies are more competitive than
> their northern counterparts. . . . Leading the charge is a new generation
> of southern multinationals, from China, Korea, India, Latin America and
> even the odd one from Africa, aggressively seeking investments in both the
> northern and southern hemispheres, competing head-to-head with their
> northern counterparts to win market share and buy undervalued assets.[31]

Also optimistic but more complex in its assessments is the Human Development Report 2013 on *The Rise of the South.*[32]

About cutting-edge globalization, there are several stories to tell. One is the rise of Asia and the growth of East-South trade, energy, financial, and political relations. General media cover much of this story, often with brio.[33] Another story that often receives mention only in patchy ways, is that EM face major social crises in agriculture and urban poverty.

The next section discusses major trends in 21st-century globalization by comparing trends during 1980–2000 and 2000–present under the headings of trade, finance, international institutions, and hegemony. A brief proposition prefaces each trend assessment. The closing section seeks to understand what the new trends mean for the emerging 21st-century patterns.

Trade

Growing East-South trade leads to a 'new geography of trade' and new trade pacts.

Through the postwar period, North-South trade relations were dominant. In recent years, East-South trade has been growing, driven by the rise of Asian economies and the accompanying commodities boom (since 2003) and high petrol prices (since 2004). According to the UN Conference on Trade and Development, a 'new geography of trade' is taking shape:

> The new axis stretches from the manufacturing might and emerging middle classes of China, and from the software powerhouse of India in the south, to the mineral riches of South Africa, a beachhead to the rest of the African continent, and across the Indian and Pacific oceans to South America which is oil-rich and mineral- and agriculture-laden.[34]

Brazil opened trade links with the Middle East, Asia, and Africa. Chile, Peru, Bolivia, and other Latin American countries negotiated trade agreements with China or received major loans from China. 'The Middle East has started looking to Asia for trade and expertise'; trade has expanded threefold in the early 2000s and the fastest growing markets for oil are China and India.[35] Growing Sino-Indian trade combines countries with 1.3 and 1.2 billion people each.[36]

During 1980–2000, American-led trade pacts such as NAFTA, APEC, and the WTO played a dominant role. In the 2000s, these pacts are in impasse or passé. Dissatisfaction with NAFTA has been commonplace, also within the US. In Latin America, Mercosur, enlarged with Venezuela and Cuba as associate members, undercut the Free Trade Association of the Americas (FTAA). ASEAN, in combination with Japan, South Korea, and China (ASEAN plus Three) reduced Asian dependence on the American market and APEC landed on the backburner. 'This group has the potential to be the world's largest trade bloc, dwarfing the European Union and North American Free Trade Association'.[37]

During 1980–2000, the trend was towards regional and global trade pacts. The walkout of the G22 in the WTO meeting in Cancún in 2003 under the heading 'no deal is better than a bad deal' upped the ante in subsequent negotiations. Advanced countries that previously pushed trade liberalization now resist liberalizing trade and retreat to 'economic patriotism'. The United States has been zigzagging in relation to the WTO (with steel tariffs and agriculture and cotton subsidies). Given WTO gridlock in the Doha development round and blocked regional trade talks (the failure of the FTAA talks in Miami followed the Cancún walkout), the US increasingly opted for bilateral FTAs, which further erode the WTO. US terms in FTAs typically include exempting American military forces from the International Criminal Court, accepting genetically modified food (GMF), and preferential terms for American multinationals and banks. The US has FTAs with 12 countries (Australia, Bahrain, Chile, Colombia, Israel, Jordan, Korea, Morocco, Oman, Panama, Peru, Singapore) and with NAFTA (Canada and Mexico) and CAFTA (Costa Rica, Dominican Republic, El Salvador, Guatemala, Honduras, Nicaragua).

In South-South trade, the trend has been towards regional and interregional combinations such as Mercosur, the ASEAN Economic Community (AEC 2015) and ASEAN plus Three. China established an FTA with ASEAN. Since 2003, there have been talks to establish a free trade zone of IBSA. The Pacific Alliance (Chile, Colombia, Mexico, Peru) is a new combination in Latin America.

The old core-periphery relations no longer hold. The global South no longer looks just north but also sideways. East Asian development models have long overtaken Western prescriptions. South-South cooperation, heralded as an alternative to dependence on the West ever since the Bandung meeting of the Movement of Non-aligned Countries (1955), is now taking shape. 'Already 43 percent of the South's global trade is accounted for by intra-South trade'. In 2013, this is 58 percent. [38]

The downside is that much of this growth is sparked by a commodities boom that petered off in 2009 and dropped in 2013. An example is the roller-coaster experience of the Zambian copper belt,[39] which experienced another upturn spurred by Chinese investments that turns out to be as precarious as

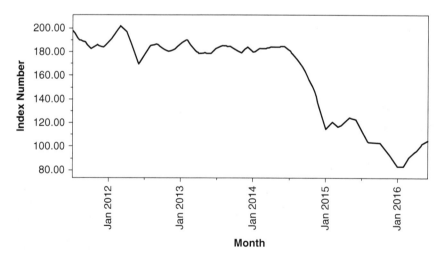

Figure 1.2 Commodity Price Index
Source: indexmundi

the previous cycle. Only countries that move up the ladder of commodity processing and technology linkages,[40] or convert commodity surpluses into productive investments in infrastructure and 'knowledge capital' stand a chance of outflanking the commodities cycle. In 2016, commodity prices showed an upward trend again (Figure 1.2 shows recent trends in commodity prices).

Finance

Imbalances in the world economy (American trade and current account deficits and Asian surpluses) are unsustainable and are producing a reorganization of global finance and trade.

During 1980–2000, finance capital played a key role in restructuring capitalism worldwide. Finance capital led from the late 19th century up to the Wall Street crash of 1929 and was then reined in by the regulations of the New Deal. In the 1980s, finance capital resumed a leading role as one of the defining features of neoliberal globalization,[41] which produced a series of crises (Savings & Loan, LTCM) and a crash in 2007 (collapse of the subprime mortgage market) and 2008 (the fall of Lehman Brothers). Financialization (the growing share of financial profits in corporate profits) involves financial innovations such as hedge funds, derivatives, and financial technologies (fintech), the maturation of advanced economies, finance as a force in globalization and as the endgame of American hegemony. The comeback of speculative capital led to diagnoses of casino capitalism and Las Vegas capitalism. Financial crises hit Mexico, Asia, Russia, Turkey, Latin America, and Argentina. In the 1990s, attempts to reform the architecture of international finance came to little more than one-sided pleas for transparency; Washington institutions should be able to read the books of developing countries.

The trend since 2000 is that NIEs hold substantial foreign reserves to safeguard against financial turbulence. EMDC held $3.9 trillion in foreign exchange reserves in 2004 and $7.9 trillion in 2013.[42] This is a lesson learned from the Asian crisis of 1997. Since then, EMs view competition in financial markets as a strategic arena. Pooling funds against financial upheaval has become necessary, such as the Chiang Mai Initiative, the Asian Bond Fund, and the BRICS Contingency Reserve Arrangement. Sovereign wealth funds also serve to maintain financial autonomy.

During 1980–2000, the IMF was the hard taskmaster of developing economies; in the 2000s, the IMF warns year after year that US deficits and policies threaten global economic stability.[43] In the IMF 2016 annual report, growing inequality looms largest among the threats facing the US economy: four forces that pose a challenge to future growth are 'the declining labour force participation rate, falling productivity, increasing polarisation in income distribution and a high share of the population living in poverty'.[44]

The US dollar is the world's leading reserve currency by a long stretch, but since 2001 there has been a gradual shift to other currencies. After the decoupling of the dollar from gold in 1971, OPEC agreed in 1975 to sell oil for dollars and a de facto oil-dollar standard emerged. Venezuela, Iran, and Russia began to price their oil in other currencies. In 2001–2005, the dollar declined 28 percent against the euro and a further 12 percent in 2006. In 2002, the world's leading central banks held on average 73 percent of world reserves in USD, which fell to 64 percent in 2015.[45] In 2009, Asian central banks cut their accumulation of dollar reserves to less than 30 percent.[46] Russia, China, and an international panel convened by the UN call for alternatives to the US dollar as reserve currency. However, a multi-currency world is still far off.

China and Japan with 70 to 80 percent of their foreign reserves in US dollars, reflecting their close ties to the American market, deviated markedly from the world average. The trend is for China to diversify its foreign reserves. For obvious reasons this diversification must be gradual. Of China's $3.33 trillion in foreign reserves, $1.73 trillion was in USD (2012). The total share of dollar assets in reserve is now approximately 55 percent.[47]

During the 1997 Asian crisis, the IMF vetoed Japan's initiative for an Asian monetary fund. Since then the Chiang Mai Initiative has established a buffer fund, followed by the Asian Bond Fund. Venezuela, backed by petrol funds, withdrew from the IMF and World Bank, and with six other Latin American countries established an alternative Bank of the South in 2009 (Banco del Sur, which since 2013 only exists as a legal entity).

Western financial markets have been dominant since the 17th century. In the 2000s, financial sources outside the West played an increasingly important role, reflecting the rise of Asia, the global commodities boom, and high petrol prices. The accumulation of petro money during 2005–2007 was three times the annual Asian surpluses from exports.[48] A new East-East financial network is emerging. China's initial public offerings no longer go just via New York and London but also via Saudi Arabia and the Dubai Bourse.[49] Wall Street has been losing its primacy as the center of world finance to London with Shanghai and Hong Kong as runners up.[50] Brexit changes this trend in favor of Wall Street and other financial centers.

East Asian countries are active investors in Latin America and Africa. Of FDI in developing countries, 37 percent now comes from other developing countries. China has emerged as a major lender to developing countries, at lower rates and without the conditions of the Western institutions. China's foreign aid competes with Western donors (Chapter 3.5).

Hedge funds have become more active international players than investment banks. In 2006, there were 10,000 hedge funds with $1.5 trillion in assets, a daily global turnover in derivatives of $6 trillion and a credit derivative market that is worth $26 trillion. In 2015, 10,149 hedge funds held $2.87 trillion in assets.[51]

Financialization has increased the risk of financial instability, and financial instruments such as derivatives and credit default swaps are increasingly opaque and out of control. Financial instability increasingly affects institutions in the West as in the collapse of LTCM (1998), the Enron episode (with WorldCom,

HealthSouth, and other corporations, 2001), Parmalat (2003), Amaranth (2006), and the crisis of American subprime mortgage lenders such as New Century (2007) with ripple effects throughout the financial system (Chapter 6). Many American economic successes were enabled by the 'Greenspan put' of low interest rates and easy money, which resumed in quantitative easing policies of the Federal Reserve as well as the Bank of Japan and the European Central Bank.

In meetings of the World Economic Forum in Davos, the American economy and the unstable dollar have long been a cause for concern. US Treasury debt at $19.5 trillion and net external debt at $14 trillion add up to interest payments of $403 billion a year (2015) and rising.[52] The United States is in the red to Asian central banks and relies on inflows of Asian capital. The dollar is upheld more by weakness of the euro (and yen and British pound) and fear of turbulence than by confidence in the American economy and appeal.

Institutions

The architecture of globalization is fragile and the clout of emerging economies is growing.

The 1990s institutional architecture of globalization was built around the convergence of the IMF, World Bank, and WTO and has been increasingly fragile. Since its handling of the Asian crisis in 1997–98 and Argentina's crisis in 2001, the IMF earned the nickname 'the master of disaster'. Argentina, Brazil, Venezuela, South Africa, Russia, and others repaid their debt to the IMF early, so the IMF had less financial leverage, also in view of new flows of petro money. IMF lending went down from $70 billion in 2003 to $20 billion in 2006.

The IMF faced constraints, laid off staff, and adopted marginal reforms (it accepts capital controls and agreed to increase the vote quota of four EM by 6 percent). In the wake of the 2008 crisis, the IMF made a comeback with G20 backing (Chapter 6). The IMF committed lending arrangements in 2016 are $159 billion.[53]

The World Bank lost standing as well. In the 1990s, the Bank shifted gear from neoliberalism to social liberalism, or structural adjustment 'with a human face' and emphasis on poverty reduction and social risk mitigation. However, to the extent that the poverty reduction targets of the Bank and the Millennium Development Goals have been met, it is largely due to developments in China and Asia, which unfolded outside the orbit of the Washington institutions. Paul Wolfowitz's attempts as World Bank president to merge neoliberalism and neoconservatism were counterproductive with an internally divisive anti-corruption campaign and a focus on Iraq. The infrastructure of power has changed as well. The 'Wall Street-Treasury-IMF complex' of the 1990s weakened when the Treasury played a minor role in the GW Bush administration.

The 1990s architecture of globalization has become brittle for several reasons. The disciplinary regime of the Washington consensus has been slipping. Structural adjustment has shown a consistently high failure rate with 'lost decades' in sub-Saharan Africa and Latin America. The 1997 Asian crisis and how the IMF handled it was a turning point. Research indicates a correlation between IMF involvement and negative economic performance, also for political reasons: because IMF involvement signals economic troubles, it attracts further troubles.[54] Zigzag behavior by the hegemon—flaunting WTO rules, fiscal indiscipline, massive deficits—weakened the international institutions. Following the spate of financial crises in the 1990s, crisis mismanagement, and growing American deficits, the Washington consensus gave way to a post-Washington no-consensus while greater economic weight and leverage backs growing momentum in Asia and EM.

Both the IMF and World Bank have engaged in self-criticism and correction. The World Bank changed its goal posts and now includes labor rights and collective bargaining among conditions for giving project aid. The IMF has criticized its handling of the situation in Greece and has insisted on debt relief as a condition for further participation in Greece's debt restructuring (after French and German banks were paid back). A paper by IMF economist Jonathan Ostry and colleagues now questions neoliberalism: 'Neoliberalism has been oversold'. In short: 'Instead of delivering growth, some neoliberal policies have increased inequality, in turn jeopardizing durable expansion'.[55] Yet extensive research of IMF lending shows that its conditionalities have not actually changed over 1985–2014.[56]

Hegemony

Rather than hegemonic rivalry, what is taking place is global realignments towards growing multipolarity.

The main options in relation to hegemony are continued American hegemony, hegemonic rivalry, hegemonic transition, and multipolarity. Hegemonic decline at the turn of the 19th century took the form of wars of hegemonic rivalry (1870–1945), which culminated in the transition to the United States as the new hegemon. Current trends look to be structurally different from previous episodes. Economic and technological interdependence and cultural interplay are now far greater than at the fin de siècle. What is emerging is not simply a decline of (American) hegemony and rise of (Asian) hegemony but a more complex multipolar field, or in Amitav Acharya's term, a multiplex world.[57]

During the 1990s, American hegemony was solvent, showed high growth, and seemed to be dynamic in the throttle of the new economy boom. The United States followed a mixed uni-multipolar approach with cooperative security (in the Gulf War) and 'humanitarian intervention' (in Bosnia, Kosovo, and Kurdistan) as leitmotivs. Unilateralism with a multilateral face during the 1990s gave way to unilateralism with a unilateral face under the GW Bush administration, a high-risk, high-cost approach that flaunted its weaknesses.[58] By opting for unilateral 'preventive war', the GW Bush administration abandoned international law. In going to war in Afghanistan and Iraq, the US overplayed its hand, a classic case of imperial overstretch. In its first out-of-area operation, NATO met fierce resistance in Afghanistan. The US is now caught up in the aftermath of its wars with the rise of ISIL, rivalry between Saudi Arabia and Iran, war in Yemen, crisis in Syria, instability in Afghanistan, and troubles in Turkey and its borders.

During the Cold War, Muslims were cultivated as allies and partners. In the 1980s, Ronald Reagan lauded the Mujahedeen in the Afghan war as 'the moral equivalent of our founding fathers'. As the Cold War waned, these allies were sidelined. Samuel Huntington's 'clash of civilizations' article in 1993 shifted the goalposts from ideology to culture and from communism to the Islamic world. He also warned against a Confucian-Islamic alliance and military cooperation between China and Pakistan. Thus, erstwhile allies were recast as enemies, and yesterday's freedom fighters were reclassified as today's terrorists.

In response to this policy shift and continuing Israeli and American politics of tension in the Middle East, a Muslim backlash took shape of which the attacks of September 11, 2001 are part. The Cold War 'green belt' and 'arc of crisis' has become an 'arc of extremism' with flashpoints from the Middle East to Turkey, Europe, and Southeast Asia. Satellite TV in the Arab world contributes to awareness among Muslims. Muslim organizations increasingly demonstrate high militancy and swift responses (for instance to the Danish cartoons and statements by Pope Benedict). The Lebanon war in 2006 showed Israel's weakness and Hezbollah's strength as part of a realignment away from American-supported Sunni governments to Iran, Syria, and Shia. The United States siding with Israel's insular stance in the region contributes to its self-isolation.[59]

New security axes have emerged, such as the Shanghai Cooperation Organization (deemed a 'counterweight to NATO') and cooperation of China, Russia, and Iran.[60] The US lost access to bases in Uzbekistan and Kazakhstan. Other emerging poles of influence are IBSA. The G77 made its influence felt in international trade and diplomacy. In response to US expansion in the Middle East and Africa, it blocked intervention in Darfur on the grounds of sovereignty, involving an Islamic government in a strategic region. China has generally backed G77 positions in UN Security Council negotiations,[61] a position that is gradually changing.

On the military frontiers of hegemony, although the United States spends 48 percent of world military spending (2005; 34 percent in 2016) and maintains a formidable 'empire of bases', the wars in Iraq and Afghanistan demonstrate the limits of American military power. As a traditional sea and air power, the US has usually been unable to win ground wars.[62] 'Globalization from the barrel of a gun' and regime change are costly propositions, also in view of the growing gap between American military and economic power.[63]

The Cold War frontiers are no longer stable. The US sponsored 'color revolutions' in the Balkans and Caucasus; Estonia, Latvia, and Lithuania joined NATO; the EU invited Ukraine to join, a major buffer state of Russia. Russia expanded into Georgia, the Crimea, and eastern Ukraine and interfered in the American elections. China expanded in the South and East China Seas.

On the economic front, the US is import dependent and 'Brand America' has lost points. The GW Bush presidency may be viewed as a failure of American brand management. The aura of American power has been fading. Rising anti-Americanism has affected the appeal of American products, and American pop culture is no longer the edge of cool. An advertising executive notes growing resentment of American-led globalization:

> We know that in Group of 8 countries, 18 percent of the population claim they are avoiding American brands, with the top brand being Marlboro in terms of avoidance. Barbie is another one. McDonald's is another. There is a cooling towards American culture generally across the globe.[64]

Besides assorted scandals, the 2016 election and the victory of Donald Trump further tarnish Brand America.[65]

The tipping points of American hegemony are domestic and external. Domestic tipping points are financialization (Chapter 6.4) and income inequality (Chapter 5.3). Financialization is crisis prone and erodes investment in the economy of goods, so in many sectors manufacturing capacity has eroded and productivity is down. Income inequality strains domestic demand in an economy that relies on private consumption for 70 percent of GDP. Low interest rates undercut the appeal of dollar assets, and rising interest rates increase pressure on the leveraged financial system. At a fundamental level, there is not much give in the structure and institutions of the liberal market economy (Chapters 5 and 8).

External tipping points are strategic debacles in the Middle East, the American legitimacy crisis, and financial markets following new money. Of the two components of the 'pivot to Asia', trade and military, with the demise of the Trans-Pacific Trade Partnership (TPP) only the military presence is left, which elicits little interest in the region.

At a general level, there are three different responses to American hegemony. One is *continued support*—which is adopted for a variety of reasons such as the appeal of the American market, the US dollar, and the shelter of the American military umbrella. The second option is *soft balancing*—such as tacit non-cooperation (such as European countries staying out of the Iraq war and declining GMF) and establishing institutions if necessary without American participation (such as the Kyoto Protocol and the International Criminal Court). Only a few countries can afford the third response, *hard balancing*—because they have been branded as enemies of the US already, so they have little to lose (Cuba, Venezuela, North Korea, Sudan) or because their leverage allows them maneuvering room (China and Russia). The number of countries that *combine* these different responses to American hegemony in diverse domains has increased. China displays all three responses in different spheres—economic cooperation (WTO, trade); non-cooperation in diplomacy (UN Security Council) and finance (valuation of the renminbi; loans to Venezuela, Zimbabwe, Sudan); and overt resistance (in Central Asia, support for Iran, and in the South and East China Seas).

Responses to American hegemony range from retrenchment (protect national or transnational interests), to reformism (contain future risk), to revisionism (overthrow US hegemony and the neoliberal order). Retrenchment policies include central banks and investors reducing US dollar holdings and G20 loans to the IMF; reformist policies seek alternatives in trade, security arrangements, and energy supplies or routes; and initiating or joining new institutions. Venezuela, Iran, and the World Social Forum have advocated revisionist policies.

Unilateralism has become too costly, and American unilateralism and preventive war have given way to multilateralism. New clusters and alignments are taking shape around trade, energy, and security. Sprawling cross-zone realignments point to growing multipolarity rather than hegemonic rivalry.

4 Trends and patterns

Is 1980–2000 and 2000–present a long enough period to identify significant changes in globalization? Why in a short period of decades would there be significant trend breaks? Essentially, two projects that defined the 1980–2000 period, American hegemony and neoliberalism—both culminating expressions of longer trends—are now over their peak. They are not gone from the stage, but they gather no new adherents and face mounting problems (stagnation, debt, military overstretch, legitimacy crises, rising inequality), and new forces are rising. The new forces stand in an ambiguous relationship to neoliberalism and American hegemony. The overall picture shows new trends in trade, institutions, finance, and hegemony, yet while the trend break with old patterns is undeniable, it is too early to speak of a new configuration. Table 1.3 reviews major trends in contemporary globalization.

Emerging economies have gone through the crises of 1990s and experienced a fast comeback after the 2008 crisis. EM had a 'good crisis', their high growth resumed, domestic and regional markets are growing, they borrow at cheap rates, and they have mostly young populations. Asian EM have grown faster than developed countries in every year since 1980 (except 1998). Their rise represents historical depth as well as a 'deeply rooted historic shift'. Since EM are new forces, theirs is a different path dependence than advanced economies. They engage in new transnational combinations that gradually reshape global dynamics.

The rise of EM, the big story of the 21st century, follows the 'East Asian miracle' of the nineties. Its features include the following:

- Growth—developing countries have been growing much faster than developed countries (which continues in phase three at a slower pace).
- Demand for commodities in China and other EM generates a cycle of high prices.
- Convergence—a gradual convergence of per capita incomes (which is now far off).

- Fast-growing middle classes—which draw Western companies and brands to EM.
- East-South turn—developing countries no longer rely on Western institutions but on markets, loans, investment, aid from Asia and other EM (Chapter 3.5).

This phase ended with the 2008 crash. When the ripple effects of crisis also affected the EU, slowdown spread to EM, and countries shifted to crisis management mode. With the shift from the G8 to the G20 came a comeback of the IMF, with loans from EM and a commitment to increase the vote quota of developing countries. American crisis management involved bank bailouts,

Table 1.3 Trends in multipolar globalization

Pattern 1990s	*Pattern 2000s*
Trade	
North–South trade dominates	Growing East–South trade
US-led trade pacts dominate	FTAA passé, APEC, WTO in impasse
Trend to regional/global trade pacts	Bilateral FTAs; regional pacts in global South
Finance	
Finance capital leads, crisis prone	EM hold dollar surpluses
IMF disciplines developing economies	IMF warns US policies threaten economic stability
US dollar leads	Marginal decline of USD as world reserve currency
US top destination of FDI	China top destination of FDI
IMF blocks Asian monetary fund	Chiang Mai Initiative, Asian Bond Fund, CRA
Western financial markets dominate	New financial flows and SWF outside the West
Investment banks lead	Hedge funds, new financial instruments, fintech
Institutions	
Convergence IMF–WB–WTO	IMF lending down; comeback after 2009
Social liberalism, poverty reduction	World Bank becomes knowledge bank
'Wall Street-Treasury-IMF complex'	Chinese loans to developing countries; NDB, AIIB
Washington consensus	Washington no-consensus
Climate change impasse	Paris climate accord, 2015
Hegemony	
US hegemony solvent and dynamic	US in deficit, in quagmire conflicts
'Clash of civilizations'	Muslim backlash; Al Qaeda, ISIL
US-led security	New security axes and poles

stimulus spending, and QE (tapering off in 2014–2016). The EU, for a complex combination of reasons, opted for austerity, which deepened slowdown. China intervened with a massive stimulus program, marking a shift from export-led to investment-led growth. EM sovereign wealth funds stepped into the liquidity gap in AE and moved in and out of financial assets (Chapter 7.5).

So far, four phases of 21st-century globalization have unfolded: (1) high growth of EM and the commodities boom of 2003–2013; (2) the crash of 2008 and recession in the US and Europe, followed by slowdown in EM; (3) from 2011, recovery in the US and repositioning of EM, especially China; (4) a trend break with Brexit and the election of Donald Trump, in which, in champions of trade liberalization, majorities reject trade liberalization. An overview is in Table 1.4.

The end of the commodities super cycle, slower growth in China, and the end of QE in 2013 and 2014 usher in phase three. Demand for commodities meant easy revenue and QE meant easy money; when both are no longer available, growth slows across EM, currencies fall, interest rates rise, and the receding tide reveals who has been bathing without trunks. With interest rates rising in the US, credit leaves EM. Because their domestic financial markets are smaller, EM rely more on foreign capital than developed countries, and foreign capital is more susceptible to fluctuations (due to political instability, reputation issues, external shocks). Debt bubbles popping in EMDC revisit a debt crisis and bring back the IMF, with the usual conditionalities.

By its nature, the global terrain is replete with grand narratives, sweeping claims, and hegemonic attempts to influence developing countries, such as the Washington consensus. Another claim is that development follows from growth and growth follows from liberalization. Still another is the narrative of 'the end of history' and liberal democracy as the yardstick of political accomplishment. In the 21st century, these claims have been unraveling and ended with the implosion of liberal market economies where majorities reject trade liberalization pacts.

Table 1.4 Phases in the rise of emerging economies

Period	Headings	Keynotes
2000–2009	Boom	High growth, commodities supercycle; Surge of East-South trade
2008–2012	Crash and rebalancing 2009–2010 stimulus	Austerity in EU; QE in US, UK, Japan, EU Advanced economies 4.2% GDP Emerging economies 6.9% GDP
2013–2015	Stormy weather	EM reorient towards regional, global South and domestic markets BRICS NDB, AIIB, new Asian trade pacts US proposes TPP, TTIP; China starts OBOR
2016	Brexit, election of Trump	End of TPP, TTIP, rise of China-backed RCEP

This chapter has mostly dealt with the first period; subsequent chapters discuss further periods. This book's central theme, multipolar globalization, concerns global dynamics. Chapters that follow take this further with oriental globalization, the East-South turn, moving complementarities, the BRICS, international institutions, global value chains, and so forth. Equally important are dynamics *internal* to EM such as the quality of growth, institutions, governance, inequality, agency, and protest. Unfolding at levels below the global, these belong to development studies and sociology, rather than global political economy or globalization. The dynamics are *intermestic,* combinations of international and domestic trends. The chapters that follow combine domestic, regional, and transnational dynamics.

Notes

1 Estimate by Morgan Stanley, *New York Times* 1/10/2010 and IMF estimate 2014. *The Economist,* When giants slow down: The most dramatic, and disruptive, period of emerging-market growth the world has ever seen is coming to its close, 7/27/2013.
2 Marber 1998; Prestowitz 2005; Agtmael 2007; Nederveen Pieterse 2008; Magnus 2010.
3 In sequence: J. Gapper, *Financial Times* 4/23/2009; E. Rigby, *Financial Times* 4/21/2010: 3; G. Silverman, *Financial Times* 10/24/2005; B. Davis, *Wall Street Journal* 1/27/2010: A9; M. W. Sadovi, *Wall Street Journal* 10/21/2008: C8; G. Tett, *Financial Times* 1/22/2010: 6; J. Booth, *Financial Times* 8/29/2007: 22; A. Wood, *Financial Times* 8/4/2008: 4; M. Mobius, *Financial Times* 11/6/2009: 24; K. Chen, *Wall Street Journal* 4/6/2010: A6; Liu Jie, *Shanghai Daily* 7/1/2010: A6; D. K. Berman, *Wall Street Journal* 9/21/2010: C1.
4 Sources, in sequence: Friedman 2005; Florida 2008; Zakaria 2008; Sirkin *et al.* 2008.
5 Morris 2008.
6 Wallerstein 1984.
7 M. Wolf, How the noughties proved to be a hinge of history, *Financial Times* 12/24/2009: 9.
8 Zoellick 2010.
9 Kose and Prasad 2010.
10 *McKinsey* 2010.
11 *Wall Street Journal* 12/6/2009.
12 Tyler Brulé, London: not as liveable as I'd like, *Financial Times* 5/1–2/2010: 20.
13 E. Heathcote, Practice makes perfect: interview, *Financial Times* 3/13–14/2010: 3.
14 Nederveen Pieterse 2009.
15 *Korea Herald* 2008.
16 Kaplinsky and Messner 2008.
17 Teslik 2009.
18 D. Oakley, Building success, *Financial Times* 11/9/2009: 4.
19 Altman 2009.
20 'Still lost in the old Bretton Woods', *Financial Times* editorial 12/28/2009.
21 A. Aslund, *Financial Times* 11/16/2009. R. Sally, The quest for a global solution is misguided, *Financial Times* 3/19/2009.
22 Nederveen Pieterse and Rehbein 2009.
23 Amsden 2003.
24 Stavrianos 1981, 1998; Nederveen Pieterse 1989.

25 Davidson 1978.
26 Huntington 1993.
27 Economic convergence: The headwinds return, *The Economist* 9/13/2014.
28 Gill and Kharas 2007; Woo 2012.
29 Rodrik 2015.
30 C. Whelan, Developing countries' economic clout grows, *International Herald Tribune* 7/10–11/2004: 15.
31 Quoted in Q. Peel, The south's rise is hindered at home, *Financial Times* 11/17/2005: 17.
32 UNDP 2013. A critical assessment is Nederveen Pieterse 2014a.
33 Marber 1998; Agtmael 2007.
34 C. Whelan, Developing countries' economic clout grows, *International Herald Tribune* 7/10–11/2004: 15.
35 M. Vatikiotis, Why the Middle East is turning to Asia, *International Herald Tribune* 6/24/2005.
36 N. Dawar, Prepare now for a Sino-Indian trade boom, *Financial Times* 10/31/2005: 11.
37 M. Lind, How the U.S. became the world's dispensable nation, *Financial Times* 1/26/2005.
38 Gosh 2006: 7. UNCTAD, South-South Trade Continues to Increase, UNCTAD Statistics Show, 12/16/2013. http://unctad.org/en/pages/newsdetails.aspx?Original VersionID=673.
39 Ferguson 1999.
40 See Morris *et al.* 2012.
41 Duménil and Lévy 2001.
42 T. Barghini and V. Pasquali, Composition of Foreign Exchange Reserves 2015, *Global Finance Magazine*, 11/20/2015.
43 E. Becker and E. L. Andrews, IMF says rise in U.S. debts is threat to world economy, *New York Times* 8/1/2004; K. Guha, IMF warns of risk to global growth, *Financial Times* 8/22/2007: 3.
44 S. Donnan, Annual report: IMF warns of four forces that threaten low growth in US, *Financial Times* 6/23/2016: 4.
45 S. Johnson, Indian and Chinese banks pulling out of ailing U.S. dollar, *Financial Times* 3/7/2005; R. Leong and A. Nag, Dollar gains share of global FX Reserves, Euro Shrinks, *Reuters* 3/31/2016.
46 D. Roman, Asia central bankers say it with gold, *Wall Street Journal* 12/28/2009: C10.
47 R. McGregor, Pressure mounts on China forex management, *Financial Times* 11/28/2006: 6. Shi and Nie 2012.
48 G. Magnus, The new reserves of economic power, *Financial Times* 8/22/2006: 11.
49 H. Timmons, Asia finding rich partners in Middle East, *New York Times* 12/1/2006: C1–5.
50 S. Tucker, Asia seeks its centre, *Financial Times* 7/6/2007.
51 S. Herbst-Bayliss, Record number of hedge funds now operating around the world, *Reuters* 6/19/2015; S. Herbst-Bayliss, Hedge funds suffer biggest quarterly drop in assets since 2008, *Reuters* 10/20/2015.
52 US Government Debt, Debts and Deficits, last modified 10/17/2016, www.us governmentdebt.us/; K. Amadeo, Who Owns the U.S. National Debt? *The Balance* 9/6/2016; Treasury Direct, Interest Expense on the Debt Outstanding, last modified 10/6/2016, www.treasurydirect.gov/govt/reports/ir/ir_expense.htm. Estimated $590 billion deficit according to Congressional Budget Office, Budget, last modified 8/2016, www.cbo.gov/topics/budget.

53 IMF, The IMF at a Glance, last modified 10/3/2016, www.imf.org/en/About/ Factsheets/IMF-at-a-Glance. Rasmus 2016 gives an estimate of $100 trillion.

54 B. McKenna, With friends like the IMF and World Bank, who needs loans, *Globe and Mail* 8/16/2005: B11.

55 Ostry *et al.* 2016.

56 Kentikelenis *et al.* 2016.

57 Acharya 2014.

58 Nederveen Pieterse 2004.

59 Mearsheimer and Walt 2005; Petras 2006.

60 The idea of a strategic triangle of China, Russia and India goes back to 1998, well before the BRIC; Titarenko 2004.

61 J. Traub, The world according to China, *New York Times Magazine* 9/3/2006: 24–29.

62 Reifer 2005.

63 Nederveen Pieterse 2008.

64 W. J. Holstein, Erasing the image of the Ugly American, *New York Times* 10/23/2005: B9.

65 F. Stockman, N. Corasaniti, U.S. example loses its sheen in ugly election, *New York Times* 11/6/2016: 1.

2 Oriental globalization

The prominent role of the West in globalization is commonplace. In the 1990s when globalization became a prominent theme it was often associated with forms of Americanization (such as McDonaldization, Barbiefication, Disneyfication, CNN-ization). What then is the role of the Orient in globalization? Is the Orient merely a bystander, a latecomer to the party?

Eurocentric views have been commonplace in relation to globalization, as in many other spheres and have been extensively criticized.[1] The critique of Eurocentrism has gone through several rounds. The first round was primarily a critique of Orientalism. Edward Said and Martin Bernal, among others, focused on cultural bias and racism in Eurocentric history, while others addressed Eurocentric bias in development thinking (Samir Amin, Paul Bairoch, Stavrianos) and history (Eric Wolf, James Blaut, Jack Goody).

In the second round, historians in the global South contributed alternative perspectives, such as Subaltern Studies in India. In addition, revisionist historical studies documented the significance of, in particular, Asia and the Middle East in the making of the global economy and world society. Marshall Hodgson focused on the world of Islam, Janet Abu-Lughod on the Middle East, K. N. Chaudhuri and Philippe Beaujard on the Indian Ocean and South Asia, Andre Gunder Frank on East and South Asia, Kenneth Pomeranz, Robert Temple, and Bin Wong on China, Eric Jones on Japan, and Anthony Reid on Southeast Asia, among many other studies. This body of work not merely critiques but *overturns* the conventional Eurocentric perspectives and implies a profound rethinking of world history that holds major implications for social science and development studies.

1 Oriental globalization past

A major thesis that runs through this body of literature is the Orient came first and the Occident was a latecomer. Frank's *ReOrient* settles on 1400–1800 as the time of 'Asian hegemony' when 'The two major regions that were most "central" to the world economy were India and China'.[2] This centrality was based on 'greater absolute and relative productivity in industry, agriculture, (water) transport, and trade' and was reflected in their favorable balance of trade, particularly in the case of China.[3] Kenneth Pomeranz's *The Great Divergence* offers meticulous comparisons of developments in China and Britain, Geoffrey Gunn draws attention to Southeast Asia as a 'first globalizer', and John Hobson synthesizes this and related literature in *The Eastern Origins of Western Civilization* and coins the term oriental globalization.

In outline the Orient first thesis runs as follows. Global connections may go back to 3500 BCE, or earlier still,[4] but, according to Hobson, 500 CE ranks as the start of oriental globalization and 600 as the beginning of the big expansion of global trade. This timing is based on the revival of camel transport between 300 and 500 CE. At the time, the global economy was centered on the Middle East with Mecca as a global trade hub. In 875 Baghdad ranked as a 'waterfront to the world' linked to China.[5] The Middle East remained the 'Bridge of the World' through the second millennium, but by 1100 (or later, by some accounts) the leading edge shifted to Song China, where it remained until into the 19th century. According to Hobson, in China's 'first industrial miracle' 'many of the characteristics that we associate with the 18th-century British industrial revolution had emerged by 1100' with major advances in iron and steel production, agriculture, shipping, and military capabilities.[6] Stretching from the Middle East to Japan, the East was the early developer—far ahead of Europe in agriculture, industry, urbanization, trade networks, credit institutions, and state institutions. Several historians note that 'none of the major players in the world economy at any point before 1800 was European'.[7] The East was also expansive: The Afro-Asian age of exploration preceded Columbus and Vasco da Gama by about a millennium.[8]

Europe was a late developer and Eastern ideas and technologies enabled European feudalism, the financial revolution in medieval Italy, and the Renaissance: 'oriental globalisation was the midwife, if not the mother, of the medieval and modern West'.[9] In Marshall Hodgson's words, the Occident was 'the unconscious heir of the industrial revolution of Sung China'.[10] Hobson dates China's central role earlier, to circa 1100, and extends it later than Gunder Frank does. In shares of world manufacturing output, according to Hobson, China outstripped Britain until 1860 and 'the Indian share was higher than the whole of Europe's in 1750 and was 85 percent higher than Britain's as late as 1830'.[11] In terms of GNP, Europe had only caught up with the East by 1870; in terms of per capita income—a less representative measure—the West had caught up by 1800.

I will discuss three specific critiques of Eurocentrism that this literature contributes and then give an assessment of this body of literature.

One of the cornerstones of Eurocentrism is the idea that China turned away from maritime trade and that this caused its gradual decline and opened the way for the expansion of European trade in Asia. The revisionist literature argues that the closure of China (and Japan) is a myth and the diagnosis of decline is likewise mistaken. It is true that China did not choose the path of maritime empire, but Western historians have mistaken the official Chinese imperial legitimation policy of upholding the Confucian ideal and condemning foreign trade with the *actual* trade relations, which continued and flourished. That China remained the world's leading trading power shows in the 'global silver recycling process' in which 'most of the world's silver was sucked into China'.[12]

Another cornerstone of Eurocentrism is oriental despotism (and variants such as Weber's patrimonialism). The revisionist literature argues, in contrast, that states such as China and Japan had at an early stage achieved 'rational' institutions, including a 'rational-legal' centralized bureaucracy, minimalist or laissez-faire policies in relation to the economy, and democratic propensities, while the European states during the 1500–1900 'breakthrough period' were far less rational, more interventionist and protectionist, and less democratic: 'eighteenth century China (and perhaps Japan as well) actually came closer to resembling the neoclassical ideal of a market economy than did Europe'.[13] Light taxation and laissez-faire attitudes to enterprise were common in the East long before the West, and throughout the period of comparison, trade tariffs were consistently far higher in Europe than in the East, which shows that the oriental despotism thesis is faulty.

A centerpiece of Eurocentrism is the judgment that other cultures lacked the European commitment to enterprise and accumulation. Weber highlighted the Protestant ethic and described Islam and Confucianism as obstacles to modern development. However, many observers have noted the penchant for commerce in the Islamic world. Viewing Confucianism as an obstacle to development involves historical ironies too: Confucianism ranked as an obstacle in the early 20th century, as in Max Weber's views, was recast as the Confucian ethic hypothesis in the late 20th century and then served to account for the rise of the Asian Tigers. An additional irony is the influence of Confucianism on European thinking. That behind Adam Smith stood Francois Quesnay and the Physiocrats is a familiar point; but the Physiocrats' critique of mercantilism was inspired by Chinese policies and the philosophy of *wu-wei* or non-intervention, which goes back to well before the Common Era.[14] Thus, Confucius emerges as a patron saint of the European Enlightenment.

What is the significance and status of the oriental globalization literature at this stage? There are echoes of dependency theory in this body of work for if it wasn't European genius or other endogenous factors that turned the tide, the role played by colonialism and imperialism in changing the global equation must be significantly larger than is acknowledged in Eurocentric perspectives. One thinks of Eric Williams's work on slavery, Walter Rodney on Africa (*How Europe Underdeveloped Africa*) and other studies. But dependency theory was structuralist in outlook whereas recent revisionist history rejects a global structural approach (such as world-system theory), reckons with contingency, and devotes attention to agency and identity formation. As Hobson notes, 'material power in general and great power in particular, are channeled in different directions depending on the specific identity of the agent'.[15] Dependency thinking came out of the era of decolonization whereas revisionist history refers to global history rather than to history viewed through the lens of a particular region and period. It looks past Fernand Braudel and his 'Mediterranean world' and past world-system theory and its preoccupation with the Low Countries and the Baltic, to far wider horizons, closer to the tradition of William McNeill's global history. These findings also match earlier history such as Cipolla's economic history of Europe and Stavrianos' work on the colonial era.[16]

At times, there is a rhetorical surcharge to this literature that reflects its character as a polemical position. This is a recurrent problem: although the portée of their findings is that the East-West divergence is a fiction and is really a continuum, some oriental globalization literature reverses the current of Eurocentrism by marginalizing the West and centering the East, and thus replays East-West binaries. Taking global history beyond East-West binaries is the thrust of another body of studies.[17]

Oriental globalization literature is uneven in that at times it presents or implies a kind of retroactive Sinocentrism and Indocentrism. For various reasons, China, India, and the Middle East have been more extensively studied and are more salient than other areas. There is frequent mention of the 'Afro-Asian global economy', but the African part remains sketchier than the Asian side. Also, Southeast Asia, Central Asia, and the Mongol Empire often fall between the cracks of the world's major zones.[18]

Oriental globalization research needs to integrate finer grained regional histories and studies such as Reid's work on Southeast Asia, Elverskog on the encounter of the trading religions Buddhism and Islam in Asia, and Hoerder on world migrations during the second millennium.[19] Janet Abu-Lughod also suggests triangulation with local histories, yet she notes 'We can never stand at some Archimedean point *outside* our cultures and outside our locations in space and time. No matter how *outré* we attempt to be, our vision is also distorted'.[20]

While the oriental globalization literature has grown rapidly and is increasingly substantial, it is by no means dominant. Most mainstream thinking continues to view the West as the early developer and Asia and the global South as laggards, or more recently, as upstarts. At the turn of the millennium—following the Soviet demise, the Asian crisis, and neoconservative belligerence in Washington—American triumphalism, though increasingly hollow, set the tone as part of an entrenched 'intellectual apartheid regime'. The Washington consensus was as steeped in Orientalist stereotypes and historical myopia as the neoconservative mission to bring freedom and democracy to the world. Eurocentric economic history à la David Landes (*The Wealth and Poverty of Nations*) and Roberts (*Triumph of the West*) rhymes with Samuel Huntington's clash of civilizations, Bernard Lewis' account of Islam (*What Went Wrong?*), Fukuyama's ideological history (*The End of History*) and Mandelbaum's work (*The Ideas that Conquered the World*). This mindset often continues to inform IMF and World Bank policies (economics without history or anthropology) as well as American aspirations in the Middle East (politics without historical depth), as if development and democracy are virtues that the West chanced upon first and only.

Besides plain ignorance and arrogance, there is something deceptive about Eurocentrism in policy, a trait that Ha-Joon Chang summed up as *Kicking Away the Ladder*.[21] In the 19th century, rising economies applied trade barriers to protect their infant industries while Britain used free trade as a means to deindustrialize colonial economies or to keep them from industrializing; and now WTO statutes and free trade agreements that uphold the intellectual property rights of multinational corporations short-circuit industrialization in the global South. Institutionalized amnesia and intellectual apartheid exist in their own right *and* serve as tools of power.

As the oriental globalization literature overtakes the self-indulgent West-centric view of globalization at an intellectual level, the global adjustments and realignments that are taking shape in the 21st century are gradually catching up with the material side of American supremacism. This diagnosis of the global confluence arrives on the scene at the time that East Asia, China, and India have been reemerging as major forces in the global economy; historiography catches up with the present just as the present is coming full circle with past trends in the world economy. A synthesis that is yet to take shape is that of historical oriental globalization with the jagged edges of contemporary globalization in the making. This is the theme of the next section.

2 Oriental globalization present

> We've had a couple of hundred bad years, but now we're back.
> Economist in Shanghai[22]

Globalization is not what it used to be. Paul Kennedy notes, 'we can no more stop the rise of Asia than we can stop the winter snows and the summer heat'.[23]

In 2011, China overtook Japan as the second largest economy in the world. China is projected to overtake the US as the number one economy in 2026.

> India, the strongest emerging market, is expected to jump to third place, with real growth averaging around 5% by 2050. Plus, Indonesia and Mexico will vault up into the top 10. On the flip side, Germany, the UK, and France will move down in rank, while Russia and Italy will shift out of the top ten.[24]

Now India already ranks as the world's third largest economy.

Several economic advantages have been moving East and to newly industrializing economies. In many parts of Asia (though not in South Korea and China), demographics include young populations—unlike in Europe, the US, and Japan—with great social densities, fast rising levels of education, growing tech capabilities, and rising levels of development. Geographical proximities in Asia and other emerging regions enable rapid learning curves. Another variable in the rise of Asia is what Abdel-Malek called 'the depth of the historical field'.[25] At times, the possibility of hegemonic rivalry and American military designs come up, as in the American 'pivot to Asia'; however, the variables mentioned above are generally not amenable to geopolitical intervention.

A different global equation is in the making and Asia plays a central role along with emerging economics such as Turkey, the Gulf Emirates, and Indonesia as part of the wider radius of oriental globalization. The question is what is the relationship between oriental globalization past and present? To what extent and in which ways does oriental globalization in the past shape and inform oriental globalization in the present? To what extent and in what sense is the rise of Asia not just a rise but a comeback? This is a question of limited status for obviously the discontinuities are as significant as the continuities. New patterns, combinations, and hybridities arising from the interactions with Western societies, global value chains, and the adoption of new technologies are as significant as continuities with the past. Yet, they are also enabled and inflected by continuities with the past, so there is merit to raising this question.

With respect to culture and civilization, continuities between oriental globalization past and present are commonly recognized. Confucianism in the circle of Sinic influence and the idea of a neo-Confucian ethic are part of this.[26] State capability and 'bureaucratically coordinated capitalism' is widely recognized as a crucial component in the rise of East Asia.[27] Dedicated public service and skillful civil servants cannot be adequately understood without the centuries-long legacy of political Confucianism.

Continuities with regard to states and nationhood are also widely recognized. China ranks among the 'continuous nations' with a national identity and state existence stretching back to long before the Common Era.[28] China is also regarded as a civilization-state. The Teen Murti School in New Delhi has also been concerned with Indic civilization, rather than just India.[29]

Besides these common points of reference, we can consider the role of trade routes, migrations, and diasporas. This kind of inquiry is not uncommon. The Annales School built on earlier studies of trade routes by Henri Pirenne and others. In Fernand Braudel's work, the *longue durée* refers to long-term changes in economic and social structures. Evolutionary economics and institutional economics address institutional legacies as part of economic dynamics, as in Douglas North's argument of path dependence. Robert Putnam argues that the success of administrative decentralization in northern Italy and its failure in southern Italy since the 1970s was in large measure attributable to the history of city states in the North from medieval times onward, in contrast to kingdoms in the South and forms of governance that involved less civic allegiance.[30] Thus, in these accounts, configurations going back to medieval and Renaissance times help to account for contemporary dynamics, even though subsequent political and economic configurations have intervened.

In language, culture, and arts, civilizational interconnections persist. The Indo-European languages are a case in point.[31] The *Atlas of World Languages* uses explanatory frameworks that range from climatic and geographical conditions and ancient population movements to intercultural borrowing.[32] History is part of the cultural and institutional capital of nations. The theme of continuity is well on the map in Asia and overseas. In Southeast Asian studies, references to the depth of civilization and the interspersion of the traditional and the modern are common, as well as the idea that the rise of Asia is a Renaissance and is one of many Renaissances.[33]

3 New Silk Roads

These continuities are materially relevant and the widespread comeback of the Silk Roads trope flags them symbolically. The theme of the Silk Road functions as collective memory, as a metaphor of depth and continuity, an invocation of times past and as a host of future projects.[34] New Silk Roads images invoke historic continuities and geographic contiguities and remind us that the links of times past ramify widely and the ripples of past waves of globalization linger on.

Asia was at the center of the world economy during oriental globalization past (OG1) in several capacities—China with silk, tea, and porcelain; India with pepper, cottons, and muslin; Southeast Asia with spices. Asian trade hubs attracted Arab merchants, followed in turn by the Portuguese, the Dutch, the English, and the French.

The new Silk Roads of oriental globalization present (OG2) center on energy (oil and gas), ports and pipelines, sea routes and rail links, infrastructures of trade and communication (fiber optic cables, satellite links), finance and investments (including sovereign wealth funds and Islamic finance). Diasporas, migrations, and geopolitical designs play a part, then as now. Conquerors have come and gone (such as Babar, the Mughals) and empires have waxed and waned along the Silk Roads. Table 2.1 sketches the main episodes of oriental globalization.

Traces of old accumulation treasure and commercial savvy persist in collective memory, circumstances, and artifacts. In many places, the remnants of old trade infrastructures and institutions still exist, and at times new trade connections reactivate ancient trade routes and nodal points. From Kaifeng and Xian in China to Damascus and Istanbul, remnants of the Silk Roads still exist: the actual roads and ports, the caravanserais, the ruins or remains of forts, palaces, and temples.[35] Through most of Asia and the Middle East, as in much of Europe, the physical remnants of thousands of years past are just around the corner.

Table 2.1 Phases of oriental globalization

Time	Place	Keynotes
Oriental globalization 1		
3000 BCE	Eurasia	Bronze Age
1000 BCE	Afro-Eurasian trade	'Commercial revolution'
500 CE	Middle East	West-East direction of trade
1100–1800	Song China, etc.	East-West direction of trade, Silk Roads
1500–1700	Southeast Asia	Spice trade
1200	Levant trade	European Renaissance
Oriental globalization 2		
1868	Rise of Japan	Meiji restoration onward
1970s	Japanese challenge	Flexible accumulation, Toyotism
1980s	Rise of Asian tigers	Developmental states
1990s	New Silk Roads, Gulf Emirates, Turkey, rise of China	Oil, pipelines, ports, fiber optic cables, satellites, economic corridors, SWF
2013	One Belt, One Road, Maritime Silk Road	Silk Road Fund, Asian Infrastructure Investment Bank, high-speed rail

The current industrial and commercial buzz in Asia was foreshadowed in the great Asian bazaar of old times, which besides the Middle East, is the world's oldest bazaar. The industriousness and savvy of Asian markets, abuzz with workshops and merchants, trade emporia, and far flung trade networks, is part of a deep infrastructure of social and institutional densities that predates Europe's Levant trade and European capitalism by hundreds of years.

Routes of migration and trade are two-way carriers of knowledge, technology, language, skills, goods, and investments. They also play a major role in Asia's resurgence. In China's rapid rise as an industrial exporter, investments by the ethnic Chinese in Southeast Asia back to the mainland played a significant part.[36] Increasingly, close economic relations between Taiwan and the mainland are part of this. In India, the role of the non-resident Indians (NRIs) as investors and intellectual and social capital has been rapidly growing and is being actively courted. These relations reactivate old migration links that wire Asian countries with worldwide links. Scholars and entrepreneurs in India are rediscovering their civilizational and economic links with the Arab world and with Persia and Central Asia.[37] The trails of Mughal conquerors and Parsi traders were two-way routes then and are so again.[38]

China and India are now reestablishing their links with Central Asia as avenues of commerce and energy supplies. China is building an oil pipeline from Iran to Pakistan and has initiated a Silk Roads Economic Belt project from Xian through Xinjiang to Central Asia and beyond to Russia and Europe. Gwadar port in Pakistan, leased by China, is a major hub in planned high-speed rail links via Kashgar to Karachi and Gwadar. India is investing in a port in Afghanistan.

'From silk to oil' is a recurrent motif across Eurasia and Central Asia. At the opening ceremony of a new oil pipeline from Baku at the Caspian Sea to Ceyhan at the Mediterranean in May 2005, the President of Turkey said 'This is the Silk Road of the 21st century'.[39] An analysis of Azerbaijan's economic future points out that 'For hundreds of years Azerbaijan's economic promise was tied to its place on the Silk Road, as that bridge between Europe and Asia. These days, it is hard to see how its plans—or promise—could lie anywhere else'.[40] The significance of Asia and its rising middle class is crucial in these assessments. Asia-Europe intergovernmental meetings have also been cast as 'new Silk Routes'.[41]

In mapping the Southwest Silk Road, Bin Yang discusses the ancient confluence of China, India, and Persia in trading and civilizational networks.[42] Ancient trade links between Yunnan, Burma, and India go back to 200 BCE. Routes of trade and migration between China and Southeast Asia also have great historical depth and carry over into present times.[43] Xiangming Chen focuses on the role of crossborder and regional social capital in Asian economies and maps processes of de-bordering and re-bordering over time. He traces trade and migration routes back to the 17th century and finds that areas of high activity in the past such as the Pearl River delta are also active now.[44] Guangzhou (Canton) was a hub in OG1 and again serves as a hub in OG2.

Cultural and economic efflorescence, past and present, has typically been a crossborder or regional phenomenon. Yet most history, particularly since the 19th century, is the history of nation states, and statistics record data primarily in nation state units.

Arif Dirlik criticizes Samuel Huntington's 'clash of civilizations' thesis and contends that the tensions between the regions refer instead to capitalist competition of different cultural and political centers.[45] Dirlik's view is more pertinent than that of Huntington, but it invites two qualifications. One is obvious: of course, the relations are not just relations of rivalry but also of collaboration. The second is that capitalism and capitalist rivalry themselves are categories with limited or contingent explanatory validity and analytical purchase. Gunder Frank's historical work eventually led him to look beyond capitalism as a central explanatory category:

> Far from arguing that capitalism is five thousand years old, I suggest that we should dare to abandon our belief in capitalism as a distinct mode of production and separate system. Why? Because too many big patterns in world history appear to transcend or persist despite all apparent alterations in the mode of production. It therefore cannot be the mode of production that determines overall development patterns. . . . World history since 1500 may be less adequately defined by capitalism than by shifts in trade routes, centers of accumulation, and the existence/ nonexistence and location of hegemonic power.[46]

In an earlier work I noted that:

> This implies a profound challenge to critical political economy; it suggests that many explanations that are held to be fundamental are in fact conjunctural and reflect not just limitations of geography but also limitations of the time frame. Global political economy may overcome the limitations of geography, but the limitations of time are of a different order; it makes a profound difference whether the time frame of explanation is from 1800 or from 1000 BCE or 500 CE.[47]

4 The global *longue durée*

The study of oriental globalization past and present shows that in economics and technology, just as in culture and civilization, taken-for-granted units of analysis—such as the nation state, capitalism—are but provisional approximations, conceptual conventions that in seeking to map the ebb and flow in time and space may lead us astray as often as they guide us. It is not surprising that the history of the *longue durée* should unsettle our analytical categories, such as the nation state and capitalism, for concepts are Zeitgeist categories that are embedded in time. Decolonization involves epistemic decolonization ('emancipate yourself from mental slavery') and the decolonization of imagination.[48] It is interesting that the road to epistemic emancipation runs as often via history as via theory.

The idea of independent invention and regional technological independence,[49] past or present, is probably a fiction. Silk production was exported from China to the Ottoman Empire and Europe, porcelain making traveled from China to Europe in the seventeenth and eighteenth centuries (with Delft blue ware, followed by Wedgwood in England, Sèvres in France, and Meissen in Germany), Chinese agricultural technologies revolutionized English agriculture, and Indian textile crafts and motifs imbued British textile production (as in Paisley, Scotland). In the late 19th and 20th centuries, industrial skills and technologies journeyed from West to East. In the late 20th and 21st centuries, Asian technologies travel West again. Japanese production methods (flexible production, batch production, and the lean firm exemplified by Toyota) and management techniques (such as quality control circles) traveled West as part of the 'Japanese challenge'.[50] Indian software enables the Walmart logistics system. All this is part of long-term movements back and forth of East-West osmosis.[51] The back and forth movement of skills and technologies and the overlaps of old and new routes of trade and migration in the *longue durée* indicate underlying affinities. Oriental globalization and occidental globalization are deeply interwoven and inseparable.

All along, oriental globalization isn't purely oriental and occidental globalization isn't neatly occidental. East-West osmosis is the leitmotiv throughout. Western architects now building modern mosques in the Middle East and redesigning urban environments, and Italian, Japanese, and Dutch architects designing iconic architecture in contemporary Asia are part of this.[52]

Between oriental globalization in the past and the present, oriental globalization has circled the globe. Eurasia was part of the terrain that was traversed (Moore traces the role of Eurasia from the 11th century).[53] Eurasia makes a comeback in the present, in Asian-European dialogues,[54] Russia's Eurasian Union, and China's new Silk Road projects (Chapter 6.5). Seen from the viewpoint of oriental globalization past and present, European development, Eurocentrism, and occidental globalization appear as episodes and phases in much wider polycentric global processes. Table 2.2 gives a précis of occidental globalization.

Throughout, oriental globalization and occidental globalization have been intertwined, with alternating leads in different epochs. The 'first industrial miracle' in China from 1100 onward was the mother of many inventions. We can distinguish several subsequent phases and types of industrialism. British and European industrialism has been craft industrialism with a high component of artisanal skills. American industrialism has been based on mass production (with Taylorism and Fordism). In the 1970s, Japan introduced flexible and batch production with microchips, high knowledge intensity, close worker cooperation (quality control circles), and lean firms. The 21st century ushers in smart production and smart services defined by high-intensity of software, and now China is in the front row, with companies such as Huawei and Xaomi (with a smartphone that uses crowd sourcing to improve its apps).

The Strait of Hormuz was central to early globalization from 800 CE when trade links with Asia and Africa formed the backbone of oriental globalization. The Silk Routes extended these links. Through most of the global *longue durée*, the global economy has been centered on the Orient, as Angus Maddison's long economic time series documents.[55] The history of oriental globalization shows that the lead of Europe and the West dates only from circa 1800, so the hegemonic role of Europe followed by the United States only refers to a brief period of 200 years. With the rise of East Asia and China, the world economy is reverting to where it has been centered through most of the history of the global confluence.

Table 2.2 Phases of occidental globalization

Time	Keynotes
1200–1400	Levant trade and European Renaissance
1500	'The conquest of the world market'
1571	Spanish depot in Manila connects the Atlantic and Pacific exchanges
1600–1850	The Atlantic economy, Triangular Trade
1800	Enlightenment, modernity
1945	The 'American century'
1960s	Multinational corporations
1980–2000	Neoliberal globalization
21C	Recentering of the global economy in Asia

The 21st century sees a comeback of oriental globalization in the emergence of a 'Chime' (China, India, Middle East) economic field. Sovereign wealth funds from the Persian Gulf and Asia play a growing role in investments and vice versa. Growing cooperation along a 'string of pearls' of Seoul, Shanghai, Hong Kong, Singapore, Mumbai, and the Gulf combine the assets of two major surplus economies—East Asia's factory economies and the oil-exporting economies of the Gulf.[56]

Since connectivity is the core of globalization, infrastructures of transport and communication are central to the rhythms of globalization. They play a key role in oriental globalization past and present. China's recent new Silk Road initiatives, One Belt, One Road and Maritime Silk Road projects, merge oriental globalization past and present. Backed by new financial and collaborative instruments, the Silk Road Fund, and the Asian Infrastructure Investment Bank (AIIB with the participation of 57 countries, 2015), they are resuming the ancient Silk Roads and Zheng He's 15th-century sea voyages. They plan to link up with the Indian Ocean, the Persian Gulf, and East Africa, as did Zheng He's voyages. They have predecessors and parallels such as Singapore's hub port in a geostrategic region (a successor to the 15th-century sultanate of Malacca) and the Gulf Emirates that have positioned themselves in geostrategic time zones and amid rising regions, notably the United Arab Emirates and Dubai with investments in a major port and hub airport, which is now the largest in the world.[57] China's One Belt, One Road seeks to connect with these hubs in various ways, with Singapore via the Maritime Silk Road and high-speed rail through Southeast Asia, and with the Gulf via Gwadar port in Pakistan. In addition, China's plans include hubs such as Tehran and Nairobi and building links with Eurasia (see Chapter 6.5). Oriental globalization past and present sets the stage for and is part of the rise of Asia, which the next chapter discusses.

Notes

 1 Amin 1989; Nederveen Pieterse 2015a.
 2 Frank 1998: 166.
 3 Frank 1998: 127.
 4 Wider discussion is Nederveen Pieterse 2012c.
 5 Hobson 2004: 40.
 6 Hobson 2004: 50.
 7 Hobson 2004: 74.
 8 Hobson 2004: 139.
 9 Hobson 2004: 36.
10 Quoted in Hobson 2004: 192.
11 Hobson 2004: 77, 76.
12 Hobson 2004: 66; cf. Frank 1998: 117; K. Bradsher, From the silk road to the super-highway, all coin leads to China, *New York Times* 2/26/2006: WK4.
13 Pomeranz 2000: 70.
14 Hobson 2004: 196.
15 Hobson 2004: 309.

16 Cipolla 1980; Stavrianos 1998.
17 Lieberman 1999, 2003; Whitfield 2003.
18 E.g., see Frank 1992.
19 Reid 1993, 1995, 1997, 2000; Elverskog 2010; Hoerder 2002.
20 Abu-Lughod 2000: 113.
21 Chang 2002.
22 Quoted in Prestowitz 2005: 225.
23 Kennedy 2001: 78.
24 Elena Holodny, China's GDP is expected to surpass the US' in 11 years, *Business Insider* 6/24/2015.
25 Abdel-Malek 1981.
26 See Tu Weiming 2000; Cohen 2000; Arrighi *et al.* 2003.
27 Weiss 1996; Katzenstein 2012; Studwell 2013.
28 Abdel-Malek 1981, Cohen 2000.
29 Kumar and Chandhoke 2000.
30 Putnam 1993.
31 Mallory 1991.
32 Haspelmath *et al.* 2005.
33 Ibrahim 1996; Goody 2010.
34 Abdel-Malek 1994; Wood 2003.
35 Broeze 1989; Whitfield 2004.
36 Chen 2005; Liu 1998; Seagrave 1996.
37 Sadhna Shanker, From the silk route to the IT highway, *International Herald Tribune* 5/25/2005: 9.
38 Nederveen Pieterse 2003.
39 V. Boland, BTC pipeline the 'new Silk Road', *Financial Times* 5/26/2005.
40 S. Donnan, Economic promise is tied to Silk Road, *Financial Times* 3/12/2015: 4.
41 Brennan *et al.* 1997.
42 Bin Yang 2004.
43 Thapar 1992; Sugiyama 1992; Dobbin 1996. On present times see e.g., Yamashita and Eades 2003.
44 Chen 2005.
45 Dirlik 2000.
46 Frank 1996: 44.
47 Nederveen Pieterse 2005: 386.
48 Nederveen Pieterse and Parekh 1995.
49 E.g., Chamarik and Goonatilake 1993.
50 Kaplinsky 1994.
51 Nederveen Pieterse 2015a devotes a chapter to East–West osmosis.
52 E.g., E. Heathcote, Western architects, FT Reports Investing in the Arab world, *Financial Times* 4/18/2016: 5; E. Heathcote, Island of urbanity in an urban desert, *Financial Times* 8/10/2016: 6.
53 Moore 2003.
54 Nederveen Pieterse 2004b.
55 Maddison 2007.
56 Simpfendorfer 2009; Niblock *et al.* 2016.
57 On infrastructure in UAE see Nederveen Pieterse 2010b and Nederveen Pieterse and Khondker, eds. 2010.

3 Asia rising

Moving complementarities

By many accounts East Asia has been the 'winner' in contemporary globalization, which adds to the trope of rising Asia that has been in the air for decades. Part of this is the Japanese challenge of the 1980s. Next was the rise of the Tiger economies, dubbed the 'East Asian miracle' by the World Bank. Soon after came the Pacific century and the Pacific Rim, 'the powerhouse of the twenty-first century', a category that excludes India and includes the American and Latin American west coast. Next came the Asian century, though many added right away that it would rather be a global century. Or, 'the next century will not be Asia's—or anybody's'.[1]

Asia's share of the global economy in purchasing power parity terms rose steadily from 7 percent in 1980, to 21 percent in 2008, and to 38.8 percent in 2014. Asian stock markets accounted for 32 percent of global market capitalization in 2010 (ahead of the US at 30 percent and Europe at 25 percent) and 33.3 percent in 2016.[2]

> Without doubt, the biggest single global shift reshaping the contours of the global economic map is the resurgence of East Asia to a position of global significance, commensurate with its importance before 'the West' overtook it in the nineteenth century. . . . The result is a shift in the center of gravity of the world economy, a shift that seems now to be on solid foundations and not a mere passing phase.[3]

High growth in Asia inspired the idea 'Asia Good, America Bad' along with 'Asian values' and a neo-Confucian boom.[4] 'Go east, young man' became the motto for bankers, MBAs, car makers, wine merchants, luxury goods traders, architects, and so forth. The refrain is familiar. With this has come a new confidence of Asians talking back, particularly after the 2008 crisis. Asians wryly echoed what Westerners had told them in the past.

> In many ways, US and European policy makers are doing the opposite of what they advised Asian policy makers to do in 1997–98: do not rescue failing banks, raise interest rates, balance your budget. Millions of Indonesians and Thais would have been better off if their governments had been permitted to do what western governments are doing now.[5]

China holds up a mirror to the United States too and voices are getting louder that the US should change course and 'shed its taboo on economic planning'.[6] A sampling of headlines of this period:

> Speak up, Asia, or the west will drown you out (Nair 2007)
> Why Asia stays calm in the storm (Mahbubani 2008)
> Lessons for the west from Asian capitalism (Mahbubani 2009)
> Asian wisdom: the US and Europe could use a refresher course in Eastern studies (Mahbubani 2010)
> The west's preaching to the east must stop (Chan 2010)
> East offers west a macro-prudential blueprint (Lyons 2010)
> Asia has had enough of excusing the west (Mahbubani 2011)
> China calls for 'responsible' US (Rabinovitch 2011)
> Chinese central banker chides U.S. (Dean and Back 2011)[7]

This rhetoric tapered off when not only the US but also Europe going into recession affected Asian economies. The US Federal Reserve policy of quantitative easing also gave a different twist to the conversation. Weaknesses of Asian economies came to the fore—the export trap, the dollar trap, China buying US Treasuries—and prompted policy changes such as boosting regional trade pacts and diversifying monetary policies.

The period 2000–07 saw the fastest growth of world trade in history. Emerging markets were driving the world economy, yet there was no decoupling of EM and the West. Asian developing countries' ratio of exports to GDP rose from 36 percent in 2000 to 47 percent in 2007. In trade balances and current accounts, East Asia has been on the upside of global economic imbalances. East Asian economies and Germany are the world's leading factory economies and exporters of manufactured goods. Energy exporters (Saudi Arabia, the Emirates, Russia, Norway) are the other main category of surplus economies. Asian EM lead multipolar globalization but are dependent on exports and are tethered to a post-bubble world economy. East Asia is a major beneficiary of contemporary globalization, but sustainable prosperity poses major challenges. China and East Asian societies aspire to be responsible stakeholders of the global system—but of what kind of global system? And on what terms does the global system let them in? How should rising Asia balance global competitiveness and domestic needs and the quantity and quality of growth?

We have entered a new phase in the interaction of capitalisms. The Washington consensus survived the crises of the nineties in tatters. In the wake of the 2008 crisis, we left its remnants behind and the question is, for what— for an East Asian model, a Beijing consensus, Seoul consensus, a Southern consensus, the Rhineland model (questionable in view of the problems of the Eurozone), the German model (questionable in view of Germany's role in the EU)? Besides high growth, do East Asian countries represent an alternative model that holds wider implications for the world economy and for developing countries? This involves disentangling the relations between rising Asia and contemporary globalization.

Why devote a chapter to Asia and not to Latin America or Africa? The reasons, in short and elaborated in this chapter are:

- Asia leads in terms of historical depth. In view of the history of oriental globalization, the rise of Asia is a comeback in a sense that doesn't apply to other world regions (Chapter 2).
- Asia leads in terms of size. The Swedish statistician Hans Rosling describes the world's pin code as '1114'—'of the planet's 7bn people, roughly 1bn live in Europe, 1bn live in the Americas, 1bn in Africa and 4bn in Asia'.[8]
- Three of the world's four largest economies are now in Asia: China first (the US is second), India third, Japan fourth.[9] China overtook the US in terms of purchasing power as the world's largest economy in 2014 (IMF assessment).
- From Meiji Japan and the Tiger economies to 21st-century China, Asia has been crucial to the rise of emerging economies and NIEs. Asian drivers have been propelling Latin America, Africa, and the Middle East.

The first section of this chapter reviews the rise of Japan and problematizes the category of Asia. The second theme is moving complementarities—Asia has risen as part of wider constellations with shifting dynamics over time. Third, the complementarities involve competition and rivalry, part of which is a clash of capitalisms. During past decades, American institutions were able to impose their influence on developing countries; are they still able to do so in the 21st century with growing deficits and weaker hegemony? Fourth, in Asia the quality of growth has become a more pressing concern than the quantity of growth. The fifth theme is the role of Asian drivers in the multipolar world and East-South relations, which is considered by examining China's relations with Africa and Latin America. Finally, what dilemmas emerge for Asia's role in the multipolar world?

1 From Asianism to Asia

When confronted with the growing might and technical lead of industrialized Western countries, several countries undertook reforms. The Habsburg Empire failed to implement reforms while Prussia succeeded. Russia under

Count Witte sought to implement reforms with heavy industry and a war navy. British interventions blocked industrialization efforts in Egypt (Muhammad Ali) and Persia. The Tanzimat reforms in the Ottoman Empire and reforms in Qing China failed (too little, too late), and in the nonwestern world only Japan's reforms were successful. Why only in Japan? This is a large question, but several elements stand out.

The first is Japan's long history of selective engagement and smart borrowing, beginning with its early relations with China. In the 16th century, Japan ousted the Portuguese, not least because of the Jesuits' proclivity for conversion to Christianity and let in the Dutch who were 'less Christian'. Dutch traders were confined to a trading post on Deshima island, which served as a source of European learning for centuries. In the 19th century, Japan sent learning missions to Western countries. Japan learned in particular from the Prussian and German examples.

In the early 1800s, Alexander Hamilton, posted in the British West Indies, saw up close the efficacy of tariff protection policies, which he later implemented in the American Republic. Friedrich List served as secretary of Hamilton and upon his return to Germany advocated similar policies, which resulted in the customs union of 1853 that prefigured the unification of the German Reich in 1871. Bismarck's policies (tariff protection, unification, national economic planning, heavy industry, military industries) served as a model for others. Like Germany, Russia and Japan built a war industry and navy. There are parallels between the Prussian Junkers, Russian Boyars, and Japan's samurai, landholding classes that were redeployed in a larger national project.

All rising powers at the time undertook aggressive projects of territorial expansion, with a view to aggrandizement and control over resources for industrialization. The American Republic undertook its 'westward march' of continental expansion. Russia sought expansion in Eurasia and Central Asia and clashed with the British Empire in Afghanistan. France colonized Algeria and expanded into the Mashrek. Germany undertook overseas colonial expansion (Togo, Tanganyika, Namibia) in the 19th century and continental Lebensraum in the 20th century. Japan incorporated adjacent territories (Ryukyu, Hokkaido in the 18th century) and sought expansion in Asia. Italy sought expansion in Ethiopia and Libya. These expansion projects came to a head in, successively, the Franco-German war of 1870, the 'new imperialism' of the late 19th century, the scramble for Africa, the Great Game in Asia, the Russo-Japanese war, and the First and Second World Wars, a long period of hegemonic rivalry with a series of wars of hegemonic succession.[10]

Facing challenges from France, Germany, and Russia, the British Empire 'subcontracted' control of the Pacific arena to the United States (which led to American colonization of the Philippines) and to Japan to serve as counterweight to Russia in the Far East. British loans and armaments supported Japan's rise and contributed to Japan's victory over Russia in 1906, which sent a shockwave through Asia and the colonized world—the first nonwestern state to defeat a Western power! It was followed by Japan's expansion in Asia in the 1930s, the Greater Asian Co-Prosperity Sphere.

Japan followed Germany's path (which shared elements with the American Republic such as protectionism and rivalry with Britain) and other Western patterns in several respects: protectionism to shield infant industries, heavy industry, a military-industrial complex, and wars of regional expansion and colonization. The emphasis on military industries matched the paths of France, Germany, and Russia. As in Prussia and Russia, the landed aristocracy was mobilized as part of the national revival project. As in Germany, Japan brought back the emperor system. Japan's trajectory also differed from Western patterns in several ways: Japan did not simply use new conquests for resource extraction (although this was the case in much of the Asian Co-Prosperity Sphere) but also established industries in colonized areas, in Korea and Taiwan.

For 18 of the past 20 centuries, Asia has accounted for over half of world output and is now returning to that position of economic dominance.[11] Oriental globalization predates occidental globalization by many centuries and stretches over a much longer time span (Chapter 2). During the 1600s and 1700s, China held the world's treasure in the form of the largest holds of silver[12] and now does so again with the world's largest current account and foreign reserves holdings. The rise of Asia is a comeback, a resurgence. A reasonable hypothesis is that the lead of the Asian Tigers has been enabled by the depth of the historical field, though just what that entails isn't clear. Given its deep history, Asia holds a special place in both historical and contemporary globalization, and its resurgence should not be underestimated.

For developing countries, 'Looking East' has been the norm for decades. East Asian societies have been able to achieve rapid development, industrialization, and urbanization while building relatively equal societies, mitigating some of the wrenching consequences of modernization. Northeast Asian experiences have been a major inspiration for the human development approach. The role of developmental states in Northeast Asia broadly parallels industrial policy and neo-mercantilism in Europe and catchup policies in Central and Eastern Europe. Chalmers Johnson coined the term developmental state originally with reference to Japan.[13]

Northeast Asian experiences involve land redistribution, proactive state institutions capable of delivering public goods and coordinating and supporting the private sector; gradual market reforms; export-oriented industrial policy; prudent macroeconomic policy in relation to the exchange rate and limiting external borrowing.[14] Beyond this profile, is there an 'Asian model'? Since East Asian societies are also arenas of struggle, what is there to emulate?[15] The heady days of Asianism—as in 'Asian values', the neo-Confucian ethic—have given way to more sober perspectives. This includes rethinking the developmental state. For developing countries seeking to emulate the Asian Tigers, the authoritarian neo-mercantilism of the seventies and eighties has evolved to a new standard of democratic, agile developmental states.

Asianism gives way to the deconstruction of Asia. As Mahathir Mohamad noted, 'Asia is only an arbitrary geographical entity. It is not a political entity.

It is not even an ethnic entity'.[16] Asia is a European construct. Asia in the plural includes the Asia of Japan's 'greater East Asian co-prosperity sphere', the Asia of decolonization and liberation movements, Asia divided by the Cold War, along with pan-Asianism, socialist Asia, Confucian Asia, multi-cultural Asia.[17]

With Asian modernization also comes theme park Asia, products of authoritarian planning: 'Every theme park is a controlled utopia, a miniature world in which everything can be made to look perfect'.[18] Mao's China, Deng Xiao Ping's model capitalist cities in China's coastal areas and Special Economic Zones, the Singapore and Hong Kong models display this trend in varying degrees and so does Seoul as 'a world capital of design'. 'We could say', according to the Dutch architect Rem Koolhaas, 'that Asia as such is in the process of disappearing, that Asia has become a kind of immense theme park. Asians themselves have become tourists in Asia'.[19] Thus, Asia is slipping away at the same time as it is rising.

Asia is a much larger geographical zone, less historically interwoven and culturally far more diverse than Europe. Europe is a much smaller, compact geographical area. The European Union is a bundle of different capitalisms—the coordinated market economies (CME) of Nordic Europe, France's state-led market economy (SME, now increasingly a CME), the patronage capitalism of Mediterranean countries, and the UK's liberal market economy (LME), until Brexit. Likewise, Asia hosts different capitalisms, still more diverse than Europe.

The state sector is large across Asia: 'state-run firms make up 40% of Asia's total and family-run firms, often conglomerates or "business houses", account for 27%' with some variation across countries.[20] Thus, in Asian countries, the state sector is the largest and comprises state-owned enterprises (SOEs), the government-linked corporations (GLC) of Singapore and Malaysia, and sovereign wealth funds. The second largest sector in most countries is the family-run conglomerates, such as the chaebol in South Korea (Daewoo, Samsung) and the conglomerates in India (Tata, Birla, Reliance, Mittal). In China, SOEs occupy this terrain. The third segment is the private sector of small family-owned and managed enterprises. A fourth domain is the informal sector, which is large from South to Southeast Asia.

In China alone, three market economies coexist: the SOEs, the private sector of family-owned and managed enterprises (characterized as 'network capitalism'), and the public-private partnership corporations of local governments.[21] Most Southeast Asian economies are hybrid CME that combine state control (GLC, sovereign wealth funds), liberal market strands, foreign companies and joint ventures, and the network capitalism of family-owned enterprises. South Korea has gradually morphed to a CME. In Japan, the CME predominates. In both, large conglomerates play a key role.

Different Asian societies face different problems. A recent headline is 'From Seoul with sorrow'.[22] Among the problems are the chaebol:

Chaebol conglomerates, the pride of the nation abroad, are considered by many to be economic bullies at home, blamed for squeezing suppliers and pushing small businesses into bankruptcy. Whatever the impressive macro-economic data suggest, more Koreans feel poor, overworked and weighed down by social pressures.[23]

'Economic democratization' is on the agenda in the 'Republic of Samsung', but path dependence makes it difficult to deliver.[24] Following the flexibilization of the labor market that was introduced under IMF pressure in 1998, contract labor is now the largest segment of the labor force at close to 50 percent.[25] Such is 'the cost of Korea's chaebol-led success: a widening income gap, struggling small businesses, and the highest suicide rate in the developed world'.[26] State-led modernization and global competitiveness have been achieved at the cost of creating a high-anxiety society. The young are under the stress of school, cramming, and 'exam hell'; workers face the stress of job insecurity; the elderly face the stress of no longer being cared for by their children and growing numbers turn to suicide.

Korea ranks high in global brands, innovation, global market reach and is export-dependent. A Wall Street view is that 'Korea is the quintessential leveraged bet on global trade . . . The moment there's any form of doubt in worldwide growth or exports or trade, the Korean market is susceptible to a selloff'.[27] According to Thomas Palley, 'the possibility of global development via export-led growth is now exhausted'. Key problems are waning consumer demand and protectionism in AE; emerging markets' exports hinder the recovery of industrialized economies and crowd out exports of other developing countries; increasing South-South competition; declining prices of manufactured goods; and the ability of multinational corporations to shift production to lower-cost countries.[28]

2 Moving complementarities

All along Asia has risen as part of wider geopolitical and geoeconomic constellations, and its development must be viewed also in relation to external forces. The following is a brief account of major transnational complementarities (brief and schematic to avoid this turning into a world history):

1   Japan's rise from the late 19th century onward occurred at the confluence of the rise and the example of Bismarck Germany and the weakening of the British Empire.[29] The victorious war with Russia (1904–05) also put Japan on a path of military industrialization and regional expansion and eventually led to the Axis of the Second World War.

2   Another major transnational complementarity unfolded during the Cold War with the Korean and Vietnam wars in which Japan, South Korea, and Southeast Asian countries served as American bases and suppliers in the war effort. American influence at this stage also involved land reform and political changes, showcasing Asian frontier economies as capitalist success stories.[30]

3   As part of the 'new international division of labor' from the 1970s onward, basic industries from the US and Europe relocated to low-wage countries in Asia and Latin America. Thus, industrialization in East Asia was a counterpart of deindustrialization in the US and Europe. Cheap manufactured goods from Asia eased the rise of postindustrial society in the West. East Asia entered industrial modernity as the West entered postindustrial conditions. Walmart capitalism and notions such as 'Chamerica' are expressions of this complementarity.

4   The relationship between industrialization and urbanization in Asia (and Latin America) and commodity-exporting developing countries that took shape in the 1990s and peaked during the commodities boom of 2003–09 is a further major phase of intercontinental complementarity. This period is associated with the Asian drivers and a surge of growth in developing countries, the rise of EM and the BRICS (with Brazil and Russia as major exporters of agro-mineral commodities and energy) (discussed in section 5 below).

5   As part of global rebalancing after the 2008 crisis, economies the world over have been repositioning. To make up for slowing demand in the West, Asian economies adjust by substituting regional and domestic demand. Growing regional cooperation in East Asia (the East Asian Economic Caucus, the ASEAN Economic Community, ASEAN plus Three, the Asian Bond Fund, etc.) strengthens competitiveness by developing economies of scale in several industrial sectors, as Gill and Kharas discuss.[31] China is the major force in this readjustment that is increasingly taking the form of a China-centric regional production and value network. China's One Belt, One Road, Silk Road Fund, and Asian Infrastructure Investment Bank are part of this reorientation (Chapter 6.5).

6   Economic stagnation and financialization in AE leads Western investors to look for yield in EM and Asia. QE in advanced economies makes liquidity available in EM (Chapter 6.4).

7   Popular opposition to liberal trade pacts in the US and EU mark the end of US-sponsored Trans-Pacific Partnership (TPP) and Transatlantic Trade Initiative Partnership (TTIP). The leadership of global trade shifts to China, which begins a new era (Chapter 10).

Moving complementarities follows from multipolarity: multiple centers and zones of influence engage in shifting relations of cooperation and competition; shifting combinations of centers generate fields that imprint epochs of development. Several points follow from this overview. First, the unit of analysis of development isn't simply the country but the economic and political field that it is part of. Second, relations of complementarity are dynamic. Third, shifting external relations are accompanied by changes in domestic institutions. Changing external conditions are not sufficient conditions but are enabling factors; domestic capabilities and institutions must rise to the occasion to make use of emerging economic and political opportunity structures. Because there is reflexivity, agency, and choice along the way, outcomes are contingent. Fourth, complementarities are multidimensional; they involve geopolitical dynamics (as during periods of hegemonic rivalry), regimes of regulation, changing technologies, and economic fortunes. The mix of geopolitical and economic variables changes over time. Fifth, complementarities entail not just cooperation but also competition, rivalry, and attempts at hegemony that seek to steer and control the next phase of complementarity. Part of this is an entanglement or clash of capitalisms, which the next section explores.

3 A clash of capitalisms

Thus, outside forces are part of the equation. According to Mahbubani, what 'the irresistible shift of global power to the East' means also depends 'on how the West reacts to the rise of Asia'.[32]

In relation to capitalism and globalization there are, with simplification, two general positions. One view holds that capitalism is a global system and institutional variations are minor in relation to its overall logic, as in world-system analysis, transnational capitalist class, and 'neoliberalism everywhere' perspectives.[33] The alternative view is, as Dani Rodrik puts it, we have globalization but we don't have global capitalism.[34] Examples of this perspective are varieties of capitalism, comparative capitalisms, new institutional economics approaches, and most development studies. In this view, capitalisms of diverse institutional stripes interact in complex ways. Comparative institutional advantage and institutional arbitrage function by virtue of diversity, sustain diversity, and keep capitalism overall ticking, as in the complementarities discussed earlier. The transnational interplay of capitalisms combines cooperation (global production and value networks, international supply chains, interfirm tie-ups, investments, finance) and competition (market share, brands, intellectual property rights, finance).

Hegemony plays a role by upholding a particular constellation of capitalism as the norm in discourse, trade regimes, credit ratings, and international financial institutions. American hegemony dominated during 1980–2000 and its influence is ongoing, without the momentum of the nineties and with the trend break of the Trump election. Then the motto was 'there is no alternative', this is the only game in town; now alternatives to Anglo-American capitalism are salient. During past decades, the 'Wall Street-Treasury-IMF complex' was able to impose its influence on developing countries and rising economies. The regime of neoliberal discipline, allegedly a regime of market forces, benefitted American MNCs and banks. We can term this a clash of capitalisms, in which friction and conflict is interspersed with cooperation. The choice of words is a spoof on Huntington's clash of civilizations and draws attention to contentions in global political economy that may be less visible and yet as important as or weightier than civilizational frictions. With shorthand simplification, in vignettes, episodes that illustrate Anglo-American attempts to dominate other economies and EM include the following:

Japan—in the 1985 Plaza Accord, the G5 agreed on an appreciation of the Japanese yen which together with the devaluation of the US dollar (the 1995 'reverse Plaza Accord') affected the trade balance between the US and Japan.[35]

Russia—Washington-inspired market-shock therapy weakened the state and unleashed the uncontrolled privatization and oligarchs of the 'wild nineties'. The Putin government brought back the security state and the 'vertical of power'.

Developing countries—the Washington consensus and structural adjustment programs of the 1990s produced 'lost decades' in Latin America and Africa. NICs that did emerge during this period were those that were *not* dependent on the IMF—the Asian Tigers, China, and India. Because they had no or little external debt, they were not part of the 'Third World debt crisis' and were under no obligation to follow Washington prescriptions. In the ensuing period, the Asian drivers play a growing role in developing countries—which is discussed in section 5.

The Asian crisis—IMF intervention in Southeast Asia and South Korea in the 1997/98 crisis imposed austerity at a critical juncture, earned the IMF the nickname 'the master of disaster', and triggered a neoliberal turn in South Korea. Chalmers Johnson used the term clash of capitalisms to describe IMF intervention in the crisis.[36] The lesson of the Asian crisis for developing countries was the importance of financial prudence and autonomy.

The Eurozone—Goldman Sachs and other banks helped the Greek and Italian governments to conceal the size of their budget deficit when entering the Eurozone. American banks operating through shell companies in Amsterdam established a 'financial Wild West' in Ireland.[37] These operations made the EU vulnerable to the crash of 2008.

Germany—the securitization of subprime mortgages culminated in the 2007–08 crisis. The subprime mortgages, derivatives, and credit default swaps were also fraud on a massive scale, a vast money laundering scam with, in Michael Lewis' words, German banks and 'Düsseldorf' as 'the mark'.[38] Austerity policies in Germany and the EU, inspired by German Ordo-liberalism and neoliberal thinking represent a 'creeping neoliberalization' of Europe.[39]

China—there has been ongoing US pressure on China to appreciate the RMB with tariffs on Chinese imports (steel, tires) and threats of further tariffs. China resisted, having learned from Japan's experience in the 1980s.[40] Restrictions on Chinese companies buying companies and assets in the US, Germany, and Australia and growing protectionism signal a different posture, also on the part of Trump.

The WTO—according to Rodrik, the WTO Agreement on Subsidies constrains industrial policy in developing countries and forces them to take recourse to monetary policy instruments (such as China's vast stimulus spending that led to its over-investment cycle).[41] Built into the WTO rules are principles of the LME, while EMDC are coordinated (CME) or SME. Rodrik advocates revision of WTO rules.

Trade pacts—the stalled Doha round of trade negotiations initiated in 2001 stalemates the WTO and other trade initiatives come to the fore. The TPP backed by the US and Japan was the latest bid to bring rising Asia within the sphere of Anglo-American capitalism. Its terms include the right of corporations to sue governments for anticipated loss of profits if governments adopt laws that impinge on their profitability, so it poses a major constraint on government policy and in effect rules out developmental states. The TTIP imposed similar rules. The TPP excluded China, but its failure puts China in the cockpit of global trade.

Banks—one reason why the six remaining megabanks in the US are so large ('too big to save'), condoned by the US government, is to secure them a front seat in the anticipated financial deepening in EM, particularly in Asia. JP Morgan and other American banks hired relatives of 'princelings' in bids to attract lucrative contracts and penetrate Chinese inner circles.[42]

Financialization—maintaining global production and value networks requires a wide financial base. EM join global finance at a time when Anglo-American megabanks rule. Asian countries have several options in relation to the megabanks. The first is to limit financial exposure and external borrowing and maintain a surplus as hedge against financial turbulence—the lesson of the Asian crisis. Second, they can concentrate financial dealings within the 'string of pearls' of Seoul, Shanghai, Hong Kong, Singapore, Mumbai (with the proviso that Wall Street and London firms are also represented there). Third, a trend is to extend this cooperation to the Gulf Emirates[43] and reduce exposure to Wall Street and London. The weakening oil-dollar system (with oil traded in other currencies), the rise of trading in RMB, the Asian Infrastructure Investment Bank, China's Silk Road Fund, and the BRICS New Development Bank and CRA point towards alternative approaches.

Neoliberalism—does the rise of China, India, and other EM uphold or bypass neoliberalism? The rise of EM is both enabled by and transcends neoliberal globalization. Liberalization and export orientation—the Washington consensus and World Bank formula—contributed to the rise of Asia.

The discussion takes place in a battlefield of paradigms, an arena in which few statistics, diagnoses and policies are ideologically neutral. Economic success and failure don't come with radio silence but are immersed in ideological noise and filtered through politics of representation. The World Bank claimed the 'East Asian miracle' as evidence of the wisdom of its policies of liberalization and export-led growth, while according to Japan it showed the virtues of capable government intervention.[44] According to Alan Greenspan, the Asian crisis demonstrated that Anglo-American capitalism was the only viable economic model. Most others have drawn the opposite conclusion that American-led finance capital is crisis prone; this has been one of the spurs of the turn of the millennium trend break in globalization patterns.

If we consider neoliberalism as cultural politics, EM surely match neoliberal trends. Middle-class consumerism and its features—marketing, commercial media, malls, and shopping culture—is a leading trend throughout EM. A headline reads 'Developing countries underpin boom in advertising spending': 'Advertising spending is soaring in the developing world, suggesting that US-style consumerism is alive and well from Brazil and Russia to Saudi Arabia and Indonesia'.[45]

If we consider economic doctrine, market fundamentalism is widely rejected. If we focus on neoliberal economics, the picture is less clear. To the extent that neoliberalism refers to monetarism and fiscal conservatism (which is contentious), many EMDC are *more* neoliberal than American fiscal profligacy. Fiscal conservatism aims to counteract inflation and avoid a deficit and financial turbulence.

EMDC must strike a cautious balance. While in most of the global South it is a cliché that neoliberalism doesn't work, international financial markets continue business as usual, so for developing countries diplomacy is in order. Deficit countries cannot afford to offend the hegemonic institutions and credit regimes. Most countries must walk a tightrope and remain on reasonably good terms with financial markets and credit rating agencies lest their cost of borrowing and doing business goes up.

These are different reasons than during the nineties. Then the main considerations were debt and dependence on the Washington institutions, which now applies to fewer countries, and a default belief in free market policies as the most dynamic and pro-growth, which has lost appeal since the crises of the nineties and 2008. If American deficits are crisis prone and inequality in the US has been growing steeply, does it make sense to follow this model? Now EM follow neoliberal policies (in the minimal sense of fiscal conservatism) to *escape* from neoliberalism (in the sense of the ideology and regime of the 'free market').

If neoliberalism refers to high-exploitation capitalism, again the picture is mixed. It does not generally apply to the Tiger economies, South Korea, Taiwan, or Singapore, at least in the sense that they have sizeable public sectors and social policies (which don't apply to migrant labor). It does apply to China where migrants from the countryside have been essential to the razor sharp 'China price' and to India where the rural economy and the urban poor support the modern sector with cheap labor, services, and produce. Thus, inequality has not been a just so circumstance or a minor quirk en route to growth but a fundamental factor in production and in establishing the international competitiveness of several EM. In China, this has begun to change since the adoption of the 'harmonious society' policy in 2005. In India, high-exploitation capitalism, buttressed by caste in the countryside, continues unabated without major changes in government policy.

'Beating them at their own game' and using market forces to develop while keeping one's identity is a difficult balancing act for competitiveness and means conforming to business standards in which, so far, some aspects of neoliberalism remain a default policy. This often means that existing structures of inequality such as caste or ethnicity are reworked.

4 The quality of growth

Limitations of growth narratives are that they are short term, subject to volatility, and growth falls short of development. Economic growth dominates media and business accounts, yet in contemporary development studies it comes only with qualifiers—sustainable growth, broad-based growth, inclusive growth, pro-poor growth, and so forth. The quality of growth has become nearly as important as the quantity of growth, because low-quality growth is a discount on the growth rate. The report of the Commission on Growth and Development set inclusive growth as standard, which is echoed in World Bank discussions on New Growth paradigms and in the Sustainable Development Millennium Goals.

While there are many measures of the quality of growth (such as gender equity, wellbeing, livability, pollution, sustainability), I focus on social inequality as an indicator of the extent to which growth is shared and development is inclusive. Measures of inequality include the Human Development Index (HDI), the HDI adjusted for inequality (IHDI), and the Gini coefficient.

The HDI for East Asia shows a major rise from 1980 to the present with South Korea in the lead. China is in sync with this trend and so is India at a lower level (Figures 3.1 and 3.2). When the HDI is adjusted for inequality, China's rank drops but drops not as steeply as that of India (Figure 3.3). China's HDI is 0.687, with a rank of 101 out of 187 countries. The HDI of East Asia and the Pacific as a region rose from 0.428 in 1980 to 0.671 (2010), which places China above the regional average.[46]

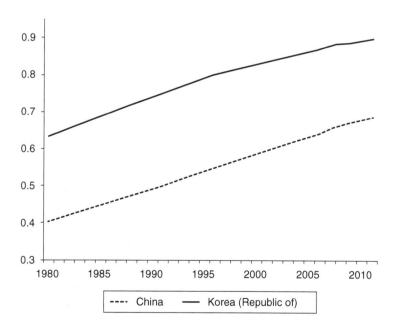

Figure 3.1 Human Development Index in China and Korea, 1980–2010

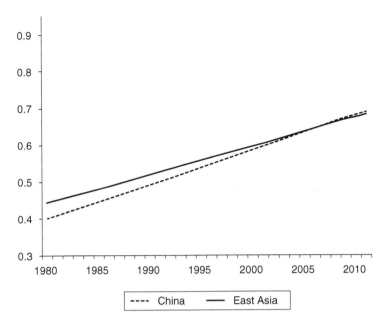

Figure 3.2 Human Development Index in China and East Asia, 1980–2010

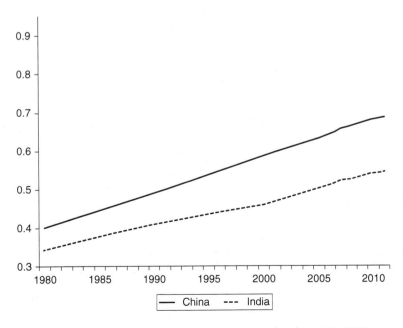

Figure 3.3 Human Development Index in China and India, 1980–2010

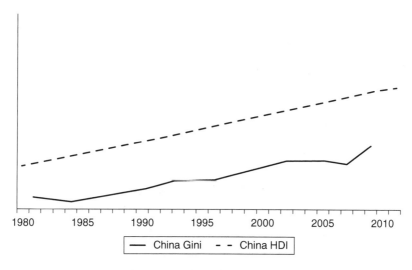

Figure 3.4 Human Development Index and Gini in China, 1980–2010

China's Gini index shows that the increase of inequality slowed from 2002, but increased again after 2007 (Figure 3.4). China's Gini index stood at 0.412 in 2000, rose to close to 0.5 in 2010 and in 2011 was 'a little higher than 2010', according to the National Bureau of Statistics. A report notes, 'The country's Gini coefficient has already reached a high, if not dangerous level. It is at a point that "is threatening" social security. Little room is left for the index to grow'.[47]

While these are only sketchy assessments, in terms of growth and inequality we can identify four broad clusters in rising Asia. First, Northeast Asian economies with steady growth, high HDI, and low Gini index. Second, China with high growth, rising HDI, and high and rising Gini index. Third, Southeast Asia tends to match the China pattern. Fourth, India with high growth, rising HDI, and steeply rising inequality.

As to how to interpret these differences there are various registers, which is beyond this discussion (Chapters 5 and 8), but brief notes follow. Northeast Asia shares features (not uniformly, but more or less) of continuous states over a long period, relative homogeneity, and high social cohesion; Sino-Confucian cultures share traditions of public service, openness, and long-distance trade, geographic proximity to Japan, and postwar land reform. Southeast Asia features greater ethnic and religious heterogeneity, profound experiences with colonialism, the enduring influence of patrimonial elites interacting with new capitalist forces, and much industry is low-value assembly production.[48] Only eight Asian names (Toyota, Honda, Canon, Nintendo, Panasonic, and Sony from Japan, and Samsung and Hyundai from South Korea) appear in the league table of the world's top 100 brands: 'the continent that accounts for nearly

30 per cent of the world economy and 60 per cent of its population boasts fewer global brands than Germany, which has 10'.[49]

Fernand Braudel distinguishes between capitalism and the market economy: the capitalist sector engages in power plays and is oligopolistic, while the market economy is competitive and juggles narrow profit margins.[50] Relations between the sectors differ by country. Capitalist forces are strong throughout Asia (keiretsu, zaibatsu, chaebol, and India's conglomerates such as Tata, Reliance, and Mittal), but the extent to which they dominate the economy and set the rules varies. Whether in China they shape institutions and dominate the articulation of modes of production is in dispute. Giovanni Arrighi views China as a market economy under the direction of state agencies, while Harvey, Dirlik and Hart-Landsberg view China's situation as simply capitalism (with Chinese characteristics).[51] To some extent the latter applied when the 'Shanghai model' was the driver of Chinese development (rapid coastal growth, FDI-intensive, deeply uneven) and although also then politics was in command, it was Shanghai-led politics, but this pattern has become less relevant after the 11th and 12th five-year plans.[52]

HDI data indicate that the overall pattern in Asia is towards higher quality growth, less so in terms of inequality-adjusted HDI, but still significant. The Gini index shows improvement in Northeast Asia but not in China and India, with rising growth and inequality increasing as steeply. China's reforms seek to reorient society from an export-led to a domestic demand-led growth path.[53] Whether these trends would add up to social development in an overall sense also depends on governance and institutional reforms in China and Asia generally.

5 Asian drivers and multipolarity

For developing countries, the Asian drivers provide an alternative to the US and Europe in markets, investment, and aid.[54] They are a 'third force', in a distant way reminiscent of the past role of the USSR. In Africa, China displaces the role of Anglo-French and American interests,[55] in Latin America it is a counterweight to US influence. 'China's rise shows developing countries that there are viable alternatives to the Washington Consensus'.[56] Since 2000, African countries have grown on average by 6 percent, a trend that is expected to last over the coming years. Ghana was the world's fastest growing economy in 2011 and Ethiopia expanded more rapidly than China in the five years to 2009, but these strides are from a low level, are marred by steep inequality, and are unstable.[57] In 2014, Ghana and Ethiopia knocked on the door of the IMF.

In several ways, contemporary multipolarity is a fulfillment of the Bandung promise (when the Movement of Nonaligned Countries was founded in 1955). South-South cooperation which has long been a rhetorical exercise is now taking shape in trade, investments, aid, international negotiations, and security, partly because of the inertia of international institutions.[58] It reinforces the position of developing countries and the G77 in international negotiations.

Twenty-first-century globalization is marked by major pattern changes (Chapter 1). The terms of trade noted by structuralist and dependency economists (rising prices for manufactured goods, declining prices for raw materials) produced growing unequal exchange; but with China as the world's leading factory economy, prices for commodities tend to be high and for manufactured goods low so there has been a reversal in the classic terms of trade. This is good news for commodities and energy exporters (such as Brazil) and for consumers (cheap products), and bad news for manufacturing sectors (such as in Mexico, Latin America's manufacturing giant) and for net energy importers also in developing countries.

The East-South turn introduces a different vortex of capitalisms. China as workshop of the world competes with other developing countries; it is not just the US, Europe, and Japan that see manufacturing jobs going to China—so do Mexico, Kenya, and Bangladesh. Garment workers from Bangladesh to South Africa have been under pressure from Chinese textile exports. In 2005, trade unions in South Africa issued a call for action against China, noting '250,000 jobs lost in African clothing, textile and leather industries'.[59]

As an instance of East-South relations, let's consider China's relations to Africa and Latin America.

A preliminary question is 'which China?', for 'China's foreign economic policies are put into practice by an increasingly diverse set of actors under pressure from a wide variety of interest groups and constituency demands'.[60] China's aim is 'foreign policy that sustains an international environment supportive of economic growth and stability in China', which involves the promotion of 'China as a responsible great power . . . a state that operates according to international rules and within multilateral institutions'. China's 'peaceful rise' (*heping juequi*) has been recast as 'peaceful development' (*heping fazhan*) to remove the sting of the 'rise'. The general formula of China's foreign economic policy is 'mutual benefit'—not unlike the approach of the USSR and the official position that guides development cooperation of the OECD. During the Hu-Wen administration Beijing viewed itself as 'the leader of the developing world' and in Hu Jintao's words, 'the biggest developing country'.[61]

Part of China's 'fragmented authoritarianism' is that different sectoral and regional agencies, each with their organizational and political goals, are involved in implementing policy. On Africa's side of the equation are diverse countries, sectors, and actors and neopatrimonial clientelism in several countries. Thus, China is plural and 'China's "Africa" is really an assortment of regimes'.[62] Methodological nationalism is a recurrent fallacy and in Africa's case 'methodological continentalism'.

Different strands of thought are viewing China as development partner, as economic competitor, and as colonizer.[63]

> Five 'images' of China are set to shape the relationship with Africa: first its image as the new face of globalization; second its role in African development success; third as a mirror for the West; fourth as a pariah partner; and finally as a responsible stakeholder.[64]

While early debates about China-Africa relations were swinging between 'euphoria (at last a power to challenge former colonizers) and hysteria (China's footprint is exploitative)', 'in recent years the debate has become more meas- ured and nuanced and overall opinion seems to be shifting to the positive side of the pendulum, albeit with reservations concerning governance issues'.[65]

In China-Africa relations, winners have been oil exporters (Angola, Sudan, Gabon) and resource-rich countries including base metal exporters (Mauritania, Mozambique, South Africa, Zambia). For resource-rich countries that are also oil importers (Botswana, Central African Republic) the China effect is mixed. Cotton exporters (Benin, Burkina, Mali) have registered modest gains from China's high import demand. Losers in the equation have been countries that are both oil importers and textile exporters; the latter suffer from the com- petition of China's textile imports in domestic and in third-country markets (Madagascar, Mauritius). Another category of losers are producers of agricul- tural commodities such as coffee (Burundi, Ethiopia, Rwanda, Uganda) and cocoa (Côte d'Ivoire, Ghana, Kenya, Malawi, Tanzania, Zimbabwe) for which Chinese demand is marginal (less than 1 percent of global consumption) and world prices have collapsed—unlike the prices of China's main agricultural imports of wheat, corn, beef, and soybeans.[66]

Chinese investment in Africa has surged in tandem with trade and has been significant in infrastructure, transport, and education. China has given Africans access to cheap consumer goods and follows a 'low-transactions-cost way of doing business', with non-interference in countries' internal affairs.[67]

Among concerns, Zafar mentions the following. First, Chinese investment 'will be based on capital-intensive natural resource extraction and will not contribute to local employment generation and . . . long-term economic devel- opment'. Second, China's effect on oil markets leads to increased energy prices for oil importers. Third, Chinese competition in manufacturing, especially in textiles, imports of cheap Chinese goods in Africa, and competition in third- country markets, undermine economic diversification in Africa and contribute to deindustrialization. Fourth are concerns over labor practices and conditions of Chinese investments, as well as human rights standards and problems of corruption and governance.[68] Land-lease arrangements are another cause for concern.[69] Some studies find that 'for many African countries, the negative may outweigh the positive ones' and call for concerted policy measures such as making African economies more competitive, investment in infrastructure through public-private partnerships, including participation of Chinese firms, local sourcing and content, and joint ventures.[70]

Later literature offers nuanced assessments. Focusing on the impact of trade of China and India in Africa, Geda and Meskel advocate a dynamic approach that looks at effects over time. For several African countries, they find in the early period, before 2000, crowding out of African production but growing complementarity in the later period (notably in Tunisia, Kenya, and South Africa). Moving from displacement to complementarity requires a proactive approach. South Africa 'has undergone a substantial structural change in the clothing industry and has moved to the next stage in industrial development', which makes South Africa a 'leading goose' in Africa. In their view, 'the overall impact of China and India seems to be that of complementarity during the later years of the study period', partly as an effect of Africa 'importing production-augmenting capital goods or skills and technology from both China and India'. They conclude 'there is a need to change from a defensive mind-set about China and India to one that is more embracing, and one in which Africans determine the terms of engagement'.[71]

This comes back in many assessments: 'African states must become more strategic and use this opportunity to build local productive capacity'.[72] Contemporary 'rivalries' are an opportunity for gains to be made by Africa 'if African governments have the strategic vision and political skills to take tactical advantage of these'.[73] This includes improving labor productivity, efficiency, and speed to market.[74] The thrust of recent China-Africa literature is that sweeping assessments are too generalizing and underestimate diversity; China's role offers both opportunities and threats, and public and private engagement is called for.[75] On China's side, security and political concerns (as in Libya, Sudan) have come to the foreground and megaprojects have failed.

Broadly similar considerations apply to 'China effects' in Latin America, with higher stakes because of much higher volumes. After Asia and Hong Kong, Latin America ranks second in Chinese trade and foreign investments, on a much larger scale than Africa, although still small as a share of China's overall exports and imports. 'Brazil, the largest Latin American exporter to China, ranks 14th among China's suppliers accounting for 1.5% of total imports'.[76]

In Latin America and the Caribbean (LAC):

> [p]roducers and exporters of raw materials . . . such as Argentina, Brazil, Chile, and Venezuela and sectors such as agriculture, agroindustry, and industrial inputs—have been the 'winners' in terms of trade with China. On the other hand, Mexico and the Central American countries specializing in commodity chains such as yarn-textile-garments, and also in electronics, automobiles and auto parts—seem to be the losers against China in domestic as well as in third markets.[77]

In Latin America, the 'China effects' in Brazil and Mexico are polar opposites: Brazil's experiences have been among the most positive and Mexico's the most negative. 'In 2002, China replaced Mexico as the second largest exporter to the US market'.[78] In recent years, Mexico has recouped its position vis-à-vis the United States.

A striking pattern is that LAC as a high-wage area is exporting primary products and importing manufactures, even though LAC is a region with a longer history of industrialization, so relations with China result in a down-grading of comparative advantage in a dynamic sense.[79] China has a labor market of 712 million who on average cost $0.61 hourly instead of $2 hourly in Mexico. In the manufacturing sector, labor costs in China are 3.7 times lower than in South America's poorest country, Bolivia, and 12.5 times lower than in Chile.[80] 'Generally, China's expansion has been economically positive for the region', but the picture is mixed:

> [w]hile China can be expected to further enhance the South–South agenda and support international demands of developing countries, it may also further enhance a globalisation that seriously neglects human rights and environmental degradation, while also making it very hard for Latin American manufacturing to survive and modernise.[81]

An essential point of rising Asia for developing countries is the example of the developmental state, which is the key difference between the Washington and the Beijing consensus:

> China never aimed at a free market and a small state, and economic liberalization has been as central to China's miraculous growth as has been the strong state and its active economic role. This difference has been crucial as shown by the wide gap between the GDP growth of China and any developing country or transition economy that reformed its state and economy according to the lines of the Washington Consensus.[82]

The challenge of rising Asia for developing countries is not the 'magic of the marketplace' of the American model but the challenge of institutions and policies. For commodities exporters, the challenge is to convert their gains into productive investments in infrastructure, education, and technology; for industrial producers, the challenge is to move up the ladder of technology, efficiency, and productivity. In meeting these challenges, a key problem in Africa is neopatrimonial politics and predatory elites. A major obstacle in LAC is the role of oligarchies, as in Mexico where economic concentration takes the form of a *nueva oligarquía* of 274 families and groups that control most of the economy[83] (discussed in Chapter 5).

There is a danger, according to Ian Taylor, that '"China" is being constructed as a scapegoat for concerns that have very little to do with Beijing' for they rather reflect the level of development of the continent and the nature of African regimes.[84] By one account, Chinese officials wouldn't be averse to discussing developmental terms for investments, but African governments don't propose them.[85] A similar consideration applies to LAC: to a considerable extent, the 'China threat' is a reflection of the caliber of political institutions, not necessarily in terms of the attributes of democracy cherished by the West, but in terms of capability and commitment according to the standards of the responsive developmental state (Chapter 8).

6 Asian dilemmas

Asian countries are involved in global value networks, interfirm tie-ups, industrial standards, technical and scientific cooperation, and a host of transnational arrangements. All are part of moving transnational complementarities. Several larger Asian countries share features in their relations with developing countries. Yet since there are glaring differences among Asian countries, they face different policy questions.

Companies such as Samsung, LG, Daewoo, Acer, Lenovo, Huawei, Haier, and Geely engage in long-term planning and strategy, and state and local governments follow policies of their own. Not just governments and corporations deal with policy questions but also trade unions, NGOs, and social movements, so multiple actors are involved.

Many 'Asias' are assembled in ASEAN plus Three. Japan and South Korea are members of the OECD, and Taiwan has observer status. All three are of investment grade in financial rankings and have established international brands. China is graduating from price competition to quality competition and is building (or acquiring) brands. Southeast Asian nations specialize in assembly production and agro-mineral exports with a growing service sector and large informal sector. India ranks high in services. Bangladesh and Pakistan rank among the 'next 11' promising growth economies (although 90 percent of Bangladesh exports is garments).

Are international institutions a major avenue of transformation? Markets change rapidly but institutions change slowly. In the G20, EME have joined the global head table, but they sit below the salt. The international financial institutions remain instruments of hegemony and the status quo, even as the status quo is increasingly wobbly. Eurozone repair efforts orchestrated by the troika of the European Central Bank, the EU Commission, and the IMF have been slow and feeble. The EME proposal for Special Purpose Vehicles to bail out the Eurozone has been sidelined. For years, the US congress stalled approving expanding the IMF vote quota for developing countries. Hence, for many EME, relations at the global level are rather mediated through regional dynamics and institutions and cross-regional combinations such as the BRICS summits (which leave out smaller emerging economies).

China, Japan, and South Korea have agreed to use their foreign exchange reserves to invest in each other's government bonds. They also plan setting up a trilateral free trade zone. ASEAN plus Three doubled the Chiang Mai financial buffer initiative to $240 billion.[86]

Should Asian countries buy US Treasuries and prop up American debt, as China continues to do at a reduced level? Should Asian countries focus on strengthening the framework of ASEAN plus Three and its financial reserves? Should they expand the Chiang Mai Initiative and Asian Bond Fund and safeguard the region against financial turbulence? Should they expand it in the form of an Asian Monetary Fund? Should they expand ASEAN to include India, Australia, and New Zealand?

Should they focus on developing financial cooperation along the 'string of pearls' of Seoul, Shanghai, Hong Kong, Singapore, Mumbai, and the Emirates? Should SWF from Asian countries pool resources to exercise influence in financial markets? Should they ring-fence the region against incursions of Wall

Street and London megabanks, should they rather build strategic links with them, or should they contain Western banks in 'special financial zones' such as Hong Kong and Shanghai's new FTZ in Pudong? Should they move towards an Asian dollar, merging the yuan, yen, and won?

Should Asian countries prop up the US and EU so they can continue their exports to these markets, or should they rather focus on strengthening regional demand and economic complementarities in ASEAN and other regional pacts; or should they strengthen their links with Latin America, the Caribbean, the Middle East, and Africa? Alternatively, should they focus on reducing their dependence on exports, strengthen domestic demand, and reorient their growth model from export-led to domestic and regional demand-led growth? Should they combine this with efforts towards sustainability, going 'green and lite'?[87] In strengthening domestic demand, should Asian countries rely on labor policies (higher minimum wage, labor security, labor laws), on social policies (social protection floor, healthcare, pensions), fiscal policies, or a combination of these, as in China's 12th five-year plan? Or, should they do all of the above at different levels and to different degrees, so they engage multiple registers at the same time?

Should the overall emphasis be on growth, or on human development, human security, and social investment? Should the emphasis be on shared growth, as advocated by the Commission on Growth and the Seoul consensus of the 2011 G20 meeting? Should this go together with policies towards deepening democracy, including economic democracy, autonomy of the state vis-à-vis mega corporations, strong trade unions, collective bargaining, and provisions for contract labor—overcoming the gap between contract workers and permanent employees that has developed in South Korea and Japan? Should it involve breaking up the chaebol and greater government support for SMEs, as in Taiwan, or should the approach be continued path dependence on the chaebol? Should services, including tradable services, receive greater emphasis in policymaking?

The growing emphasis on regional cooperation in Asia reflects multiple registers.[88] First, it is part of a general regional turn: since the late 20th century, regionalism has been a major political articulation of globalization. Second, the macroeconomic rationale of regional cooperation is scale and leverage in market size and investment and reducing dependence on exports to the US and Europe, which is the backdrop of the East Asian Community and ASEAN plus Three. Third, East Asian cooperation is propelled by grouping around China-driven supply chains. 'Asia's China-centric supply chain has become a new and important source of panregional growth for most of its major economies, especially Japan, Korea, and Taiwan'.[89] This carries the risk of China dependence, or as long as China is okay, Asia is fine. Fourth, another meaning of East Asian regional cooperation is regional cocooning, particularly on the part of middle powers—seeking shelter from (neoliberal) globalization under a regional umbrella. This clashes with the region's reliance on global trade. China has long broken out of the shell of regional cocooning. Finally, regional cooperation is a stepping stone towards global engagement and governance, pooling regional resources that serve as negotiation platforms in wider international forums.

Experiencing globalization for decades as a juggernaut that comes from outside and following American hegemony for as long has created a habitus of passive globalization, so taking up proactive global agendas is a difficult transition. Now the era of passive globalization is past. While a proactive agenda of shaping globalization is indispensable for governments and major corporations in EME and in macroeconomics, international relations, and political science (mostly according to narrow agendas and frameworks), civil society may lag behind in global reflexivity.

In sum, Asia is rising but Asian wellbeing is not. The quality and the quantity of growth are out of sync. The high and rising Gini index in most Asian countries signals a growth path short of social development that is not sustainable. Rising Asia is a mixed blessing: in several respects, it has been positive for developing countries generally, yet it poses challenges in Asia and beyond. Asian market economies are distinctive in terms of institutions and regulations, yet they share the general preoccupation with growth and GDP, join the rat race of Anglo-American capitalism, and transform cities such as Shanghai into spaghetti bowls of concrete expressways. Whether China can transition towards a more balanced development path, Northeast Asian countries can resuscitate their path of relatively equitable growth, and Southeast Asia can rise above the middle-income trap, is in question.[90]

Notes

1 Chandra Nair, We should stop talking of our Asian century, *Financial Times* 3/7/2012: 11.
2 Zoellick 2010.
3 Dicken 2011: 525.
4 Reid 1995.
5 Kishore Mahbubani, Why Asia stays calm in the storm, *Financial Times* 10/29/2008: 11.
6 K. Mahbubani, US needs to shed its taboo on economic planning, *Financial Times* 5/6/2011: 9.
7 In sequence: Chandra Nair, Speak up, Asia, or the west will drown you out, *Financial Times* 1/4/2007: 13; K. Mahbubani, Why Asia stays calm in the storm, *Financial Times* 10/29/2008: 11; K. Mahbubani, Lessons for the West from Asian capitalism, *Financial Times* 3/19/2009: 9; K. Mahbubani, Asian wisdom: The US and Europe could use a refresher course in Eastern studies, *Newsweek* 12/6/2010: 34; Ronnie Chan, The west preaching to the east must stop, *Financial Times* 1/6/2010; G. Lyons, East offers west a macro-prudential blueprint, *Financial Times* 7/28/2010: 18; K. Mahbubani, Asia has had enough of excusing the west, *Financial Times* 1/26/2011: 11; S. Rabinovitch, China calls for 'responsible' US, *Financial Times* 7/12/2011: 2; J. Dean and A. Back, Chinese central banker chides U.S., *Wall Street Journal* 8/4/2011: A12.
8 Cited in G. Rachman, War and peace in Asia, *Financial Times* 8/6–7/2016: 1–2.

 9 Ibid.: 2.
10 Arrighi 2007; Nederveen Pieterse 1989.
11 Zoellick 2010; Maddison 2010.
12 Frank 1998.
13 Johnson 1982.
14 Studwell 2013.
15 See e.g., Goodman *et al.* 1998; Booth 2002.
16 Mahathir Mohamad, Dawn of an Asian century is a myth, speech at Malaysia-China Partnership, *New Straits Times* 8/27/1996.
17 Wang 2005.
18 Buruma 2003: 55.
19 In Buruma 2003: 54.
20 Business in Asia, *The Economist* 5/31/2014: 9.
21 Redding and Witt 2010.
22 Tudor 2012.
23 D. Pilling, Thriving South Korea wallows in existential angst, *Financial Times* 9/27/2012: 13.
24 Kim 2016.
25 Lee 2012; Lee and Jeong 2011.
26 Yoon 2012.
27 Quoted in E. Ramstad, Global woes land a punch in Korea, *Wall Street Journal* 8/17/2011: C5.
28 Palley 2011: 4–5.
29 Quigley 1966.
30 E.g., Cumings 2010.
31 Gill and Kharas 2007.
32 Mahbubani 2009: 5.
33 Peck and Tickell 2002.
34 Rodrik 2005.
35 Bello 1992.
36 Johnson 1998.
37 O'Toole 2009.
38 Lewis 2010.
39 Streeck 2013; Germany and economics, *The Economist* 5/9/2015: 46–47; Blyth 2013.
40 Gong 2012.
41 Rodrik 2010.
42 H. Sender and T. Mitchell, Plugged into the Party, *Financial Times* 11/8/2013: 7.
43 Simpfendorfer 2009.
44 Wade 1996.
45 G. Silverman, Developing countries underpin boom in advertising spending, *Financial Times* 10/24/2005; Ciochetto 2011.
46 UNDP 2011.
47 Quoted in J. de Parle, New plan to reduce income inequality, *China Daily* 5/23/2012.
48 Discussed in Nederveen Pieterse 2015b.
49 K. Brown, Why Asian companies need a brand new start, *Financial Times* 9/22/2010.
50 Braudel 1984.
51 Arrighi 2007; Harvey 2005; Dirlik 2006.
52 Roach 2009; Chi 2010; Li 2012; Chen and Ping 2012.
53 Roach 2009.
54 Kaplinsky and Messner 2008.

55 Zafar 2007.
56 Fernández Jilberto and Hogenboom eds. 2012a: 27.
57 African Progress Panel report, Anan 2013.
58 Wade 2009.
59 ITGLWF-Africa press release, Call for action against China grows, *Cape Town* 10/11/2005.
60 Taylor 2009: 3.
61 Taylor 2009: 4, 15.
62 Taylor 2009: 13.
63 Alden 2007, quoted in Cheru and Obi 2010: 6.
64 Alden 2007, quoted in Shaw 2010: 20.
65 Draper *et al* 2010: 107.
66 Zafar 2007: 112–113; cf. Geda and Meskel 2010; Wild and Mepham 2006.
67 Zafar 2007: 126.
68 Zafar 2007: 126.
69 Manji and Marks 2007; Ademola *et al.* 2009.
70 Ademola *et al.* 2009: 503–4.
71 Draper *et al.* 2010: 104, 104–5, 106.
72 Draper *et al.* 2010: 119.
73 Keet 2010: 32.
74 Broadman 2007.
75 Broadman 2007; Taylor 2006, 2009; Cheru and Obi 2010.
76 Jenkins and Dussel Peters 2008: 237.
77 Jenkins and Dussel Peters 2008: 248; Dussel Peters 2012.
78 Dussel Peters 2012: 22.
79 Ibid.: 20.
80 Ibid.: 22.
81 Ibid.: 7, 26.
82 Ibid.: 26.
83 Hogenboom 2012: 65.
84 Taylor 2009: 19.
85 Keet 2010: 25.
86 Gosset 2012.
87 Roach 2009.
88 E.g., Kim 2012; Sakamoto 2000.
89 Roach 2009: 399.
90 Roach 2009; Nederveen Pieterse and Kim 2012; Traub-Merz 2012; Pettis 2013; Nederveen Pieterse 2015b, 2017.

4 BRICS are in the eye of the beholder

1 BRICS skepticism
2 Omni-channel politics
3 Bricolage

To focus the mind on the BRICS phenomenon, its sprawl and changes over time, the following is a chronological sample of headlines:

Illiberal capitalism: Russia and China chart their own course (*Financial Times* 1/9/2008)

New champions, emerging leaders: The end of western dominance of commerce looks nigh (*Financial Times* 9/26/2008)

BRIC leaders take their place at the top table (*Financial Times* 9/26/2008)

Rising stars buffeted by global storm: Emerging economies have been unable to escape the contagion (*FT* 12/24/2008)

Emerging powers want fair global economic order (*FT* 6/17/2009)

BRICS balance shared interests with rivalries (*FT* 4/14/2010)

Consumption starts to shift to China, India and Brazil (*FT* 4/21/2010)

Building BRICS: Promise of growth lures carmakers (*FT* 1/21/2010)

Building BRICS: Bankers sense shift in capital flows (*FT* 1/22/2010)

BRIC nations grow weary of G20's rhetoric of co-operation (*FT* 10/21/2010)

Are cracks forming the in the BRICS? (*Wall Street Journal* 2/16/2010)

How the BRICS are building on their history (*FT* 6/10/2011)

BRICS nations voice money-flow fears: Leaders call for shift away from reliance on dollar, warn on risks from developed nations' loose monetary policies *Wall Street Journal* 4/15–17/2011)

Emerging markets are more than just the BRICS (*New York Times* 10/7/2012)

Beware membership of this elite club: Growth will be barely more than 1 per cent because micro meddling has damaged business confidence (*FT* 12/5/2012)

From this sample several points are apparent: (a) long-term trends underlie the rise of the BRICS, (b) BRICS boosterism and skepticism alternate, (c) skepticism grows over time, (d) the BRICS are part of the wider cluster of emerging economies, and (e) they represent a crisscross of trends in trade, development, consumption, finance, geoeconomics, and geopolitics. To put this in a wider perspective, Table 4.1 gives a brief chronology of the BRICS.

According to *The Economist*, the BRIC are 'The trillion-dollar club':

> [t]he only developing economies with GDPs of more than $1 trillion per year . . . have provided 45 percent of economic growth worldwide since the financial crisis began in 2007 . . . The BRICS nations together command nearly 26 per cent of the world's geographical area, and 43 per cent of the world's population. The bloc commands 17 per cent of global trade and are recipients of 11 per cent of global FDI. The five nations also command 25 per cent of global GDP in terms of purchasing power parity and approximately one fifth of global nominal GDP (over 19 per cent).[1]

The chorus is familiar. Brazil, Russia, India, and China are the leading emerging economies and the four largest economies outside the OECD. Their combined GDP is $16 trillion (2016). Together their foreign reserves are six times the assets of the IMF. Their share of world GDP has grown from 12.4 percent in 1999 to 15.45 percent in 2009 and, with the inclusion of South Africa, approximately 20 percent in 2016.

Together BRIC countries comprise more than 40 percent of the world's population and a quarter of the world's land mass. The populations of BRIC societies are Brazil 201 million, Russia 143 million, India 1.2 billion, and China 1.35 billion (2013). They totaled 2.8 billion in 2013 and are projected to rise to 3.2 billion by 2050. Russia is one of the few countries where the population shrank, from 143 million in 2003 to 139 million in 2010; from 2009, the population increased again for the first time in 15 years.[2]

Table 4.1 Chronology of BRICS

2001	O'Neill, Goldman Sachs coins the term as investment category
2003	Goldman Sachs paper, BRICs will dominate in 2050, larger than G6 in dollar terms
2009	BRIC are resilient after 2008 crisis
	First of annual BRIC summits, Yekaterinburg
2010	BRIC adds South Africa and becomes BRICS
2014	BRICS establish New Development Bank & Contingent Reserve Arrangement
	BRICS trim US dollar and Treasury holdings
2015	Recession in Brazil, Russia, slowdown in China (6.9%), outstripped by India (7.3%)
2016	O'Neill: 'I got 2 out of 4 countries right'

The BRIC originate as an investment meme as part of EM and a lengthy list of acronyms, which come and go quickly (a sample in loose chronology is in Table 4.2). 'The fad for giving group labels to emerging markets is just a geo-economic form of Scrabble for the family'.[3]

Dimensions of the BRIC that matter are their regional role, their international role, relations among the BRICS, and domestic relations such as governance and inequality. This chapter takes up several lines of argument. First, it addresses BRICS skepticism and the reasons why the category is questioned. Next, it argues that their importance is nevertheless enduring. Their growing cooperation at international levels where the BRICS engage in multi-channel politics at multiple fronts simultaneously reflects this importance and momentum.

Since the BRICS are also major developing countries, their domestic development is part of this momentum. With export markets shrinking, domestic demand is a condition for sustainable prosperity, which refocuses attention on low-income majorities and government policies. These questions are important in EM generally. To probe this, we turn to inequality within the BRICS and focus on rural majorities and peasants, on inequality because it is a major element in assessing the quality of growth (Chapter 3.4) and on peasants because while they are often overlooked they are central to how the rise of EME affects the rural and urban poor and the informal sector. If given slowdown in the OECD, the era of export-led growth (at any rate based on exports to developed countries) is winding down, domestic demand and consumption is a priority in emerging economies' agenda. The focus is also on middle classes because they are central to how business and Western media perceive EME (Chapter 8.1).

Table 4.2 Investment memes

EM, EME	Emerging markets, Emerging market economies
CIVETS	Colombia, Indonesia, Vietnam, Egypt, Turkey, South Africa
MINT	Mexico, Indonesia, Nigeria, Turkey
MIST	Mexico, Indonesia, South Korea, Turkey
PINEs	Philippines, Indonesia, Nigeria, Ethiopia
N-11	Next 11 growth economies (Bangladesh, Egypt, Indonesia, Iran, South Korea, Mexico, Nigeria, Pakistan, the Philippines, Turkey, Vietnam)
EAGLES	Emerging and growth-leading economies
7 percent club	Countries that have averaged growth of at least 7% a year
E7	Seven largest emerging economies (BRIC, Indonesia, Mexico, Turkey)
'Fragile five'	India, Indonesia, Brazil, South Africa, Turkey, 2013
Growth markets	Indonesia, South Korea, Mexico, Turkey
SICS	Systemically important countries (BRIC, Mexico, South Africa, Turkey, South Korea)
VARP	Vietnam, Argentina, Romania, Pakistan, 2016

1 BRICS skepticism

BRIC boosterism precedes BRIC skepticism. Jim O'Neill who coined the idea, kept it going over the years, as in the following headlines of his articles, which give a sense of BRIC boosterism:

> The BRICs economies must help form world policy
> BRICS could point the way out of the economic mire
> Why it would be wrong to write off the BRICS
> How Africa can become the next BRIC[4]

Media in BRICS such as in China also have their share of BRICS boosterism:

> BRICS nations to work together to reform world financial system: 'Developing countries produce goods and services, while developed countries produce problems and headaches' (*China Daily* 6/18–19/2011)
> BRICS can build optimism: Despite their slower growth, emerging economies will remain the engines driving the global recovery and future development (*China Daily* 10/18/2012)
> BRICS and mortar: The BRICS provide a big market for China (*China Daily* 3/25/2013)
> 'Time is ripe' for BRICS' own bank (*China Daily* 7/8/2014)
> Putin: Emerging powers must play bigger role in world affairs (*China Daily* 7/12–13/2014)
> Xi urges efforts of BRICS to improve global governance (*China Daily* 9/5/2016)

There are ample reservations against using the BRIC as a category. Some view it as just banking industry spin, hype, and marketing. Analysts criticize the focus on the BRIC for limiting foreign investment to just four countries among EME.[5] The reservation raised most often is that they are too diverse to be lumped together. Unlike previous categories such as the Indian Ocean, the Mediterranean world, the Baltic, the Atlantic, and the Pacific Rim, they share neither a contiguous geography nor a common history. Apart from being large in GDP, population, and territory, they are quite diverse as economies and polities. Russia relies strongly on energy exports, China on manufactures' exports, India on services' exports, and Brazil on a combination of these.[6] Brazil has become an agricultural superpower, a fast rising agro-mineral and industrial exporter with a social structure shaped by slavery, race, and property owners with large holdings. At times, its inclusion in the BRICs is questioned.[7]

The contribution of manufacturing to GDP is highest in China at 48.7 percent and below 20 percent in the other three countries.[8] The BRIC do not only follow different modes of development, they also compete with each other, as in the mixed relations between China and India.[9] While trade between China and Brazil has grown steeply, China's industrial goods compete with domestic manufactures in Brazil, as they do in other emerging economies. China and Russia increasingly engage in a strategic relationship.[10]

The BRIC are countries 'that suffer from having a brilliant future'.[11] What is the validity of the BRIC as an analytical category?

> Although all are federal states, only India and Brazil are well-institu-tionalized democracies, one of which is parliamentary and the other presidential, respectively. Russia is a declared democracy moving towards authoritarianism, while China is a Marxist people's republic. Each of the four embodies distinct cultural and linguistic traditions, though they share the characteristic of having been recognizable political entities for centuries.[12]

That India and Brazil are democracies while Russia and China practice 'illiberal capitalism' is a recurrent theme.[13] 'What many realist scholars fear is the rise of a powerful anti-western and anti-liberal values coalition, led by China but possibly also including Russia'.[14] Realist sources refer to the surge of EME and the BRIC as 'a World Without the West': 'Inviolable sovereignty in the World Without the West rejects key tenets of "modern" liberal internationalism and particularly any notion of global civil society or public opinion justifying political or military intervention in the affairs of the state'.[15] The new forces fail by the standards of the old order such as modern institutions and 'liberal internationalism'. In fact, part of the problematic of emerging economies is whether the terms set by the old order are valid yardsticks or are exercises in containment that reflect the thinking of the incumbents.[16]

Brazil and Russia have significant natural resources and their per capita ecological footprints are quite low: Brazil's is 3.1 hectares and Russia's 5.7 hectares, while their national ecological reserves are 6 and 1.1 respectively. The population giants have lower per capita footprints, India's is 1.2 hectares and China's is 3.4 hectares, but the size of their populations neutralizes this advantage. Their national ecological reserves are −0.7 for India and −2.4 for China. In comparison, the US has the highest level of consumption, a per capita footprint of 8.2 hectares and a negative ecological reserve of −4.5.[17]

Russia, a past superpower, and China are members of the UN Security Council while India and Brazil aspire to join. Among the four, Brazil is a newcomer to international influence.

The story of 'BRICS without mortar', one of the recurring BRICS jokes, is one of lack of cohesion among the BRICs. Clearly, what holds the BRIC together, or at any rate sets them apart is not cohesion but size and momentum. Size matters:

The four do not share domestic political institutions, international goals, or economic structures and challenges. If the category, nonetheless, provides insight it must be because this set of countries holds similar implications for the *larger* system—the international political economy—within which it is embedded.[18]

In addition, they are regional economic leaders—Brazil in Latin America and the Caribbean (and Lusophone influence extending to Angola, Mozambique, and Timor-Leste), Russia and the Eurasian Union, India in South Asia, South Africa in southern Africa, and China's radius that extends through Asia and worldwide.

A fundamental crack in the BRICS as a category is that it is conceived in multiple time frames—a long time frame in which by 2030 or 2050 they will be on a par with advanced economies, or will rank among the world's leading economies, and a short time frame in which it functions as an asset class and is supposed to deliver growth in the time frame of finance. If it does not, the category flunks. Hence, the recurrent tweaking of the BRICS—only two remain standing, or just one, and BRICS jokes. In the time frame of finance, the BRICS are to deliver at a time when AE are stagnating, a low yield environment in which QE and austerity further depress yield, which both adds to the pressure to deliver and diminishes BRICS opportunities to deliver since demand in AE is low. Thus, the BRICS are an economic and finance paradox. The time frame of finance is impatient while the time horizon of the BRICS themselves is long. At the same time, in view of the constraints of global governance and international institutions, their actual cooperation is timely.

They are the largest economies outside the OECD, the largest emerging economies, economies of near continental size and as such, they are major players in the long run—no matter what the short horizons of finance and market analysis indicate. The enduring importance of the BRICS hinges on these elements:

- Size—their large internal market provides them with economies of scale and makes them less exposed to external volatility. Because their national economy is large, their leading firms are also large. Market size makes them attractive to FDI and gives them leverage in negotiating the terms and conditions of FDI.
- Regional leadership—in trade, production, services, and possibly finance. They play a key role in regional formations, economic and political. For foreign investors, they may serve as regional gatekeepers.
- International profile—their size gives them standing in international negotiations such as the WTO and climate change and in groupings such as the G77 and G20.
- Their growing cooperation—in new institution building (NDB, CRA), international forums (G20, G77, WTO), and relations among one another (IBSA).

Other variables—such as state capability, the strength of social forces and civil society, historical depth, and soft power—either don't hold over time or don't apply to all BRICS, so the above are the key components.

2 Omni-channel politics

A *China Daily* report on China's new government in 2013 is headlined, 'Leaders work for a stable world'. The report cites Premier Li Keqiang's media debut: 'There are more than 1.3 billion people in China and we are still on a long journey toward modernization. That requires an international environment of lasting peace. Even if China becomes stronger, we will not seek hegemony'.[19] This casts China as a responsible stakeholder in global relations, not as a revisionist power.

There are obvious reasons why BRICS should act as stakeholders in the existing order and equally obvious reasons why they would transcend the order. They depend on advanced countries as markets and for technology, FDI, interfirm cooperation, global value chains, and so forth. On the other hand, while they have emerged as major players they are underrepresented in international institutions. The EME have risen in the context of the contemporary world order, not thanks to but despite neoliberalism and American hegemony. For 200 years, advanced countries have dominated the world order, a world of incumbents. Probably the most significant discrepancy is that while the BRICS and EM are now drivers of the world economy, they are also developing countries.

In the ongoing process of global rebalancing, will emerging economies join the club of the old order, the global plutocracy, or will they act as an emancipatory impetus on the global scene (Chapter 6)? The question is worth asking, but may also be too simple and the options too narrow. According to John Ikenberry, 'All the great powers—old and new—are status quo powers. All are beneficiaries of an open world economy and the various services that the liberal international order provides for capitalist trading states'.[20] This rose garden version of international order glosses over the T&C, terms and conditions. The way the US has treated China over the years shows another side of the liberal international. Amitai Etzioni describes this treatment as multifaceted containment. The US put strenuous conditions in the way of China's admission to the WTO; Congress stalled for years to approve a higher vote quota of developing countries in the IMF; the US opposed the IMF granting the RMB reserve currency status; it warned countries against joining the AIIB; and excluded China from the TPP.[21]

A realistic script for the BRICS is multi-channel politics. First, participate in the existing order as a responsible stakeholder; the existing international institutions will not go away and, whatever their limitations, they remain relevant to global stability. Second, seek reform of international institutions to ensure better representation of developing countries. The contributions of BRICS and EM in the G20 and IMF have been conditional, not carte blanche.

In 2010, emerging economies contributed $100 billion to the IMF, along with pressure for more representative governance of international institutions and a higher vote quota of developing countries. Third, initiate new institutions such as the Chiang Mai Initiative Multilateralization (CMIM) and the BRICS NDB and CRA. New institutions require a long gestation time. For countries that seek to access more than 30 percent of their maximum credit, the CMIM outsources enforcement of conditionality to the IMF because of its analytical capabilities,[22] which is a bit ironic for an institution that represents the nucleus of an 'Asian Monetary Fund'. Fourth, develop cooperation frameworks that are outside of or at least not dependent on the old networks, such as the Shanghai Cooperation Organization, the AIIB, IBSA, and other forms of South-South cooperation.

Woven into BRICS DNA is a shared goal of 'global realignment' away from the advanced countries.[23] Yet more important still is their acting across a wide register, across the spectrum of cooperation, withholding cooperation (soft balancing), and resistance (hard balancing). Since it concerns a third of the world's population with diverse interests and complex engagements, wide-register multi-channel politics makes sense. Hard balancing carries a price. The Shanghai Cooperation Organization, blocking the growth of American influence in Central Asia since the Afghan war, and Russian and Chinese (and later Turkish and Brazilian) support for Iran (until the US and EU arrived at a settlement with Iran in 2016), are cases in point. China's expansion in the South China Sea is another. Loud defiance and confrontation (such as North Korea, Venezuela, Ahmadinejad in Iran) are not relevant options for countries that represent a third of the world population.

Wide-register multi-channel politics implies heterogeneity and complexity. Sweeping monochrome assessments make little sense. Even matters of degree (what is the overall position on the spectrum from status quo to transformation) are difficult to assess.

The time frame also matters. The time frame of finance, business, and much geopolitics is short with frequent fluctuations, while the time horizon of social development and structural transformation is long. Emerging economies have long and complex histories of power, defeat, and comeback behind them. The contemporary place of China and Russia at the global head table is a comeback. The contemporary role of East Asia in the world economy is a resurgence as well. India holds great civilizational depth. While Brazil and South Africa are newcomers to global influence, both carry complex histories. China, India, Russia, Brazil, Egypt, Turkey, Iran, Mexico, Peru, Japan, Korea, Indonesia, Thailand, Cambodia, Tibet, among others, have an imperial past. Against this backdrop, many social forces in emerging economies take into account a long time frame.

A further consideration is the general dearth of global public goods. Global governance has a record that is both lengthy and limited. The *Governance Report 2013* illustrates the impasse. Its most momentous contribution is to call for another UN high-level commission on 'responsible sovereignty'.[24] Thus, it is not realistic to expect the BRICS to break an impasse that is structural and has been decades in the making. According to Paolo Nogueira Batista, deputy president of the NDB, 'one reason for the creation of the NDB is undoubtedly the slowness of the reform process in the Washington-based institutions'. This also applies to the creation of the AIIB.[25]

There are widely divergent perspectives on the role of the BRICS, all the way from sub-imperialism to transformationalism. According to Patrick Bond, the emerging forces act as 'deputy sheriffs' for the old powers.[26] One of the analytics is the 1960s theory of subimperialism. The assessment is extreme, data are interpreted through one lens only, and current developments point in opposite directions. Sources such as the *Wall Street Journal* offer a diametrically opposite view and bemoan 'the rise of the regional hegemons': 'Russia, Iran and China are advancing as the US retreats'.[27] Bond's view is an application of David Harvey's approach that posits a relationship between capitalism and imperialism (along with 'primitive accumulation').[28] It may lead to the blanket assessment of 'neoliberalism everywhere'.[29] At another extreme is Manoranjan Mohanty's perspective of global restructuring, according to which the new forces provide the impetus for major civilizational and democratic transformations.[30]

These assessments carry strong normative overtones. One view is completely top-down (hegemony rules) and the other is bottom-up (civil society constrains hegemony). These are instances of wide divergence in the assessments of globalization and capitalism. This is worth reflecting on because BRICS is in the eye of the beholder. The eye of the beholder matters because data are heterogeneous and in flux, multiple trends are in play and data are theory-dependent. Since trends and data are open to diverse selections and interpretations, a broad, wide-angle view makes sense.

Given post-crisis impasse in the US, Europe, and Japan, and the BRICS as new players, expectations in some quarters may be high. A guiding principle may be that a country's external relations will not usually exceed its internal, domestic relations. There are many instances when foreign policy provides a distraction from domestic pressure (popular imperialism is an example, nationalist fervor is another), but generally nations are less magnanimous abroad and spend less political capital in a cluttered arena that offers limited maneuvering room. Ultimately then, an important guide to the BRICS' international role is their domestic conditions. If we consider not just growth but the quality of growth and the quality of governance, it may be sufficient to temper expectations.

Among new BRICS initiatives are the Contingent Reserve Arrangement and the New Development Bank:

> In essence, the currency reserve pool seeks to partly replicate the role of the IMF, which helps stabilise economies facing a liquidity crisis in the short run. In a sense, the BRICS bank will act like the World Bank and

the currency reserve pool could play a financial stabilisation role, like the IMF. The creation of a new financial architecture in a South-South context is the most concrete idea that has emerged from the four BRICS summits held since 2009. . . . The central banks of the US and Europe have effectively pumped close to $5 trillion of fresh money since 2008 without any significant output growth. This scale of fresh currency injection has created multiple bubbles in real estate assets and commodities all around the world. The BRICS economies are particularly vulnerable to this. The proposed BRICS currency pool is therefore relevant in this very context.[31]

While the NDB may be 'an auxiliary funding institution', it is aligned to the BRICS' development agenda. The BRICS also plan to establish their own credit rating agency, given that the credit rating agencies that affect developing countries' credit standing are privately owned American companies (the big three are Standard and Poor's, Moody's, and Fitch).

3 Bricolage

The BRIC stand out for several reasons. While they are the leading EME, they are also developing countries with major poor majorities. With a total population of 2.8 billion, BRIC societies comprise nearly half the world's population of 7 billion. They also comprise almost half of the world's poor. The total number of people living in poverty in BRIC societies is 376 million, less than half the 'bottom billion'. In other words, should the BRICs address their problems of poverty it would meet almost half of the world's problems of poverty. They include countries that combine the world's largest growing resources with the greatest social need.

It is not clear at this stage to what extent the emerging economies are add-ons to the status quo or are game changers and what the nature of their game is. An important predictor of their external influence is their internal conditions. Here social inequality is a better gauge and more sensitive indicator than liberal democracy, human rights, the use of Internet and social media, or assorted cultural changes—common yardsticks from Western points of view. Thus, while most international attention focuses on economic and political equations (as in 'emerging markets' and 'emerging powers'), the social dimension in the BRICS matters as much.

The BRIC are starkly different in their histories and approaches to poverty and inequality. Since 1949, China has experienced the greatest victory over poverty in history. Incomes in China have risen 400 percent since 1980 and the estimated number of people living in poverty was down to 1.9 percent in 2013. China still has low levels of per capita income ($7,924 in 2015) compared to the US ($55,863 in 2015). The poverty level in Brazil is high at 21.4 percent (48 million, 2009), but since the mid 1990s programs such as

Bolsa Família have raised living standards by providing the poor with financial and medical support. India with 21.2 percent living in poverty (2011) is at a similar level of poverty. In Russia poverty increased in the decade after 1989, but shrunk during the last decade to 13.4 percent or 19.2 million (2016), nearly back to 1989 levels.[32]

Russia and China have experienced major social revolutions while India, Brazil, and South Africa have only experienced political transformations. The yardsticks of democracy and inequality do not move in tandem. The democracies, India, Brazil, and South Africa, are marked by the BRICS' highest rates of inequality and their combating poverty combines with a low priority for addressing inequality. In India, electoral democracy exists alongside caste and communalism, and India's poor are larger in number than in all of sub-Saharan Africa. India's literacy rate of 74 percent of the adult population is the lowest among the BRICS (the adult literacy rate in Brazil is 93 percent, in China 95 percent, Russia 99 percent, South Africa 93 percent, 2012). In Brazil, the threshold for political parties to enter parliament is low and governance involves coalitions with numerous parties (25), including landholding and business groups.

Measuring the income distribution, comparing the proportion of national income received by the top 10 percent of the population to that received by the bottom 10 percent, illustrates patterns of difference. China comes out the most equal of the BRICs with the bottom 10 percent earning 3.5 percent and the top decile earning 15 percent; proportions in the other three are closer together, with Brazil showing the widest social inequality. Table 4.3 shows that between 2010 and 2016 inequality increased in all BRIC except India.

Whether the BRICS can integrate the poor majority, rural and urban, holds major ramifications. Inequality matters for several reasons. First, if EM opt for inclusive rather than polarizing growth, their development is likely to be more sustainable, both according to classic human development perspectives and recent assessments. Second, inequality is crucial in assessing the quality of growth. The monumental numbers of GDP growth in China cannot be taken

Table 4.3 Proportion of national income of top 10% and bottom 10% of BRIC population

BRIC		Top 10%	Bottom 10%
China	2010	15.0%	3.5%
	2016	30.0%	1.7%
Russia	2010	30.4%	1.9%
	2016	42.4%	5.7%
India	2010	31.1%	3.6%
	2016	31.1%	3.6%
Brazil	2010	43.0%	1.1%
	2016	42.9%	0.8%

Source: CIA 2010, 2016.[33]

at face value because the prices of labor, land, and environment have been kept artificially low. The sacrifice of the rural and urban poor is the flipside of emerging economies' growth. Third, if social inequality is addressed, it is likely that addressing political and ecological constraints follows suit; policies with regard to inequality are an indicator of wider dynamics. Fourth, as EM step onto the world stage, their problems increasingly become global problems. If the overall choice is for narrow growth, the likelihood of capitalisms converging towards a Davos-style capitalism and global plutocracy (now more centered in the East) is greater, which poses risks of wider instability over time. Fifth, inclusive development in the domestic sphere will inform emerging economies' relations with developing countries. If 'frontier capitalism' is contained domestically, it may also be constrained in external economic relations.

Barrington Moore Jr voiced the classic position that the modernization of the agrarian sector is a necessary condition for a stable democracy.[34] The failure to integrate the rural majority into modernity was a contributing factor to the rise of fascism and Nazism as coercive ways of achieving modernization. Soviet communism was another alternative. Most EME are also developing countries with a poor majority.

The peasant question has been either the undoing or the foundation of social revolutions—a factor in the undoing of the Soviet revolution and a foundation in the case of China. The Soviet industrialization debate during the New Economic Policy (1921–1929) first favored agriculture with policies that advantaged rich peasants (kulaks). Stalin's forced, rapid, and massive collectivization of the peasantry short-circuited this, which led to a steep fall in agricultural output, famine, and flight from the land. The worker-peasant alliance, the hammer-and-sickle, was elusive.[35]

Gandhi and Gramsci were contemporaries and both sought to address the peasant question.[36] Gandhi with his dhoti dress, cultivation of rural virtues and rural industries such as the spinning wheel, and espousal of rural causes as in the Salt March; and Gramsci with his interest in the role of the church and popular religion because it was the church that was able, unlike any other institution, to reach Italy's peasant majority.

Contemporary trends show 'the continuing relevance of the agrarian problem'.[37] The rural majorities in developing countries make rural development a key concern. The 'peasant question' has loomed large in development studies. Development policy has been an arena of 'agrarianists', proponents of 'agriculture first' and 'industrialists', proponents of 'industry first'.[38] Arthur Lewis took up the Dutch economist Boeke's thesis of the dual economy, the divide between the modern and traditional sectors. 'Industry first', the position that dominated postwar modernization polices, came with euphoria about industrialization and viewed agriculture as a sector that should transfer resources to industry, with cheap agricultural produce for workers, in effect, an 'industrial trickle-down' approach.

In China, Mao's 'walking on two legs' or developing both industry and agriculture, including building rural industries such as steel production in

Township and Village Enterprises (TVEs), was an early attempt at balanced development (which followed Marx's ideas).[39] It was marred by the disastrous failure of the large-scale experiments of the Great Leap Forward and the Cultural Revolution. Nevertheless, the Chinese revolution placed the peasantry center stage and Mao's approach contributed to China's development, also in the countryside.[40]

The peasant question loomed large in decolonization movements and in Frantz Fanon and Amilcar Cabral's work. According to Fanon:

> The peasantry is systematically disregarded for the most part by the propaganda put out by the nationalist parties. And it is clear that in the colonial countries the peasantry alone are revolutionary, for they have nothing to lose and everything to gain.[41]

The rural majority has been a key element in decolonization struggles, in insurgency, and counterinsurgency. It was part of American Community Development in India in the 1950s. American national security doctrine targeted 'village modernization' in Cold War arenas, land reform in South Korea, 'strategic hamlets' in South Vietnam, and low-intensity conflict in Nicaragua.[42] Mobilization of the peasantry was part of the Vietnam War and the 'protracted people's war' that raged on several fronts. In Lin Biao's 'peasant revolution', the world's peasantry would surround the cities.[43] Che Guevara's focismo and his rallying cry 'Two, Three, Many Vietnams' echoed this perspective.[44] In Bolivia, Che sought to mobilize the peasantry, in vain.

The growing problems of import substitution industrialization (ISI) in developing countries and health, education, and infrastructure policies that favored urban areas, gave rise to Michael Lipton's thesis of 'urban bias', a notion that long remained influential, as in the World Bank's argument of agriculture for development (2008).[45] Development strategies often sideline the rural majority. In South Africa, Black Economic Empowerment has barely any provision for the peasants in the Bantustans. The argument of urban bias, however, understates the role of class and underrates urban poverty; what is at issue is not space but *class*. Peasants are differentiated between rich and poor, and class alliances across the rural-urban divide produce a class bias in public policies, so the actual bias, rather than an urban bias, is often a 'landlord bias'.[46]

In development studies, the wider agenda is broad-based development, rather than narrow growth paths that benefit limited strata. In human development perspectives, the case for integrating the peasantry in development is straightforward: the more of society's members that make productive contributions, the more all of society benefits. Interest groups contest economic priorities, strategic groups seek to capture state power, and cultural and historical legacies affect the relations between middle class and peasants, between urban centers and the countryside. Uneven development and internal colonialism are interspersed with histories of conquest, ethnic domination, religious divides, and regional imbalances. Several legacies are well known such as caste and communalism in India, apartheid in South Africa, and colonial conquest and slavery in Latin America.

With major strides of industrialization and urbanization in EME, it is no surprise there are growing frictions between insecure middle classes and peasants in the process of 'de-peasantization', migrating to towns, adding to the working class. New class configurations are taking shape with a vast expansion of the global working class, a shift of working class into the middle class, and some of the middle class entering higher strata. Development projects (dams, mining, forestry, industrial agriculture, infrastructure, urban expansion) affect local populations, indigenous peoples, and their livelihoods. Land issues and ecological frictions and conflicts are part of the changing equations between the middle class and peasants. Environmental changes and problems of conservation, watersheds, and access to cultivable land affect agriculture and the rural poor.

Japan, South Korea, and Taiwan achieved integration of the rural majority with land reform, broad education policies, fiscal reform, industrial policies, and rural industries.[47] This laid the foundations in human and social capital and institutions that made the later success of export-oriented industries and economic liberalization possible. As city states, Singapore and Hong Kong have not had to deal with a peasant hinterland and are outside this picture. These questions loom large in India, Pakistan, Bangladesh, and most of Southeast Asia. In India, 71 percent of the population is rural, of which 29 percent (more than 200 million people) lives below the poverty line. In the Philippines, land reform has long been a major hurdle. High concentration of landholding also applies to Thailand and Malaysia. In this regard, Southeast Asia resembles Latin America more than Northeast Asia.

Turkey and Bolivia are countries in which the (former) peasantry is in power. In Turkey, rural migrants from Anatolia, the power base of the AKP, the governing party have gained major influence. In Bolivia, highland indigenes supported the Evo Morales government, which followed earlier policies of decentralization.[48]

From unbundling the middle class (Chapter 8.1), it follows there are no general scenarios of how middle classes respond to the social aspirations of the poor. Empirical findings in different countries point in multiple directions. Would the growing middle classes of Asia and Latin America welcome the emancipation of the poor majority? They would as long as they are deemed an asset to economic growth. To what extent this is the case is a function of public discourse, which is shaped by media, political institutions, economic models, and cultures of emancipation, or the public standing of egalitarian traditions (Chapter 5.2). In each of the BRICs, there are egalitarian traditions and emancipation discourses that hold different standing over time, in public culture and local environments.

Practically all emerging economies face major rural and agricultural crises. In China, this takes the form of pressure on land, deepening rural poverty, pollution, village-level corruption, and urban migration. In Brazil and the Philippines, land reform drags on because the political coalition to confront landholding oligarchies is too weak. In South Africa, the apartheid legacy, poor soil, and weak agricultural base in the former Bantustans contribute to rural crisis.

These are classic problems of modernization. EM need balanced development and 'walking on two legs', yet urban bias (low agro prices, inadequate support for agriculture) and the intrusion of transnational market forces in agriculture (land appropriations, multinational agribusiness) are crisis prone, as in India.

The impact of poor peoples' movements and social struggles in the 2000s has been greater than during 1980–2000, notably in China and Latin America. In China where 'a social protest erupts every five minutes', social crises led to 'harmonious society' policies adopted in 2005. In Latin America, poor peoples' movements contributed to the election of leftwing governments in Venezuela, Bolivia, Ecuador, Uruguay, and Nicaragua and to policy adjustments in Argentina and Chile. In the wake of the Great Recession, the 'pink tide' has been receding.

While China has abandoned the 'Shanghai model' of fast-growth policies that are geared to attract foreign investment, it is pursued with fervor in India. A case in point is the 'Shanghaing of Mumbai' and the growth of special economic zones.[49] What is the relationship between the India of Thomas Friedman (*The World Is Flat*, 2005) and P. Sainath (*Everybody Loves a Good Drought*, 1996), between celebrating growth and deepening poverty, between Gurgaon's Millennium City of Malls and abject poverty kilometers away, between dynamic 'Cyberabad' and rising farmer suicides nearby in the same state of Andhra Pradesh? According to official figures, 100,248 farmers committed suicide between 1993 and 2003. Armed Maoist struggles spread to 170 rural districts, affecting 16 states and 43 percent of the country's territory and have become a major security problem.[50]

> For every swank mall that will spring up in a booming Indian city, a neglected village will explode in Naxalite rage; for every child who will take wings to study in a foreign university there will be 10 who fall off the map without even the raft of a basic alphabet to keep them afloat; for every new Italian eatery that will serve up fettuccine there will be a debt-ridden farmer hanging himself and his hopes by a rope.[51]

India's economic growth benefits a top stratum of 4 percent in the urban areas with little or negative spinoff for 80 percent of the population in the countryside. The software sector rewards the educated middle class. The IT sector has an upper-caste aura—brainy, needs good education, English language—and extends upper-caste privileges to the knowledge economy with low-cost services from the majority population in the informal sector.[52] Public awareness in India is split between middle-class hype and recognition of social problems, but there are no major policies in place to address the problems of rural majorities and the urban poor.

China with its long history of peasant revolts and mobilization adopted the 'harmonious society' platform in 2003 with policies of tax relief, clinics in the countryside, and urbanization.[53] Latin America and Brazil experienced peasant rural-urban migration earlier than in Asia and have absorbed the rural majority, but in the informal rather than in the formal sector.[54] In Brazil, the urban poor, the favelas, and the informal sector are as important as urban-rural relations.

In addition to rural crisis, EME face profound urban poverty as part of the 'planet of slums'.[55] Rural crisis feeds into the sprawling world of the favelas, bidonvilles, and shantytowns. Urban policies are at best ambivalent to the poor and often negligent. Bangkok's glitzy monorail mass transit system connects shopping areas, but not the outlying suburbs. As India's rural poor are driven out of agriculture, they flock to the cities while clampdowns on informal settlements, hawking and unlicensed stores, and land appropriations squeeze the urban poor out of the cities, a scissor operation that leaves the poor with nowhere to go.

What is the standing of egalitarian traditions and cultures of emancipation in the BRICS? In India, egalitarian traditions include Gandhi and Ambedkar, Nehruvian socialism, Marxist-Leninist parties, the Dalit movement, participatory development in Kerala, Karnataka, and forms of decentralization, village self-rule (panchayat raj) and grassroots democracy.[56] Except for Nehruvian socialism and the Congress Party, none of these has been mainstream and none is now salient in public culture. Although India holds a vibrant tradition of popular protests, strikes, civic activism, and active democracy, eradicating poverty and undoing social inequality have never been a major public priority. A headline sums it up: 'Strong growth yet to improve lives of the poor'.[57] Part of the impasse is a crisis of governance, a tide of corruption scandals, and a growing shadow economy.[58] The Naxalite rebellion affects a sizable part of India's territory, is an expression of acute rural unrest, and involves shifting coalitions of Dalits, Adivasis, and impoverished farmers. The Naxalites are as marginal to India's mainstream preoccupations as is MST, the movement of the landless and the urban poor in Brazil, and more so because it presents an acute security threat.[59]

China draws on a long history of peasant revolts and peasant mobilization.[60] From the Jenan Way and Mao's peasant-based revolutionary strategies, the policy of the Township and Village Enterprises (TVEs) and building rural industries, the countryside has been central to China's revolutionary process. This changed with Deng Xiaoping's 'four modernizations' and its emphasis on rapid coastal industrialization, attracting FDI, and an export-led economy built on vast rural migration to the industrial belt. Deng's modernizations built on the foundations laid during the Mao era, just as India's liberalization built on foundations going back to Nehruvian socialism.[61]

That labor standards in China lag far behind ILO norms is widely recognized, but recent trends show improvements.[62] The 'harmonious society' framework adopted in 2003, for all its limitations, produced significant changes. Today's rural migrants are the second generation of peasant workers. Worker suicides in spring 2010 at the Foxconn and Honda factories have led to 25–30 percent wage increases, protest actions at many other factories, new militancy among rural migrants (coordinated by mobile phone and SMS), improvements in labor conditions, moving factory production inland where wages are lower, and higher working class wages in China. The labor contract law that went into effect in 2008 with its stronger protection of worker rights enables some of these changes.[63]

Brazil has long been associated with extreme inequality. It has stood out as a negative example of pauperizing growth. 'Brazilianization' has been international shorthand for steep social inequality.[64] Brazil has also been the site of major social movements: a strong abolitionist movement, strong labor, indigenous and environmental movements, and the movement of the landless (MST), and trendsetting forms of participatory democracy such as Porto Alegre's participatory budget.[65] Brazilian social movements host the World Social Forum in Porto Alegre. The PT government initiated significant changes with a strong increase of the Human Development Index and a sharp decline of the Gini index by .5 since 2000, a rare and remarkable achievement.[66]

In Russia, egalitarian traditions go back to the *mir*, the peasant community, to 19th-century emancipation movements, the Bolsheviks, and the Soviet era. After the collapse of the USSR and market shock therapy, Russia has 'raced to the top of the listing of most unequal societies'. 'Egalitarian ideas still have many adherents in Russia, while the economic elite despises demands for egalitarian policies and prides itself on being a true meritocracy'.[67] Market shock therapy weakened the state and generated a cohort of tycoons, many of which later aligned with the 'vertical of power' of the security state. The 2004 bill that converted Soviet-era social entitlements into (limited) cash payments met with widespread popular opposition.[68]

Finally, there are also various transnational dimensions to rural issues in the BRICS. Liberalization and the entry of multinational agro-industries in fertilizer, agricultural equipment, seeds, and produce markets affect rural livelihoods, as in the 'green revolution' and its effects over time on Indian agriculture.[69]

Agricultural subsidies in the EU and US carry negative consequences for the rural poor in developing countries. 'US and EU subsidies of agriculture mean that developing countries such as those in Africa find it harder to export their products'.[70] This is a matter of relations between the affluent middle class and cultivators on a transnational scale. Countries such as the Emirates, Saudi Arabia, and South Korea lease agricultural land in Sudan, Pakistan, Mozambique, and other developing countries, acquiring millions of hectares for long periods at meager or nominal rates, to the detriment of locals.[71] Offshore agriculture is a contention between the affluent middle class and peasants at a transnational level.

City-states without a peasant hinterland (such as Singapore, Hong Kong, and the Gulf Emirates) are hosts of rural migration flows from other countries. Thus, not only rural-urban but also transnational migration is part of the global equation.[72]

Many migrants come to high-income economies from the countryside; crossborder migration is an extension of internal migration, such as construction workers from Kerala, Baluchistan, and Afghanistan working in the Emirates, West Africans working in Europe, and Hispanics from Central America in the United States. The ensuing cultural and social tensions don't just reflect xenophobia or religious differences but also class and cultural frictions between the middle class (urban, Western, 'modern') and peasants (rural, nonwestern, religious, ethnic), articulated in differences in cultural style and outlook. Peasants may be the bearers of national identity (as in Palestine, Egypt, Turkey, Cambodia, Laos), but that does not make peasant cultural styles appealing. Peasant cultural vocabularies typically hinge on ethnicity and religion and are not particularly appealing to urbanites. The pathos surrounding headscarves and the burka in France and other European countries reflects not just secularism and the 'chauvinism of prosperity' but also middle class disdain for rural styles.[73] Tensions also followed in the wake of the Great Recession, such as new restrictions on immigration in Australia and the Syrian refugee crisis.

Each of the BRIC has implemented social policies in recent years, with state provisions and legislative changes in China, conditional cash transfers to the poor in Brazil, and paid work programs in India's Rural Livelihood program. Only Brazil has managed to dent inequality significantly.

In 2007, *The Economist* wrote, 'In some ways Brazil is the steadiest of the BRICs. Unlike China and Russia it is a full-blooded democracy; unlike India it has no serious disputes with its neighbours. It is also the only BRIC without a nuclear bomb'.[74] In 2015, however, Brazil slipped from a growth rate of 7.5 percent to a recession of −3.5 percent and in 2016, a governance crisis ended the 13-year rule of the labor party (PT).

This illustrates the vulnerability of the BRICS. The collapse of energy and commodity prices in the years after the 2008 crisis triggered recession in Russia with negative growth of −3.5 percent (2015). In South Africa, the ANC, the governing party since 1994, suffered major losses in elections and lost governing majority in major cities (2016). China, the 'muscle' of the BRICS, faces a growing overhang of debt. India remains fragile as an uneven collage of states with fragmented regulation and inadequate infrastructure.

In sum, the BRICS unfold at the confluence of several variables:

- The rise of emerging economies, following the rise of Asia.
- The rise of China (especially since joining the WTO in 2001), which pulls along EMDC.
- Economic stagnation in advanced economies affects China and Asian EM with ripple effects in EMDC.
- Financialization in advanced economies and institutional investors and hedge funds looking for yield represents the demand side of return, and BRICS are on the supply side. The BRICS and other EM asset classes have been created to meet this demand.
- In view of the dearth of global public goods, inadequate global governance, and underrepresentation of EM in international institutions, the BRICS' new institutions have emerged and contribute to a multipolar world order.

The next chapter examines inequality on a global canvas. Chapter 6 turns to the 2008 crisis. While the crisis is experienced globally, its impact is by no means uniform, and there is wide variation in how societies cope with these challenges, which sheds light on the institutional variation among capitalisms.

Notes

1 The BRICs: The trillion-dollar club, *The Economist* 4/15/2010; C. Giles, J. Anderlini, I. Gorst, J. Wheatley, and J. Leahy, BRIC quartet defined by differences, *Financial Times* 6/15/2009.
2 CIA 2010; US Census 2010.
3 A. Beattie, When is a BRIC not a BRIC? When it's a victim, *Financial Times* 1/22–23/2011: 9.
4 In sequence, *Financial Times* 2/23/2007, 9/23/2008: 28, 1/6/2009 and 8/27/2010.
5 T. Gray, Emerging markets are more than just the BRICs, *New York Times* 10/7/2012: 10.
6 L. Denning, Are cracks forming in the BRICs? *Wall Street Journal* 2/16/2010: C10; D. Oakley, Different strokes for different folks? *Financial Times* 12/1/2008: 17.
7 Armijo and Burges 2010; Sotero and Armijo 2007.
8 Chen and Zhang 2010: 49.
9 Chen and Zhang 2010.
10 E.g., Lo 2008.
11 Desai 2007: 781.
12 Armijo 2007: 8.
13 G. Rachman, Illiberal capitalism, *Financial Times* 1/9/2008: 9.
14 Armijo 2007: 27.
15 Barma *et al.* 2007: 27; cf. Gat 2007.
16 Cf. Nederveen Pieterse 2009; Vukovich 2010.
17 The Global Footprint Network, Ecological Wealth of Nations. Last modified 2016. www.footprintnetwork.org/ecological_footprint_nations/ecological_per_capita. html. Accessed 10/18/2016.
18 Armijo 2007: 39
19 Zhang Yunbi and Wu Jiao, Leaders work for a stable world, *China Daily* 3/18/2013.
20 2011, quoted in Etzioni 2016: 185.
21 See Etzioni 2016; cf. Feldman 2015.
22 Hertie 2013: 93.
23 J. Singh, BRICS at risk of crumbling under weight of individual agendas, *The Indian Express* 3/24/2013.
24 Hertie 2013.
25 IMF governance: one step forward, one step back, *Bretton Woods Observer* winter 2016: 5.
26 Bond 2013.
27 Rise of the regional hegemons, *Wall Street Journal* editorial 5/26/2015: A12.
28 Harvey 2004.
29 Peck and Tickell 2002; a critique is Nederveen Pieterse 2014b.
30 Mohanty 2015.
31 M. K. Venu, Laying new BRICS in Durban, *The Indian Express* 3/25/2013.
32 World Bank, Poverty & Equity, http://povertydata.worldbank.org/poverty/country/CHN. Accessed 10/24/2016. Central Intelligence Agency, World Factbook, www.cia.gov/library/publications/the-world-factbook/fields/2046.html. Accessed 10/24/2016; AFP, Millions more Russians living in poverty as economic crisis bites, *The Guardian* 3/21/2016.

33 Central Intelligence Agency, Household Income by or Consumption by Percentage Share, www.cia.gov/library/publications/the-world-factbook/fields/2047.html. Accessed 10/25/2016.
34 Moore 1996, quoted in Thompson 2010: 201.
35 Lewin 1985; Kay 2009.
36 Pantham 1995.
37 Kay 2009: 104.
38 Kay 2009.
39 Meisner 1977.
40 Rodrik 2001; Arrighi 2007.
41 Fanon 1967: 47.
42 Cullather 2006.
43 Lin Biao 1965.
44 Guevara 1967.
45 Lipton 1977; Kay 2009: 105. World Bank Development Report 2008.
46 Kay 2009: 110-114.
47 Kay 2002, Kim 2008; disputed by Hart-Landsberg 1993, Chang 2010, Jeong and Westra 2010.
48 Nederveen Pieterse 2001.
49 Mahadevia 2006.
50 Jo Johnson, Insurgency in India—how the Maoist threat reaches beyond Nepal, *Financial Times* 4/26/2006: 13.
51 Tejpal 2006.
52 Krishna and Nederveen Pieterse 2008.
53 Li 2010.
54 Kay 2009.
55 Davis 2006.
56 Gore 1993; Mohanty *et al.* 2007.
57 J. Lamont, Strong growth yet to improve the lives of the poor, *Financial Times* 1/27/2011: 1.
58 Reed 2010; Kumar 2013.
59 Roy 2010.
60 Zhou 2007.
61 Bramall 1993; Guthrie 2006; Rodrik 2001.
62 Chan 2001; Chan and Siu 2010; Breslin 2009.
63 'The LCL gives workers a private right of action to enforce their own legal rights. In other words, employees may now sue their employers directly, without the aid of the state'. Harris and Luo 2008.
64 It has produced neologisms such as Brazilionnaires; Cuadros 2016.
65 Burity 2009; Seisdesos 2010.
66 E.g., Petras 2009 disputes this.
67 Oversloot 2006: 75.
68 www.russiajournal.com/node/18256.
69 Bryceson *et al.* 2000; Bernstein 2004; Akram-Lodhi and Kay 2009; Sainath 1996; Nanda 1999.
70 Stiglitz and Schiffrin 2004: 4; Kay 2009: 114.
71 World Bank 2010; Margulis *et al.* 2013.
72 Nederveen Pieterse 2010b.
73 Nederveen Pieterse 2007.
74 Land of promise, *The Economist* 4/12/2007, quoted in Piper 2015: 9.

5   Social inequality

Multicentric perspectives

In advanced economies, globalization and technological change are blamed for rising inequality while in emerging economies globalization and tech change are credited with lifting millions out of poverty. In the US and UK, inequality has grown steeply over past decades while in Nordic European countries inequality has increased only marginally. The same variables, tech change and globalization, yield widely different processes and outcomes of inequality. The disparities reflect different initial conditions and different institutions, so it follows (a) goldilocks globalization has changed place and (b) it's the institutions, stupid! In China, poverty is accepted (it's still a developing country) but inequality is not (it undercuts the legitimacy of the party). In India, inequality is accepted but poverty is not (it is a blight on national pride). Instead of a generalizing macro approach that focuses on global trends and global perspectives, we need multicentric perspectives that are attuned to diverse initial conditions, different institutions and cultures of inequality, which means a fundamental shift in the conversation. General trends (such as globalization and tech change) affect different conditions in different ways.

This chapter first disentangles poverty and inequality. Poverty as a theme is widely accepted while inequality is politically volatile. The second argument is that global inequality as a theme belongs to an earlier cycle of globalization and has receded with the rise of emerging economies, so it is time to move on and unbundle inequality by regions and countries. The chapter discusses trends in social inequality in emerging economies, developing countries, and advanced economies. Section 4 seeks to explain patterns of inequality in terms of institutions and discusses how global trends affect countries and regions differently. The closing section addresses ongoing policy debates.

1 Poverty yes, inequality no

There are global perspectives on poverty and poverty reduction, such as the UN Millennium and Sustainable Development Goals. There is an international working consensus on the importance of reducing poverty, but there is no consensus and no global perspective on inequality. The reason is simple: inequality is a political and ideological football. Addressing poverty has been possible under the most unequal and hierarchical conditions, as in grain disbursements in imperial China, alms, zakat, poor relief, soup kitchens, and charity. It is possible to palliate poverty without sacrificing privilege; but taking up inequality targets the structures of privilege and hierarchy and right away presents hefty political and ideological concerns because they overlap with the organization of accumulation.

Arguably, inequality is more important as a theme than poverty. 'Most of the poorest people in the world (70 per cent of those living on less than $1.35 per day—2010) live in middle-income countries',[1] so the key issue is inequality, rather than poverty per se. But inequality is politically sensitive while poverty as a theme is widely acceptable. Perspectives on inequality diverge more widely and are more contentious than perspectives on poverty.

According to a 1996 report, 358 billionaires own as much wealth as 2.3 billion people. According to a 2005 report, the world's richest 50 people are earning more than the 416 million poorest. According to a 2014 report, 85 billionaires own almost as much as half the world's population and a 2016 report updates this to a mere 62 billionaires.[2]

Several institutions have raised questions of social inequality, but when it comes to policy international institutions consistently settle on poverty. The *Poverty Guidance* (2000) of the British Department for International Development puts it plainly:

> Lower inequality can be achieved directly by redistributing . . . assets, such as land and income. Such redistribution can be politically difficult and may reduce growth. A less direct approach is to build the assets of the poor and increase their ability to participate in growth.[3]

'May reduce growth' is the key trope.

The outcome in international development policy is, as usual, hegemonic compromise.[4] We live in the era of this compromise. The UN Development Goals are a hegemonic compromise and reflect 'difficulties' and fundamental disagreements (whether inequality is necessary for growth or hampers growth).

Meanwhile much ingenuity goes into devising policies that address poverty *without* affecting inequality and the structure of wealth and power. Seriously addressing poverty *does* dent inequality. 'When the poor get literate and educated, the rich lose their palanquin bearers'.[5] But usually anti-poverty approaches (such as the 'war on poverty' in the US) fall way short. Poverty as a theme matters, but inequality cuts deeper and has become increasingly urgent.

In recent years, inequality has leapt high up the agenda. Two presidents called it their main challenge, Obama in the US and Michelle Bachelet in Chile. Pope Francis highlights it in his Apostolic Exhortation *Evangelii Gaudium* (2013).[6] The World Economic Forum recognizes that inequality has become dramatic. Its 'Outlook on the Global Agenda 2014' ranked 'widening income disparities as the second greatest worldwide risk in the coming 12 to 18 months'. Inequality is 'impacting social stability within countries and threatening security on a global scale'.[7] Stagnant wages in developed countries, banking scandals, spectacular statistics of rampant inequality, the 2008 crash, social movements such as the Indignados in Europe, Occupy Wall Street, and the slogan of 'the 1% and the 99%' have contributed to the salience of inequality.

Earlier discussion focused on global inequality and the relationship between globalization and inequality. A recap is as follows. Postwar capitalism from 1950 to the 1970s combined growth and equity. Although overall North-South inequality widened, growth went together with growing equality among and within countries. Neoliberal economics during 1980–2000 produced a sharp trend break: now growth came with sharply increasing inequality within and among countries. The exceptions to the trend were the East Asian Tiger economies.

Debates on globalization and inequality—whether globalization does or does not increase inequality—were prominent in the late 1990s and early 2000s. Global inequality loomed large as a sequel to the North-South gap, now under the heading of globalization.[8] Chairing a UN meeting on global disparities in 2000, Juan Somavía, then head of the ILO, said: 'We can no longer give globalization the benefit of the doubt. The results are in, and it flunked'.[9] According to Mahathir Mohamed in his goodbye speech as prime minister of Malaysia in 2003, 'Globalization is recolonization'.

In the 21st century, with the rise of emerging economies, especially China and India, there is no longer any doubt that globalization *has* reduced global inequality. This is a general assessment: 'The world's Gini index fell between 2002 and 2008—perhaps for the first time since the industrial revolution'.[10] At the same time, 'while global income inequality has fallen, within countries— rich and poor alike—inequality has been rising almost everywhere'.[11] Thus, overall inequality between advanced economies and emerging economies is narrowing while inequality within EM and AE is increasing. It follows that the discussion moves on. In the discussion of globalization and inequality the data are aggregate, the units of analysis large and discourse unfolds at a macro level. This provides limited insight so the issue is to shift to a finer-grained level of discussion. Adopting multicentric perspectives means no longer focusing on global inequality (or globalization and inequality) but on inequality within regions and countries.

If by a global perspective on inequality we mean a transnational perspective coherent enough to inspire international policy, there is *no* global perspective on inequality. If a global perspective means a perspective that takes into account the diversity of inequality across nations and regions, then it refers to perspectives that differ according to regional and national trends. The second section reviews perspectives on inequality across a sample of developing and developed countries. The discussion is exploratory and seeks to be indicative of the diversity of perspectives on and institutions of inequality. The third section discusses the global interplay of diverse institutions and how global trends affect countries and regions differently. The closing section concerns ongoing policy debates and their political subtext.

2 Patterns of inequality

There is a wide variety of policies and outcomes in relation to inequality, across and even within countries. Sri Lanka's Human Development Index (HDI) of 0.757 (2012) is close to that of wealthy Saudi Arabia (0.782). Adjusted for inequality, Sri Lanka's IHDI is higher than that of Saudi Arabia.[12] Bangladesh has a higher HDI and literacy rate than its mighty neighbor India.[13] In India, Kerala, Tamil Nadu, and Karnataka have higher HDI, literacy rates, and female participation in the labor force than other Indian states. In per capita GDP, the United States is at the world top, but its profile of inequality and poverty matches that of Romania.

In other words, poverty and inequality don't line up. A variable that goes some way to account for this variation is different perspectives on inequality. Perspectives on inequality reflect historical patterns and shape policies along with other dynamics. Elisa Reis notes, 'elites everywhere have a crucial role in the shaping of distribution policies'.[14] Perspectives on inequality are not uniform or homogeneous; they are mixed and layered, often contradictory, and reflect diverse interests and subjectivities.[15] This section reviews perspectives on inequality in Asia, Latin America, Africa, the Middle East, and developed countries. This overview makes use of Gini index, HDI, and inequality-adjusted HDI data (rather than indices of poverty) as estimates of income inequality. These are not effective measures of wealth inequality; data on assets such as land and property are not readily available. While we discuss perspectives, the assumption is that what matters are institutions of inequality and perspectives shaping institutions, social norms, and expectations.

Asia, the largest and most diverse world region, shows a wide diversity of approaches to inequality. In India, inequality is widely accepted but poverty is not. Inequality is viewed as a given because of social heterogeneity (region, religion, rural-urban differences) and cultural legacies (caste). Poverty is not accepted because it is viewed as a blight on national pride and an obstacle to progress. According to Bhikhu Parekh:

> [t]he insecure and self-absorbed Indian middle class, which want to get on with the task of development, see the poor as a drag and an embarrass-ment, and do not want to hear about them. The media, therefore, say little about poverty and popular films do the same.[16]

Because of the reservations policy, the poor have organized as castes and a policy that was intended to mitigate the effects of caste has in effect reinforced caste. India's literacy rate of 71 percent of the adult population (2015) is the lowest among the BRIC (the adult literacy rate in Brazil is 93, China 96.4, Russia 99.7). India accounts for the largest number of poor in the BRIC with 29.8 percent or 366 million living in poverty (2010).[17]

Bangladesh scores better than India on many indicators because of its pro-people development approach, the major role of NGOs, and policies such as micro-credit. The country's elite is of recent formation and rather than blaming (and 'othering') the poor, views poverty as part of the problem of development.[18]

Former socialist countries in Asia, Vietnam, and China, show markedly higher literacy, life expectancy, and HDI than other Asian countries. The adult literacy rate in Pakistan is 56.4 (2015), in Bangladesh 61.5 (2015) while in Vietnam it is 93.4 (2012) and in China 96.4 (2016).[19] A similar pattern exists in life expectancy and HDI.

China's rapid growth has lifted millions out of poverty and has tilted global poverty statistics, yet inequality and the rural-urban income gap have also grown steeply. China's Gini index of 0.421 is now higher than in any other Asian society (except Singapore and Hong Kong).[20] Maoist China repudiated inequality, whether feudal or bourgeois. The revolutionary era has bequeathed a social ethos of egalitarianism that continues to manifest in matters small and large. Since the Deng Xiaoping era ('to get rich is glorious'), inequality has become acceptable as a price of growth. This carries the implication that (a) inequality is viewed as an efficiency factor, (b) inequality that is unrelated to growth or hampers growth (such as corruption and market rigging) is unacceptable, with social media increasingly acting as public watchdogs, and (c) as growth slides, campaigns that target inequality may flare up.

Fast-track growth in coastal China under Jiang Zemin (the 'Shanghai model') was followed by efforts at rebalancing under Hu Jintao and Wen Jiabao (under the headings of 'harmonious society' and the 'scientific outlook on develop-ment') with major infrastructure and social investments in the countryside. Improving labor laws and labor conditions, strengthening the social safety net and urbanization have aimed at redirecting China's export- and investment-led growth model and boosting domestic consumption.[21]

Today's rural migrants are the second generation of peasant workers. The worker suicides in spring 2010 at Foxconn and Honda factories have spurred protest actions in many other factories, new militancy among rural migrants (coordinated by mobile phone and text messages), moves to improve factory labor conditions, moves to take factory production inland where wages are lower, wage increases of 25–30 percent, and a trend towards higher work-ing class wages in China.[22] A new pattern has developed in which the central government and party-state shore up their legitimacy by seeking to coopt or even foster protest, at times against local government, while at the same time controlling and containing its effects.[23]

These efforts continued under Xi Jinping with campaigns against government and CCP conspicuous consumption and corruption, also by relatives of government officials. The rural–urban divide in income and inequality remains salient. The Hukou system of household registration that restricts urban residence rights for rural migrant workers remains a major component of structural inequality. In sum, tolerance of inequality in China has grown but is conditional, and egalitarian values continue to influence public perceptions and inspire social movements and protests.[24]

Southeast Asia continues to be affected by feudal legacies and patrimonialism, particularly in land ownership and styles of governance, which intersect with lingering colonial influences. The Philippines, according to Joe Studwell, 'has never moved on from the colonial era and the patterns of amoral elite dominance that it created'.[25] Trading minorities (such as the ethnic Chinese) who stepped into the vacuum left by the colonizers could gain wealth in settings with weak institutions. Add in as well the Singapore model of industrialization led by foreign direct investment of multinational corporations, the outcome of which has been characterized as 'technology-less industrialization'.[26]

Northeast Asia followed Japan's model of industrialization (land reform, developmental state, industrial policy, investment in heavy industries) while in Southeast Asia weaker states leaned towards American influences and FDI. This combination of factors has produced stark differences between Northeast and Southeast Asia:

> The Gini coefficients of Japan, South Korea and Taiwan are 0.25 (0.38 in 2011), 0.32 (0.30 in 2014) and 0.24 (0.34 in 2014) respectively. In southeast Asia they begin at 0.34, 0.381 (2013) in Indonesia, and track quickly out to more than 0.5 in Hong Kong and Singapore.[27]

Cambodia is at 0.36 (2013) and Malaysia at 0.462 (2013).[28]

It is remarkable that the Gini coefficients of Northeast Asia match those of Nordic Europe (Norway and Sweden at 0.25, Belgium and Germany 0.28, the Netherlands 0.30, 2013)[29]—and do so largely *without* welfare states and mostly because of structural reforms.

To consider one country, South Korea underwent a career from developmental state to post-developmental state, followed by a neoliberal turn in the wake of the Asian crisis of 1997 and IMF intervention. South Korea has been increasingly burdened by the success of its champions, the chaebol that stifle competition and squeeze small and medium businesses. A further concern is the relationship between inequality and democracy. The growing gap between permanent and contract labor (as in Japan) contributes to social inequality.[30] Yet welfare spending has grown (average growth has been 13.1 percent over the last ten years while OECD average growth has been 5 percent).[31] According to Judith Teichman, 'The strength of civil society and labor . . . has been instrumental in Korea's social welfare expansion since the late 1990s'.[32]

Rapid growth across much of Asia has come with a widening wealth gap; through the 1990s and 2000s the Gini index of Asia rose about 1 percent each year. Thus, as Asia rises it converges with Latin America, the world's most unequal region.[33] But in such assessments the category Asia is too sweeping; in terms of inequality we can identify four broad clusters in Asia (Chapter 3.4).

According to the Human Development Report 2013, 'Latin America has seen income inequality fall since 2000, but it still has the most unequal distribution of all regions'.[34] In **Latin America**, at one extreme is Cuba where the top decile of income earners garners no more than 19.7 percent of national income and the Gini index is 0.30, and at the other extreme is Brazil where the top decile takes 42 percent of national income and the Gini index is 0.547 (2013), which places it among the world's most unequal societies.

In Brazil, inequality and poverty are usually conflated and when it comes to policy elites clearly favor policies that reduce poverty. Elisa Reis notes that Brazilian elites:

> [r]eject the idea of the restructuring of distribution . . . economic growth ought to be the strategy for dealing with the enormous shortfalls faced by Brazilian society, without penalizing the rich . . . Redistribution through more progressive taxation is accepted only by approximately 10 per cent of the elites.[35]

The preferred solutions are economic growth (i.e., trickle-down) and state action to alleviate poverty. According to Elisa Reis:

> In the official party line of the government the emphasis on stamping out inequality has been increasingly replaced by stressing the eradication of poverty. Despite its high profile image, the 'Zero Hunger' campaign, which is the social program that epitomizes the new trend, seems to lean more toward philanthropy than to notions of equal rights.[36]

Chile's Gini index of 0.521 (2013) is almost as high as that of Brazil. An assessment in Chile is 'We've had economic growth . . . with social malaise'. President Michelle Bachelet aimed at a tax overhaul to mitigate social inequality.[37] Several Latin American countries are clustered at a high level of inequality, such as Mexico with a Gini index of 0.472 (2013), Peru 0.481, Costa Rica 0.507, and Colombia at 0.559.[38] Cultures of conquest, colonialism, and slavery have produced enduring inequality, a color line, and a divide between those of European descent and indigenes. A new middle class is growing in urban Peru while poverty has been increasing in the impoverished highlands,[39] a tale of two economies that is echoed in other Latin American countries.

In **Africa**, apartheid South Africa was one of the world's most unequal societies, and post-apartheid South Africa is no different, with a Gini index of 0.63 (2013), higher than Brazil (0.547) and Haiti (0.592). The top decile of income earners captures half the country's income. The elite views inequality as necessary and as a boon for economic growth and is in denial about the extent of poverty, in particular rural poverty.[40] Since inequality is typically blamed on the apartheid legacy, the response has been policies such as Black Economic Empowerment, which has expanded inequality within black communities:

> Africa still has the smallest middle class as a share of the total population of all emerging regions . . . While economic growth in the continent has averaged nearly 6 per cent over the past decade, the upper middle class—those earning $10-$20 per day—has grown at a rate of less than 2 per cent.[41]

Angola is an example of polarizing growth with a Gini index of 0.427 (2013). Angola is 'a country with thousands of millionaires but where more than a third of its 25m people live below the poverty line'.[42] Nigeria's Gini index is 0.488. Oil wealth has not made a dent in inequality.[43] The fast-growing economies of Ghana and Ethiopia have Gini indices of 0.428 and 0.336 respectively.

Gini indices in the **Middle East** range from the lowest in Afghanistan at 0.278 to Qatar at 0.411 (2013) as the highest. Yemen with 39 percent of the population living below the poverty line is the poorest country in the Middle East. Several Arab states rank as high-income societies but their HDI is low. Populations in the Middle East and North Africa (MENA) are young and the region shows the world's widest gap between educated school leavers and job opportunities. According to a UNDP report:

> Recent social upheavals show that a mismatch between education and economic opportunity can lead to alienation and despair, especially among young people. Of the 20 countries with the largest increases in mean years of schooling over 1980–2010, 8 were in the Arab States . . . In most of these countries, employment opportunities failed to keep pace with educational attainment.[44]

Gender inequality in the region is well above the world average. In the Gulf Emirates, a steep divide runs between citizens and migrant workers who make up between 80 to 90 percent of the population, work in miserable conditions, shorn of labor rights, and have no chance at citizenship rights.[45] Alvaredo and Piketty observe:

> There is no doubt that income inequality is extremely large at the level of the Middle East taken as whole—simply because regional inequality in per capita GNP is particularly large. According to our benchmark estimates, the share of total Middle East income accruing to the top 10% income receivers is currently 55% (vs. 48% in the United States, 36% in Western Europe, and 54% in South Africa). Under plausible assumptions, the top 10% income share could be well over 60%, and the top 1% share might exceed 25% (vs. 20% in the United States, 11% in Western Europe, and 17% in South Africa).[46]

Among developing countries, a distinction runs between those with low Gini index and high GDP and per capita income (notably Northeast Asia) and those with low Gini index and low GDP and per capita income (such as Afghanistan, Bangladesh, Niger); the latter can be a matter of 'shared poverty'.[47]

A marked difference between *perspectives* on inequality in developing countries and developed countries is the timeline. In developing countries discussions of inequality often hark back to precolonial and colonial times. Preindustrial legacies and institutions intersect with postcolonial trends and globalization.[48] In developed countries discussions of inequality are mostly concerned with recent trends, the postwar era (associated with Keynesian economics), and the period after 1980 (associated with globalization, tech change, and neoliberalism).

Among **developed countries** there are marked differences between liberal market economies (LME), in which market forces lead, or are supposed to lead, and coordinated market economies (CME), in which government plays a coordinating role with other major stakeholders. Arguably, state-led market economies (SME) such as France and South Korea have gradually become CME. LME, CME, and SME are the main categories in the varieties of capitalism approach, a literature that mainly concerns the period from the 1980s to the 1990s. Related approaches are comparative capitalisms and modalities of capitalism (see Chapter 8.4).[49]

Since the late 1970s, inequality has grown generally but most steeply in LME (the US, UK, New Zealand, Australia). The combined effects of deregulation, financialization, managerialism, and CEO super salaries have resulted in the stagnation of incomes for the majority and a steep rise in inequality, especially steep, off-the-charts in the United States. In the US, not only inequality but also poverty is generally acceptable. Poverty is acceptable also because it is largely invisible with patterns of urban segregation and policies that reinforce it.[50] An additional factor was the GW Bush administration's tax cuts for the wealthy, which has been termed 'inequality by design'.[51]

The American 'drift towards oligarchy' is reinforced by trends such as the growing concentration in commercial media and the Supreme Court decision to remove caps on political campaign contributions by wealthy donors (2013). 'At the very top of the scale, plutocrats can shape the conversation by buying up newspapers and television channels or funding political campaigns'.[52] American democracy is a 'democracy fit for the 1 per cent'.[53] JK Galbraith deemed 'countervailing powers' (such as trade unions, civic organizations, social movements, public forums) necessary to balance the power of corporations, and these have eroded over the past decades in the US. This has been a general trend in postindustrial societies,[54] but is particularly pronounced in the US. Given the weakness of countervailing forces, the gains of rising productivity have accrued to corporations and shareholders, not to workers. The ethos of 'greed is good' that became dominant since the 1980s has given rise to practices of 'elite deviance', or in plain language, corporate crime.

The middle class's 'fear of falling' that was a looming specter in 1990, increasingly does mean falling into precarious conditions.[55] 'Will work for less' is a new adage.[56] Fifteen percent of Americans live below the poverty line.[57] 'Stagnant incomes, rising taxes, the pocketing of productivity gains by the corporate elite, a surplus of available credit, globalization, privatization, and labor market changes have altered what it means to be part of the American middle class'. It has given rise to 'post-industrial peasants' who keep up consumption habits on the basis of credit and live in debt peonage.[58] In Manhattan, 21.4 percent of the population lives below the poverty line, 46 percent live in or near poverty, and the Gini index is 0.60.[59]

CMEs include Germany, the Netherlands, Scandinavia, in short Nordic capitalism, and Japan. Here generally neither inequality nor poverty is acceptable. In European CME, the social contract—upheld by social democratic and Christian democratic coalition governments—has weakened because of 'creeping liberalization'[60] and growing immigration since the 1970s. Options with regard to immigration are combining welfare disbursements with 'citizenship integration' programs and making welfare benefits subject to stricter conditions. In most of Europe a growing number of immigrants have entered 'the precariat', working and living in precarious conditions.[61] Another option in relation to immigration is a double standard for citizens and migrant workers as denizens (as in Singapore, Hong Kong, Japan, and the Gulf Emirates).

The welfare state has stayed in Nordic Europe, has partly gone in the UK and Australia, and has become residual in the US. While CME have undergone 'variegated neoliberalization'[62] and austerity cutbacks, arguably (and it's not an easy argument) many social institutions remain robust. Robust enough for two EU finance ministers to caution that 'Europe accounts for just over 7 per cent of the world's population but 50 per cent of global social welfare spending'. They immediately add that 'Reform is the key'.[63]

3 Explanations, institutions

The variety of patterns of inequality across regions and countries generates two questions: how do we explain this variety and how does it relate to general trends such as globalization and tech change? The key variable is institutions. In short, weak institutions are correlated with weak overall economic performance and with high inequality.

In Mexico, a *nueva oligarquía* of 274 families and groups control most of the economy.[64] In Pakistan, '22 families' have exercised major control.[65] In the Philippines, large landowning families have long been the mainstay of the political elite. Concentrations of economic power are documented in many countries. Weak governance and weak institutions enable elite capture, which generates patches of wealth while leaving the economy as a whole behind and the majority in poverty.[66]

Why do institutions matter and why are they weak? According to Acemoglu and Robinson, economic development is almost entirely dependent on a state's institutions.[67] Development studies increasingly views governance as *the* most important variable that determines development (Chapter 8).

State governance may be strong in some spheres but not in others. In Pakistan, the military has been the mainstay of the power elite throughout the country's regime changes. The bureaucracy, the second major elite, has been dominant during civilian governments. Yet while strong in security and administration, Pakistan has an extremely low tax-to-GDP ratio of 9 percent, 'the lowest in the world'.[68]

Development policy distinguishes high, middle, and low-income countries, and subdivisions within each category (such as high, middle, and low middle-income countries). Travel in, for instance, Southeast Asia and the distinctions become viscerally clear in infrastructure, urban design, and level of organization. Singapore is a high-income country with world-class infrastructure (port, airport, urban design) and public services. Malaysia is a high middle-income country with excellent infrastructure and urban design, while in Cambodia (middle middle-income), Laos and Myanmar (low middle-income), infrastructure, urban planning, and overall organization are at a lower level. Besides, there are differences between urban and rural areas, cities, and small towns in each country. The World Bank's Index of Doing Business combines these national income levels with *weak and strong institutions* at *each* level.[69]

Why are institutions weak? General reasons why institutions are weak or weaken are (1) historical legacies, (2) authoritarian and military governments, (3) ideological interventions (such as free market thinking since the 1980s), and (4) gaps between new technologies and regulation (Chapter 8.4).

Some institutions go back to feudal legacies, such as large landholdings in Southeast Asia. Some date back to colonial times, such as large landholdings in Latin America and the Philippines. Or, institutions are weak because the national formation has been weak from the outset with regional and ethnic divisions, instability, and frequent regime changes, as in a number of African countries, the most recently decolonized region. Yemen is an example of 'intractable instability', divided and with frequent regime changes.[70] Some weak institutions go back to governance transitions upon decolonization. In East Asia, particularly Singapore and Hong Kong, when the colonizers left a vacuum of power, trading minorities stepped into the breach, occupied key economic positions, and established monopolies, in league with governing elites. The rise of Li Ka-shing, the Hong Kong business magnate, the richest person in Asia, illustrates an 'anti-competition and regulatory failure'.[71]

Classic instances of weak institutions are mining and petro economies. Part of the 'resource curse' is that resources can usually be more easily controlled by a strategic group and are more amenable to elite capture than farming and industry. African resource economies are an example.[72] Several petro economies are high-income countries with weak institutions and high inequality such as the Emirates, Saudi Arabia, Brunei, Uzbekistan, Kazakhstan, Nigeria, and Russia. Norway shows that this is not a necessary combination.

A further source of weak or weakening institutions is the regulatory lag in response to new technologies and economic opportunities. Technological, economic, and political changes produce new growth opportunities and changes in class relations which, after a time lag, produce adjustments in governance and institutions. In Marx's perspective, changes in the forces of production lead to changes in relations of production, usually as the outcome of new technologies such as navigation (compass, lateen sail) and long-distance trade, the steam engine and industrialization, and in the 20th century, computer chips and global value chains, containerization, and the expansion world trade, and so forth. Changes in the forces of production followed by changes in relations of production are perennial features of political economies. At each juncture, new accumulation opportunities bring new economic actors to the fore (merchants, industrialists, banks, telecoms, IT firms) that sideline incumbents (aristocracy, monarchy, industrialists) so the structure of privilege changes and new inequalities emerge. New accumulation requires new regulation, but institutional adjustments come about after a time lag and are subject to political maneuvering.

Since the Second World War, there have been major technological changes in production (integrated circuits, flexible production, digital turn), the organization of firms (MNCs, TNCs, lean firms), logistics (containerization, Walmart, Amazon distribution networks), and marketing (global brands, e-commerce). Major developments of the last 50 years include accelerated globalization, ICT, and financialization. As ever, institutions lag behind. The institutional lag is structural (in the sense of a perennial feature) and mutable in that it changes form according to the conjuncture and economic transformation. First-mover advantage also enables accumulation. Reforms develop in response to elites and strategic groups repositioning, social pressure, and class struggle. The lag in regulation involves power shifts between incumbents and new forces, new rapports de forces, a reshuffling of strategic groups, alliances, and hegemony. Both incumbents and new forces try to use regulation to protect their position, enhance advantages, extend monopoly rents, keep out newcomers and SMEs, and create regulation so cumbersome that only large corporations can comply.[73] Establishing loopholes becomes a side-industry of regulation. Consider a schematic sketch of dynamics over time, with emphasis on Europe and North America (Table 5.1).

Telecoms in the 1970s and 1980s opened up vast new accumulation opportunities and many billionaires hail from this economic niche.[74] Carlos Slim's wealth, the richest man in the world (2014), 'derives from establishing an almost complete monopoly over fixed line, mobile, and broadband communications services in Mexico'.[75] Thaksin Shinawatra, the Thai billionaire, derived his wealth from a telecoms monopoly, as did Silvio Berlusconi in Italy and Rupert Murdoch in Australia and the UK. The digital economy accounts for the fortunes of Microsoft, Apple, Google, Facebook, etc. Recent accumulation frontiers are the Internet and Silicon Valley (along with e-commerce, Ali Baba, apps, Uber, Airbnb).

Table 5.1 Economic transformations and institutional change (Europe and the West)

Time	New economics	New institutions
12–15C	Levant trade, merchants	Town rights, rise of city states
16–17C	Expansion of trade	State centralization, absolutism, mercantilism
17–18C	Triangular trade, colonialism, plantations	Rise of bourgeoisie, French Revolution, people's sovereignty
19C	Industrialization	Unions, parties—suffrage, social reforms
1890–1929	Finance and monopoly capital	Anti-trust laws, state monopolies
1930s	Great Depression	New Deal, fascism, Nazism
1945–1980	Oil majors, MNCs, TNCs, GVC	Keynesian policies
1980s	ICT, telecoms, financialization	Deregulation
1990s	Financial crises	Chiang Mai Initiative, Asian Bond Fund
21C	Hedge funds, credit default swaps, fintech	Basel III, Dodd-Frank bill, Vickers Report, Central Banks QE
	Emerging economies, SWF, OBOR	G20; BRICS NDB, CRA; AIIB

In the 1980s, in response to the economic stagnation of the 1970s, liberal market policies became dominant. According to liberal market views, inequality is welcome and necessary. In Margaret Thatcher's words, 'it is our job to glory in inequality and see that talents and abilities are given vent and expression for the benefit of us all'.[76] According to efficient market theory, inequality is a necessary part of an incentive structure that enables innovation and enterprise. A flexible labor market keeps wages low. Redistribution means interfering with the market and should be avoided. With the Thatcher and Reagan administrations in the UK and US came neoliberalism with deregulation, privatization, and liberalization as dominant trends.

A further twist is strong regulation for the weak and weak regulation for the strong. The Reagan administration cut social spending and expanded the security state, which kept state spending as a share of GDP as high as it was before and over time turned the US into the country with the highest incarceration rate among developed countries. The security and law and order apparatus disproportionally targets the poor and minorities while lobbies in Congress orchestrate loopholes and institutionalize corporate welfare. Deregulation (also of campaign financing) reinforces this tilt.

After major crises such as the savings and loan banks, the dotcom bubble bursting, and the Enron series of crises in the US, virtually no significant institutional reform has taken shape. The subprime crisis of 2008 has led to re-regulation such as Basel III, the Dodd-Frank bill in the US, and the Vickers Report in the UK, but many provisions are so complex and opaque that their actual impact is marginal or nearly imponderable. Or, they only concern banks while the main problem are shadow banks. Central Bank policies such as QE have been monetary holding operations, rather than structural reforms (Chapter 6.4).

Review Table 5.1, and major differences between economic changes and regulatory responses in the past and during the last 50 years become visible. Major economic changes of the last 50 years—such as the rise of MNCs, TNCs, global value chains, tax evasion, tax havens—are transnational in nature. Financialization comes with new financial instruments (quantitative investment, algorithms, derivatives, credit default swaps, high-frequency trading, etc.) and new actors such as hedge funds and sovereign wealth funds. Overall there has been little regulation in response. The combination of new tech (telecoms, chips), new economic opportunities (accelerated globalization), and deregulation generated the vast wealth gaps of our era. Given the magnitude and scope of recent tech and economic transformations, the inequalities that have developed have also been unprecedented. The governance gap is wider than ever. Ours is an era of digital capitalism and analog regulation. Often the response is not just political inaction but political maneuvering that deepens the effects of tech and economic changes.

In sum, the past 50 years have seen momentous expansion of tech capabilities and economic opportunities that enable global reach and scope, and governance institutions that are out of step with accumulation opportunities. The mismatch between the momentous increase in tech capabilities and economic transformations and institutions of governance is a core problem. Two related problems intertwine. Many changes unfold at a transnational level and fall outside the range of national institutions. Because of the neoliberal turn, also broadly since the 1980s, deregulation has been in vogue ('the market knows best', efficient market theory), and not just the capacity but the political will to regulate has diminished.

The variety of institutions accounts for the variety of patterns of inequality. Political capture and elite capture are general headings that involve different elites and different patterns of inequality. Research in Pakistan distinguishes traditional elites (landowning and religious), modern elites (military and bureaucracy), and emerging elites (corporate and international).[77] The enduring role of traditional elites accounts for the persistence of the 'rural idiom' in Pakistan politics.[78] In Europe a similar pattern is 'the persistence of the old regime', which according to Arno Mayer ended with the First World War and the onset of industrial warfare.[79]

With regime changes come shifts in dominant elites, such as the rotation of military and civilian governments (in which bureaucratic elites dominate) in Pakistan. With each type of government, the status of different business groups rotates and each involves coalitions with traditional elites. Shifting patterns of elite collusion affect the concentration of ownership of business groups and firms.

These patterns raise several points: (a) arising from specific initial conditions (conquest, decolonization), the effect of institutions may be long lasting;

(b) weak institutions can occur at every stage of development, in preindustrial, industrial, and postindustrial societies, and at high, middle, and low national income levels; (c) much discussion focuses on democracy, but democracy does not preclude weak or weakening institutions (though these are more likely to occur in the absence of democracy); (d) much discussion and mobilization is concerned with policies and politics, but should they not rather concern institutions since weak institutions can sidetrack good policies? (Chapter 8); and (e) several patterns are transnational in their ramifications.

The momentous increase in tech capabilities and economic opportunities comes with global reach. Deregulation is transmitted transnationally through various mechanisms. Multinationals and global value chains pass on market imperatives that may override national regulation and create conditions of exception (FTZ, SEZ, tax incentives, etc.). In agricultural futures, 'speculators accumulate as risks rise for the world's poor'.[80] Structural adjustment weakened state regulation in developing countries. The admonition to lift capital controls made them more susceptible to crisis. FTAs with the US and TPP and TTIP trade pacts include clauses that override national institutions.

Part of the global condition is global neomedievalism, a baffling maze of crisscrossing jurisdictions, authority structures, treaties, international trade rules, regional bodies, and national factions and interest groups. Deregulation has increased the concentration of wealth and power—hence the 62 billionaires who own half the world's wealth (2015). Oxfam International's 2014 report highlights the contemporary situation as follows:

- Almost half of the world's wealth is now owned by just one percent of the population.
- The wealth of the one percent richest people in the world amounts to $110 trillion. That's 65 times the total wealth of the bottom half of the world's population.
- The bottom half of the world's population owns the same as the richest 85 people in the world.[81]

In many developing countries, deregulation, liberalization, and privatization—hallmarks of the Washington consensus—reinforced virtually all patterns of inequality—traditional, modern, and emergent. With government rules and oversight turned back, elites could reoccupy accumulation niches. The policy turn to 'good governance' that occurred in 1997 attempted to clean up a mess that was partly the making of international development agencies.

The Economist captures plutocracy in emerging economies in a 'crony capitalism index': 'Developing countries contribute 42% of world output, but 65% of crony wealth'. Hong Kong and Singapore score highest on the index.[82] However, political capture does not merely exist as a peripheral problem in developing countries. This account glosses over the extent to which markets are rigged also in the US where crony capitalism is institutionalized—in the military-industrial complex, big oil, big pharma, agro-industry, too-big-to-fail banks, lobbies in Congress, and campaign financing. Because it has been institutionalized, it doesn't look like crony wealth.

Political scientists document that the steep inequality of recent decades in the US has been politically engineered in Congress.[83] Political coalitions in government have enabled banks to develop as a rent-seeking racket. But media and movies portray misdeeds as individual crazies (as in *The Great Gatsby*, *The Wolf of Wall Street*), not as socioeconomic institutions.

> From the 1980s onwards, the financial and banking sectors pumped millions of dollars into undoing regulations put in place after the stock market crash and Great Depression of the 1930s. Deregulation has had two major ramifications: corporate executives associated with the banking and financial sectors have become exceptionally wealthy, and global markets have become much more risky, culminating in the global economic crisis that began in 2008 . . . there is a direct correlation between financial deregulation and economic inequality in the US.[84]

Deregulation is most advanced in LME and ties in with the varieties of capitalism discussed earlier. The *conjunction* of accelerated globalization, tech change, the digital economy, neoliberalism, and financialization is responsible for the steep and pervasive increase in inequality over recent decades. The effects are amplified because it is a package deal. Each of the above per se may hold diverse ramifications, but in combination with deregulation as common denominator, the benefits overwhelmingly accrue to corporations and elites.

How does the variety of patterns of inequality relate to general trends such as globalization and tech change? Do general trends override differences among regions and countries, as in convergence theories? Accounts of inequality hold that inequality is necessary for growth, and globalization and tech change foster inequality by altering the balance between capital and labor.

In advanced economies, globalization and tech change are blamed for growing inequality. In emerging economies, globalization and tech change are credited with growth and lifting people out of poverty. In least developed highly indebted countries, globalization and tech change are blamed for marginalization and growing inequality. Global trends affect different zones differently. Globalization doesn't work the same way in different settings.

James Rosenau gave an optimistic assessment of global trends according to which rising human development indices, urbanization, and growing social and communication densities are producing a general 'skills revolution'.[85] This is valid, yet the flipside of knowledge economies is that with rising skill levels come widening skills differentials and urban–rural disparities.

Globalization needs unpacking. In shareholder capitalism (LME), it means outward investment and domestic deindustrialization, while in stakeholder capitalism (CME) outward investment tends to be balanced by inward investment in plants, technology, and incremental innovation. This is why Toyota and Volkswagen are the world's first and second major car sellers.

As Rafal Soborski shows, the 19th- and 20th-century ideologies—liberalism, socialism, social democracy, anarchism—continue to work through globalization, so liberal globalization (emphasis on free trade and growth) is quite different from social democratic globalization (emphasis on growth with equity).[86] Institutions and perspectives mediate globalization effects. We say 'globalization', but it means different things in different registers such as freedom (for Davos elites, banks, MNCs), opportunity (for EM and premium-skilled labor), risk and marginalization (for least developed countries), outsourcing and marginalization (for low-skill strata everywhere), and so forth.

Advocates of globalization such as Jagdish Bhagwati blame growing inequality on tech change: 'Technology, not globalisation, is driving wages down . . . the culprit is not globalisation but labour-saving technical change that puts pressure on the wages of the unskilled'.[87]

Tech change needs unpacking too. Tech change is central to transformation agendas and is often driven by business groups as an imperative that overrides existing institutions. Innovation is the key trope. According to Edward Conard, 'U.S. innovators have produced Intel, Microsoft, Google, Facebook, etc. The rest of the world has contributed next to nothing'. In this view, risky investment drives improved productivity, which in turn drives wages and living standards for rich and poor—the standard refrain of trickle-down.[88] New Labor and New Democrats deployed innovation and tech progress to ease the way for neoliberal reforms, sideline trade unions, privatize public assets, and lay off workers.[89]

In LME, the gains of innovation and higher productivity accrue to shareholders and CEOs; in CME they are more widely distributed. What matters then isn't innovation and tech change per se but the *institutions* of economic coordination according to which the gains of transformation are allocated. 'Technology itself does not dictate the outcomes. Economic and political institutions do'.[90]

In view of institutional diversity, general scripts don't apply, or are too thin to carry much weight. Diversity pulls the rug from under macro theories and introduces complexity into 'the global'. Standard explanations for growing inequality, globalization, and tech change, miscast enabling trends as determining trends. Analyses of social inequality in different zones show that what matters is not simply globalization and automation, or other general variables, but the institutions that channel their effects. Macro theories fall flat. The Kuznets curve—inequality rises under early industrialization and then flattens over time—doesn't hold.

In LME, wages for the majority have been stagnant. In emerging economies, middle classes are growing; in LME the middle class is shrinking. A 'flat world' and a 'spiked world' have been developing simultaneously. A flat world in which development and tech change enable competitive infrastructure and skill levels in low-wage countries, and a spiked world in which tech change enables new opportunities (centers of excellence, industrial and science parks), North and South.[91]

Similarities crosscut the diversity of institutions of inequality: inequality has been rising everywhere, also in middle-income countries, and governance everywhere is out of step with tech capabilities and accumulation opportunities, particularly in finance. Planet plutocracy and the planet of slums coexist as part of global interplay.[92] Both illustrate the shrinking middle class, the global hourglass.

4 Policies

> Part of the beauty of me is that I am very rich.
> Donald Trump

In the late 1990s, the World Bank changed course from structural adjustment to Poverty Reduction Strategy Chapters (PRSP), a significant shift. In the 2000s, perspectives moved on further, also at the IMF. Arthur Okun's classic argument on the tradeoffs between efficiency and equity (1975) is now found too broad-brush. An IMF staff discussion notes, 'we are all familiar with win-win policies that have potential both to promote efficiency *and* equality'. It mentions 'public investments on infrastructure, spending on health and education, and social insurance provision' as examples of policies that 'may be both pro-growth and pro-equality'.[93] These kinds of policies have been part of the productivist approach to welfare in Scandinavia and Nordic Europe for decades, as in Gunnar Myrdal's work and the human development approach.

Growth matters, but trickle-down is no longer generally accepted in economics. Trickle-down is a self-serving assumption. 'The size of the cake does not ensure its equitable sharing'.[94] Pursuing growth rarely comes with concern for the quality of growth. In retrospect, much of what has passed for economics turns out to be ideology and politics, just as critics of Chicago school economics argued all along. Analyses of the relations between growth, inequality, and poverty reduction have become more precise and meticulous.[95]

Education as an anti-poverty approach is problematic because (a) without special policies education reproduces rather than overcomes stratification, (b) the relevance of education to development is under discussion,[96] (c) there is often a mismatch between school curricula and jobs, as in India, and (d) the gap between getting a degree and getting a job is a major cause of inequality and unrest, especially in the MENA.

Social policies range widely, from NREGA in India to subsidies for rice growers in Thailand, and become targets at election time. Conditional cash transfers to the poor, as in Mexico's Opportunidades and Brazil's Bolsa Família, have become widely accepted and embraced by international development institutions. However, limitations of social policies are that they are typically disarticulated from growth policies; they are often short term, depend on market and political fluctuations, and as reparation policies they fall short of a new social contract. To be effective and sustainable, social reforms should be part of the *overall* growth model and engage macroeconomic imbalances. They should include structural reforms: land reform, fiscal reform, wealth tax, restructuring growth towards broad-based development, infrastructure, public services, and social investments for the majority.[97]

Arguably, among developing countries China comes closest to a structural approach to combating poverty with major social investments in the countryside (tax relief, infrastructure, clinics, pensions) and reforms that seek to reorient the growth model to domestic demand-led growth—a rebalancing that goes back to 2003, but remains work in progress that is yet to bring inequality down.[98]

In **advanced countries**, inequality gives rise to fierce debates, particularly in LME. In the US and UK, inequality has grown so dramatically that the other side of the equation pops to the foreground—the awareness that inequality *slows* economic growth. The crash of 2008 intensified debates with a dramatic sense of inequality, slowdown, and dim prospects. It introduced new discourses (the 1 percent and the 99 percent, billions for banks), movements such as Occupy Wall Street, caused disarray in mainstream economics and sent paradigms and ideologies to the cleaners. Part of the equation is a growing literature on plutocracy and on poverty and economic decline.[99]

In a bestseller in the UK, Wilkinson and Pickett make a persuasive case about the damage that inequality does to collective wellbeing and show that all, also the rich, benefit from greater equality, in less crime, greater security, social stability, and cohesion.[100] Economists argue the case of the interdependence of the 1 percent and the 99 percent. Neo-Keynesians argue that the American problem is inequality and low wages (Robert Reich proposes a better distribution of income to boost middle class purchasing power, wage insurance, a severance tax on employers, etc.).[101] Financialization and CEO remuneration—major variables of income inequality—are much further advanced in LME than in CME.

Thomas Piketty's work shifts the focus from income inequality to wealth inequality and documents that over 200 years the return on capital has exceeded the rate of growth ($r > g$), so inequality is structurally embedded and is wont to increase unless it is counteracted by a wealth tax.[102] A conservative comment on 'the Piketty age' maintains: 'A country can be equal and dismal. Markets bring wonders as well as stratification'.[103] In typically Anglo fashion, this overlooks that societies can be dynamic, innovative *and* egalitarian, as in Nordic Europe and Northeast Asia.[104]

While inequality in the US has risen far higher than in the UK, public debate in the UK is ahead of that in the US, social consciousness is stronger and progressive voices (such as the Equality Trust, Compass, One Society, the Fairness Commission in the Labour Party) are more embedded in society and hold a larger public platform. According to the Archbishop of York, excessively high incomes have become as 'socially unacceptable' as racism and homophobia. The Tory government charged the Hutton Review to examine pay differentials in the public sector, and the High Pay Commission report recommended that every British corporation be required to disclose the ratio between top executive and median worker compensation. Thus, debates in the UK focus on the *pay ratio* between CEOs and median employees[105] while policy debate in the US mainly concerns raising the minimum wage—which meets resistance in Congress, and raising taxes on the wealthy stands even less of a chance.

The US, where liberal market views have been promoted mostly loudly, is also where they have been disproven most clearly. A *New York Times* headline asks: 'Growth has been good for decades, so why hasn't poverty declined?'[106] The link between growth, jobs, and wages—which still existed when J.F. Kennedy proclaimed 'a rising tide lifts all boats'—broke by the mid 1970s. If growth does provide job growth, wages remain low—because most jobs are in low-end services, minimum wages are low, and trade unions have weakened. What follows is a vicious circle of weak consumer demand, weak economy, little investment, no job growth. Many economists no longer accept the argument that inequality fosters growth and find that inequality is not necessary for growth and threatens growth: 'Not only does inequality damage growth, but efforts to remedy it are, on the whole, not harmful'.[107] The principle of shared growth that has been the norm in development studies for a decade has crept into American discourse: 'without broad-based income growth, no recovery can be self-sustaining'.[108] In Stiglitz's words, 'Inequality holds back the recovery'; 'our economy won't come back strong unless it also becomes more fair'.[109]

There is ample pushback against such views. According to Harvard economist Greg Mankiw, 'Yes, the wealthy can be deserving'. Since CEOs and superstars add outsize value, they deserve their multimillion dollar remuneration.[110] According to another Harvard economist, Mullainathan, 'anger at the very wealthy should be channeled into better policies to help the poor'. He criticizes 'a top-heavy focus on income inequality' and seeks to shift the agenda back from inequality to poverty: 'by always talking about the top 1 percent, we aren't talking about the bottom 20 percent'.[111] A sample of commentary headlines illustrates the drift of pushback:

> Inequality is irrelevant if the poor are growing richer (Deirdre McCloskey, 2014)
> If you tax the 1 per cent it is the middle class who will suffer (2014)
> Corporatism not capitalism is the root of inequality (Edmund Phelps, 2014)
> The wages of fear are policies that risk hurting the poor (2014)
> Bad luck, not policy, is the scourge of the young (Janan Ganesh, 2014)[112]

A hidden variable in the US is that billionaires and oligarchies exercise outsize influence on public policy and debates. They do so mostly indirectly through 'stealth politics', through board memberships of think tanks, foundations, and institutions.[113]

A sideshow of plutocracy in the US is philanthropy and a cottage industry of helping the poor while getting richer. Corporate social responsibility helps corporations clean up their reputation. 'Impact investment' serves the wealthy to help the poor and get richer. Prahalad's focus on the 'bottom of the pyramid' seeks to do the same for MBAs under the heading 'eradicating poverty through profits'.[114] In Silicon Valley such efforts often come with an aura of self-congratulation.[115] A canyon wide gap in many efforts is that they rarely come with better pay and work conditions for employees and other stakeholders and often go together with tax avoidance. Under the heading of philanthropy, foundations provide channels for the circulation of wealth among elites.

In CME in Northwest Europe, policy debates are of a fundamentally different character. They concern rolling back austerity, disciplining the financial sector, and how to be globally competitive while maintaining social protection. A further question is how to rebalance the Eurozone. Policy debates in Scandinavia concern jobs and immigration (Sweden) and the role of the sovereign wealth fund (Norway).

The 2008 crash has not changed the situation. Luigi Zingales notes:

> [t]he capture of regulatory bodies by those whom they are supposed to regulate. . . . The 2010 US Dodd-Frank financial 'reform' was 2,139 pages long and popularly known as the 'Lawyers' and Consultants Full Employment Act'. The complexity serves to hide the loopholes . . . The biggest obstacle to reform is that insiders can devote time and energy to maintaining their position.[116]

Oxfam concludes, 'Left unchecked, political institutions become undermined and governments overwhelmingly serve the interests of economic elites to the detriment of ordinary people'.

Why has inequality leapt to the foreground in recent years? In EMDC, issues are the cumulative effects of unbalanced growth, international policies, and slowdown after 2011. In European CME, austerity is the central issue (i.e., creeping liberalization). In LME, consumption on credit (including second mortgages) made up for stagnant wages, but the 2008 crash busted credit dreams. Even the *Wall Street Journal* notes that rising wealth in the US (since 2000) doesn't boost the economy because it mostly goes to wealthy savers. Comments zero in on policy:

Inequality is not inevitable (Joseph Stiglitz, 2014)
We do not have to live with the scourge of inequality (Jonathan Ostry, 2014)
Policy, not capitalism, is to blame for the income divide (James Galbraith, 2014)[117]

On the other side of ideological and political gridlock, Paul Ryan advocates 'the Founders' vision, which puts individuals, their families and their communities—not government—at the center of American life . . . this vision favors choice and competition over government-run solutions'.[118] According to Neel Kashkari, Republican nominee for governor of California, 'the best social program in the world is a good job'. He bemoans 'over-regulation and over-taxation that drive jobs out of state'.[119] On Wall Street, economists and attorneys make 'The case for crony capitalism'.[120] The Trump administration and its cabinet of billionaires and plutocrats adds the step from reality TV to reality politics and back to the Gilded Age.

According to Judith Teichman, determining variables of policies in relation to inequality are the historical role of the state, mediating the effects of globalization, and the strength of civil society and labor. The latter explains 'Korea's social welfare expansion since the late 1990s' while the comparative weakness of civil society and labor in Chile and Mexico has meant slower social progress.[121]

The upshot of this discussion is that inequality is not inherent in capitalism or the market economy but is a political choice. The main actors are the state, civil society, and organized labor. Across the spectrum of capitalisms there is wide variety of responses to general trends. Reforms depend on the quality of institutions, the public sphere, civic organizations, and the role and ownership of media. The next chapters continue this discussion. Chapter 6 deals with the 2008 crisis and Chapter 8 discusses institutions, governance, and protest.

Notes

1 J. Lefroy, letter to *Financial Times* editor, 4/22/2014: 8. 'In Indonesia, China, India, Pakistan and Nigeria—all lower middle-income countries except for China, which is now classed as upper middle-income—the richest 10 percent of the population have acquired a much greater share of national income than the poorest 40 percent over the past 30 years, with the trend set to continue'. See www.worldbank.org/en/topic/poverty/overview; cf. Oxfam International 2014.
2 Speth 1996; UNDP 1996; UNDP 2005; Oxfam International 2014.
3 Quoted in Edwards 2001: 6.
4 Nederveen Pieterse 2010a.
5 Sainath 1996: 50.
6 How inequality became a household word, *Business Week* 12/16/2013: 16–17.
7 Oxfam International 2014.
8 E.g., Wade 2004; Nederveen Pieterse 2004; Milanovic 2005.
9 E. Olson, UN finds 1.2 billion mired in poverty: Assailing globalization, Meeting calls for cutting total in half by 2015, *International Herald Tribune* 6/27/2000.
10 J. Gapper, Capitalism: While the income gap in industrialised societies grows inexorably wider, global inequality is shrinking, *Financial Times* 12/24/2013: 6
11 C. Giles, Growing income gap gives blueprint for action, *Financial Times* 10/17/2007: 8.
12 HDI figures for 2014 are Sri Lanka 0.757, Saudi Arabia 0.837. Inequality-adjusted HDI figures are closer, 0.774 and 0.762, and Sri Lanka has higher IHDI than Saudi Arabia.
13 Khondker 2011.
14 Reis 2006: 200.
15 De Swaan *et al.* 2000.
16 Parekh 2011: 123.

17 CIA 2016. Of the total Indian population, 29.5 percent or 363 million were living below the poverty line in 2011–12. R. Katyal, India census exposes extent of poverty, CNN 8/2/2015. www.cnn.com/2015/08/02/asia/india-poor-census-secc/. Accessed 10/25/2016.

18 Khondker 2011: 41, 42; Hossain and Moore 2005.

19 UNESCO Institute for Lifelong Learning, National Literacy Programme. Accessed 10/25/2016. UNICEF, At a glance: Viet Nam. Last modified 12/31/2013. Accessed 10/25/2016. Central Intelligence Agency, The World Factbook: Literacy. Accessed 10/25/2016.

20 Khondker 2011: 40, 45; Nederveen Pieterse 2014a.

21 Chi 2010.

22 Breslin 2006, 2009.

23 Friedman 2014; Liu 2015.

24 Wider discussion is Nederveen Pieterse 2014a.

25 Studwell 2007: 181

26 Studwell 2007: 192.

27 Studwell 2007: 191. World Development Indicators, World Bank 2012.

28 UNDP 2013.

29 UNDP, Income Gini Coefficient, last modified 11/15/2013. Accessed 6/2016.

30 Lee 2012; Im 2014.

31 Hwang and Lim 2016.

32 Teichman 2014: 72.

33 D. Pilling, Rising inequality is a blemish on Asia's growth story, *Financial Times* 4/10/2014: 9.

34 UNDP 2013: 30.

35 Reis 2006: 205, 208.

36 Reis 2006: 217; cf. Fleury 2014, Pelfini 2011.

37 N. Miroff, Chile taxes to tackle inequality, *Guardian Weekly* 5/16/2014: 33.

38 World Bank estimate (data.worldbank.org/indicator/SI.POV.GINI), http://hdr.undp.org/en/content/income-gini-coefficient. Accessed 6/2016.

39 H. Weitzman, High growth masks Peru's two diverging economies, *Financial Times* 7/28–29/2007: 5.

40 Kalati and Manor 2005.

41 J. Blas, Inequality in Africa weighs on new class of consumers, *Financial Times* 4/19–20/2014: 14

42 J. Cotterill, Angolans prepare for life after autocrat as ruling party reasserts authority, *Financial Times* 12/6/2016: 6.

43 A. England and J. Blas, Angola: Gulfs apart, *Financial Times* 6/5/2014: 7; T. Burgis, Nigeria unraveled, *Financial Times* 2/14–15/2015: 15.

44 UNDP 2013: 93; cf. Achcar 2013.

45 Khondker 2010.

46 Alvaredo and Piketty 2014.

47 Khondker 2011.

48 E.g., Beteille 1969; Kumar 2013 on India.

49 Discussion in Nederveen Pieterse 2014b; Amable 2003.

50 Abramsky 2013.

51 Hacker and Pierson 2010.

52 Tim Harford, How the rich make sure they stay on top, *Financial Times* 8/16/2013: 7.

53 Edward Luce, America's democracy is fit for the 1 per cent, *Financial Times* 3/31/2014: 9.

54 Fraser 2013, 2015.

55 Ehrenreich 1990; Standing 2011.
56 S. Franklin, Will work for less, *Chicago Tribune* 1/22/2006.
57 Rana Foroohar, The truth about the poverty crisis, *Time* 9/26/2011: 24.
58 Leicht and Fitzgerald 2007: 11.
59 S. Roberts, Nearly half of New Yorkers are struggling to get by, *New York Times* 4/30/2014.
60 Streeck 2013.
61 Standing 2011.
62 Brenner 2002; Brenner *et al.* 2010.
63 George Osborne and Wolfgang Schäuble, The eurozone cannot dictate Europe's rules alone, *Financial Times* 3/28/2014.
64 Hogenboom 2012: 65.
65 Haq 1968, cited in Shoukat 2016: 42.
66 Acemoglu and Robinson 2012.
67 Acemoglu and Robinson 2012, quoted in Ezrow *et al.* 2016: 67.
68 Shoukat 2016: 288; cf. N. Mangi, The shadow economy *is* Pakistan's economy, *Bloomberg Businessweek* 4/9–15/2012: 19–21.
69 Camarate *et al.* 2016.
70 Ezrow *et al.* 2016: 120.
71 See Studwell 2007.
72 Burgis 2016.
73 Derber 2007.
74 Schiller 1999.
75 Oxfam International 2014.
76 In Greig *et al.* 2007: 24.
77 In Shoukat 2016: 31–32.
78 Shoukat 2016: 134.
79 Mayer 1981.
80 T. Jackson, *Financial Times* 5/12/2008.
81 Oxfam International 2014.
82 Planet Plutocrat, *The Economist* 3/15/2014: 57–58; cf. Studwell 2007.
83 Hacker and Pierson 2010.
84 Oxfam International 2014.
85 Rosenau 1999.
86 Soborski 2013.
87 J. Bhagwati, Technology, not globalization, is driving wages down, *Financial Times* 1/4/2007: 13.
88 Conard 2012; Lowenstein 2007.
89 Nederveen Pieterse 2004, chapter 1.
90 M. Wolf, Enslave the robots and free the poor, *Financial Times* 2/12/2014: 9.
91 Friedman 2005; Florida 2008.
92 Davis 2006.
93 Okun 1975; Ostry *et al.* 2011.
94 Parekh 2011: 123.
95 A meticulous discussion is Donaldson 2008.
96 Mehta 2014.
97 Nederveen Pieterse 2012a.
98 Chi 2010; Li 2012; Nederveen Pieterse 2017.
99 E.g., Frank 1999, 2006; Rothkopf 2008; Freeland 2012; Vogel 2014; Abramsky 2013.
100 Wilkinson and Pickett 2009.

101 Frank 2007; Reich 2010; Krugman 2003, 2009; Noah 2012; Stiglitz 2013.

102 Piketty 2013.

103 J. Ganesh, Tory tax on property is perfect for the Piketty age, *Financial Times* 5/6/2014: 13.

104 Cf. Moene 2013; Partanen 2016.

105 Pizzigati 2011.

106 N. Irwin, *New York Times* 6/4/2014; cf. S. Greenhouse, Fighting back against wretched wages, *New York Times* 7/28/2013: 7; Wage stagnation, *The Economist* 9/6/2014: 71–72; J. Sparshott, Hiring booms but soft wages linger, *Wall Street Journal* 1/11–10/2015: 1–2.

107 M. Wolf, A more equal society will not hinder growth, *Financial Times* 4/23/2015: 7.

108 E. Luce, Avoiding poverty pay is the tonic America needs, *Financial Times* 12/2/2013: 13.

109 J. E. Stiglitz, Inequality impedes recovery, *New York Times* 1/20/2013: 1, 8.

110 G. Mankiw, Yes, the wealthy can be deserving, *New York Times* 2/16/2014: 6.

111 S. Mullainathan, A top-heavy focus on income inequality, *New York Times* 3/9/2014: 4; Bennet 2010.

112 In sequence: McCloskey, *Financial Times* 8/12/2014: 7; R. Robb, *Financial Times* 5/16/2014: 7; Phelps, *Financial Times* 7/25/2014: 9; K. Murphy and R. Topel, *Financial Times* 8/16–17/2014: 7; J. Ganesh, *Financial Times* 1/7/2014: 9.

113 See Winters and Page 2009; Page 2009.

114 Prahalad 2004.

115 E.g., J. Steinberg, The people's mogul: The Benioff doctrine, *San Francisco Magazine* 5/2014: 72–75.

116 Zingales 2012; S. Brittan, Nil desperandum in the fight against crony capitalism, *Financial Times* 7/6/2012: 9.

117 J. Galbraith, *Financial Times* 5/27/2014: 7; J. Ostry, *Financial Times* 3/4/2014: 11; J. Stiglitz, *New York Times* 6/27/2014.

118 P. Ryan, A better way up from poverty, *Wall Street Journal* 8/16–17/2014: A11.

119 Neel Kashkari, Brother, can you spare a job? *Wall Street Journal* 7/31/2014: A13.

120 Paul H. Rubin and Joseph S. Rubin, The case for crony capitalism, *Wall Street Journal* 7/8/2014: A11.

121 Teichman 2014: 72.

6 Crisis and the East-South turn

Dynamic imbalances

1 Crisis and opportunity
2 Global rebalancing, global plutocracy?
3 Multipolarity, global restructuring?
4 After crisis
5 One Belt, One Road

> I made a mistake in presuming that the self-interest of organizations, specifically banks and others, was such that they were best capable of protecting their own shareholders.
> Alan Greenspan, US Congress, October 2008

Why is this theme important? The present juncture is an in-between condition. The old hegemony is no more, its frailties pose growing risks and a new constellation isn't available yet. Current trends can be read in two ways, towards recalibrating the old order, or as the emergence of new logics, which can be simplified as a tale of two scripts. One scenario is global plutocracy with American capitalism and financial markets in the West back in the lead, EM joining the club, and the G20 as the de facto governing board of the IMF. An instrument for achieving this is the discourse of global rebalancing, which functions as a hegemonic ideology and policy framework. A scenario way on the other end of the continuum is emancipatory multipolarity, considering that countries that represent the majority of the world population have come to the global head table (G20) and initiate new international institutions. That the rise of EM is a major turn in globalization is not controversial (Chapter 1); the question is what this bodes for global restructuring and whether it holds an emancipatory potential, which is highly controversial.

Let us consider as a guiding image the global situation as a giant see-saw or teeter totter. The middle position is multipolarity—that is, not just New York, Berlin, Tokyo matter, but also Beijing, New Delhi, Sao Paulo, Moscow, Seoul, Jakarta, Istanbul, etc. Multipolarity is a given and is noncontroversial. What *is* controversial are the terms and conditions of multipolarity and its ramifications. In Table 6.1 multipolarity is the middle position and is by its nature unstable and constantly oscillating.

Table 6.1 Multipolarity

Global plutocracy	Multipolarity	Global restructuring
US capitalism leads, EM join, comeback of IMF, TPP and TTIP	Global rebalancing	EM at the global head table; initiate new institutions

The G20 talk of global rebalancing has gradually waned in importance. What were major issues such as China resisting appreciating its currency faded as time wore on. Nevertheless, I spell out the argument of hegemonic rebalancing as an arena of contention.

Plotlines in this chapter are the 2008 crisis, its development over time, and how the crisis works out in global relations. Global rebalancing is an ongoing empirical process with diverse meanings as well as a hegemonic ideology, on the argument that since the crisis is a global systemic crisis, EM should chip in and provide financial support to the IMF ($100 billion in 2010).

The first section reviews the sequence of the 2008 crisis. Section 2 discusses global rebalancing according to G20 platforms, actual adjustments, and new emerging multilateralism, and scenarios of global plutocracy such as neoliberalization, the role of the IMF, and trade pacts such as TPP. Section 3 discusses multipolarity and the scope for emancipatory multipolarity, the mixed record of East-South cooperation, and forward notions such as global restructuring. Section 4 considers after-crisis policies in AE and EMDC. The closing section focuses on China's One Belt, One Road (OBOR) as a major alternative approach.

1 Crisis and opportunity

The sequence of the 2008 crisis is broadly as follows. In August 2007, the American subprime mortgage market collapsed, the derivative securities that were built on them also folded, which triggered a crisis of investment banks. This culminated in the fall of Lehman Brothers in September 2008 and then spread to commercial banks. Banks in the UK came also under pressure and some folded. Crisis then shifted to German banks and continental Europe. Despite bailouts and stimulus efforts, this prompted recession in the US and Europe, which in turn led to slowdown in Asia and China, and ripple effects across EMDC.

Initially, the crisis was a North Atlantic crisis, confined to the US, UK, and Europe.[1] In Europe, crisis exposed the weaknesses of Greece, Portugal, Spain, Italy, and Ireland. EM had a 'good crisis' and were not affected. Eventually, when not only the US but also the EU slowed down, the Great Recession affected China and Asia, not because their banks were affected but because of slowing demand for their exports. From 2010, slowing growth in China and Asia spread recession to primary commodities exporters in Australia, Latin America, Africa, Southeast Asia. The commodities boom that had tapered off from 2009 came to an end. In 2014, the oil price collapsed from over $100 per barrel to below $50, which affected oil exporters and financial instruments tied to energy markets. Three factors precipitated this collapse—low demand because of recession and high supply because of shale oil production in the US and the Saudi and OPEC decision to keep oil production high.

Debates on the crisis unfolded in stages as well, with no debate ever quite ending and each turn adding new twists. The first discussion concerned finance and banking—are banks too big to fail? What kind of regulation is needed? In the US, should the barrier between commercial and investment banking be reinstated? Was the subprime mortgage crash an unpredictable freak event (a black swan, in Nicholas Taleb's term); was it a white swan, part of a pattern of boom and bust, predictable and predicted (as in the crisis economics of Roubini and others), or was it a grey swan, with a bit of both?[2] Was the crisis a liquidity crisis, a credit crunch, financial in nature, or was it also a deeper solvency crisis that reflects economic fundamentals and structural problems?[3] What are the relations between the financial sector and the real economy of goods? What is the role of shadow banks and financial technologies (fintech) such as high-frequency trading and automated settings? Next, the emphasis shifted to underlying global imbalances between deficit economies (in trade and current account) and surplus economies, first in relation to the US and China, then in relation to Germany and the EU. Grexit and Brexit on the horizon revealed imbalances in the Eurozone. Lengthy negotiations with Greece involved austerity, Germany's position in the EU, and the rules of the Eurozone. This took a further turn with the British referendum in favor of Brexit. The Panama papers (a large cache of documents from one of Panama's largest companies holding secret offshore accounts, 2016) brought tax havens, fiscal offshoring, and the fine line between tax avoidance and tax evasion high on the agenda.[4]

2 Global rebalancing, global plutocracy?

> Playbooks are not readily available when it comes to new systemic themes. This leads many to revert to backward-looking analytical models, the thrust of which is essentially to assume away the relevance of the new systemic phenomena.
> Mohamed A. El-Erian, How to handle the sovereign debt explosion,
> *Financial Times* 3/11/2010: 9

When in the early 2000s American trade and current account deficits grew ever larger, economists honed in on global imbalances[5] and several argued the imbalances were unsustainable and would produce an orderly or a disorderly adjustment, a soft or a hard landing. Gradually, the perspective widened to include not just American deficits but also Asian surpluses, especially of China.[6] A comment noted, 'global economic imbalances' are 'code, as everyone knows, for the US current account deficit and the Chinese surplus'.[7]

The crisis brought the imbalances in trade and current accounts (the twin deficits of the US) into the headlines. According to a widely held view in

Wall Street and Washington, the 'savings glut' in Asia prompted the crisis. In Krishna Guha's words:

> [t]he current crisis is in the strictest sense a crisis of globalization, fostered and transmitted by the rapid and deep integration of very different economies. Fast-growing developing countries with underdeveloped financial systems were exporting savings to the developed world for packaging and re-export to them in the forms of financial products . . . the claim that this was sustainable assumed core financial centres—above all New York and London—could create the financial products efficiently and without blowing up. They could not.[8]

Thus, the culprit was the 'savings glut' in Asia that overwhelmed American financial institutions. Perhaps we should add that three decades of deregulation had enhanced the vulnerability of these institutions, and the Federal Reserve's low interest rates relayed the inflows through an easy money regime that created a credit bubble society.[9]

A major post-crisis script discussed in G20 meetings, Davos, and business media has been global rebalancing. If global imbalances are the underlying cause of crisis, managing crisis means addressing the imbalances. In the US and EU—where this was the dominant discourse—rebalancing essentially meant that China should appreciate its currency, the yuan (RMB), and surplus countries (East Asia and oil exporters) should fund the IMF so it can resume its role of managing world economic stability.[10] Further prescriptions are that Asia should export less, save less, and consume more, and the US should consume less, save more, and export more. Since these prescriptions involve not just policy changes but structural changes, they landed safely on the backburner.

The threat behind the agenda is protectionism. As the US and EU put steady pressure on China to appreciate its currency, China accused them of protectionism and 'restricting China's development'. The situation is reminiscent of the 1985 Plaza Accord in which the G5 agreed on an appreciation of the Japanese yen that was followed years later by devaluation of the US dollar (Chapter 3.3). This time, China has learned from the Japanese experience, the US has less leverage, and China, the US's major creditor, expresses its concern about American deficits and policies.

The argument of rebalancing presents several problems. It upholds an abstract model and recycles a neoclassical idea of equilibrium. The dominant ideas of rebalancing reflect the perspectives of advanced economies, several of which are deficit countries; they seek to restore a balance that is unrecoverable (if it ever existed) and has been overtaken by economic trends. It also assumes more capacious global governance than is realistic given the existing imbalances and the past record.

In economics, there have been as many ideas of balance as there have been political and economic systems. Each political and economic transition is marked by a redefinition of balance. In neoclassical economics, the price mechanism is supposed to balance supply and demand. Efficient market theory, the lead paradigm during recent decades, also assumes that markets are self-equilibrating. The 2008 crash debunked this assumption. In Keynesian economics, when demand falters, the role of government is to stimulate and rebalance the economy through demand management. Richard Nixon's adage 'We're all Keynesians now' made a comeback. However, Keynesian policies work differently in a high-connectivity world than in a national setting because stimulus spending easily leaks to economies where yield is higher, and in a context of financialization.

If equilibrium models don't apply in economies generally, they apply even less in the world economy. Major imbalances such as the triangular trade, relations between colonial and colonized countries, gunboat diplomacy, unequal exchange between manufactured goods and raw materials have been at the foundation of the contemporary world economy. The 'American century' doesn't evoke a global balance either. The US dollar as world reserve currency, the oil-dollar system, the role of Wall Street, steep differences in levels of development, the debt crisis in the global South, and IMF conditionalities display glaring structural imbalances:

> The blunt fact is that at no point in the past century has there been anything resembling a global economic equilibrium. . . . When officials and economists today speak of correcting global imbalances, it is unclear what benchmark they have in mind.[11]

Global imbalances are embedded in domestic imbalances. The emphasis on global rebalancing diverts the attention from domestic reforms. When during 1980–2000 American consumption drove world economic growth, private consumption was 72 percent of US GDP (comparative rates in 2005 were 57 percent in Europe, 51 in Asia, and 36 in China). As American consumption levels were rising, median wages did not, in part because American workers compete with low wage, no-union labor in the American South and with low wage labor overseas.[12] The combination of rising productivity, stagnant wages, and rising consumption was made possible by Americans working long hours, two-earner households, imports of cheap Asian consumer goods, and vast expansion of credit with deferred payments, credit card debt, home equity loans, and adjustable rate and subprime mortgages. These were abided by Federal Reserve low interest policies and external borrowing, which from the nineties onward absorbed 70 to 80 percent of world net savings. The financialization of the American economy and the credit bubble in real estate, then, primarily reflect the conjunction of rising consumption and stagnant wages in the US, rather than global imbalances or a 'savings glut' in Asia.

So balance has no precedent in the world economy, imbalance is common, yet balance is a recurrent rhetoric. Global economic balance is a hegemonic utopia. Besides, the actual significance of an appreciation of the RMB is doubtful.

It doesn't affect the American trade deficit, which stems from its offshoring production across borders where profit margins are higher, and it would not fix America's import dependence. According to Min Gong, the American trade deficit would broadly remain what it is and imports would rather be sourced from other East Asian countries and Latin America.[13] China de-pegging the RMB from the US dollar, begun in 2005 and resumed in 2010, barely affected the Sino-US trade imbalance. As the *China Daily* stiffly noted, 'It is the sovereign right of a country to decide the value of its currency. And it should not change to suit another country's need'.[14] When in the run-up to a G20 meeting in 2010 China resumed its de-pegging of the RMB from the dollar (appreciating the RMB by 0.53 precent), presumably to deflect tensions with the US Congress, American attention shifted to Germany with calls that Germany should increase consumption, cut exports and savings, and adopt policies to stimulate demand, which the German government promptly declined.

'Global rebalancing' is code language for shifting the burden of reform onto China and other surplus economies; in other words, keep the 'free market' in the West courtesy of adjustments in Asia. There is no need for reforming American ways as long as there are external remedies. But in fact it shows that the global fault lines no longer run between North and South, but between trade (and current account) deficit countries (such as the US, UK) and surplus countries (East Asia, Germany, and energy-exporting countries). Actual ongoing global adjustments are dynamic imbalances, i.e., transitions from one type of imbalance to another.

Further considerations are, first, that the global imbalances reflect long-term changes in the world economy, so beyond immediate effects we must consider long-term trends. Second, the 2008 crisis was not a cause of imbalances but a manifestation. Crisis is a prism through which global rebalancing is perceived and a process through which it unfolds. The crisis was not an 'ordinary systemic crisis'. It was a financial and banking crisis at one level and an economic crisis at another, both of which were embedded in global imbalances. Third, global rebalancing is multidimensional. Although it is primarily discussed in economic and financial terms, it is as much a political, institutional, social, and cultural process. Ideas of rebalancing depend on narratives of crisis, which are influenced by the nature of the recovery; what emerges as the dominant crisis narrative will affect the idea of balance.[15] Fourth, what is needed is to compare narratives of crisis and imbalance and adjustments in societies located at different places on the spectrum of global imbalances. Global adjustments must be viewed not merely from the viewpoint of AE but also from the viewpoint of EMDC.

Will there be a global convergence of capitalisms on the American model? Will American capitalism gobble up emerging economies and will emerging economies join the club of big powers as franchises of American ways with a different interior design? This is under discussion worldwide. I will present perspectives on both sides of the equation.

Figure 6.1
Source: Mike Keefe, *The Denver Post* and InToon.com.

Martin Sorrell, chief executive of the British global marketing group WFF, expects adjustments and the end of the era of super consumption, and expects the pendulum will swing back, albeit with a different geographic balance of power and a new capitalism with an Asian-Pacific and Latin American flavor.[16] The tenor is: let regulations come, they will fail again, incorporate the new capitalism, and the London City will be back in business. Others observe a merger of elites, with business elites and ruling elites West and East forming a new global 'super class'.[17] World-system analysis and transnational capitalist class perspectives argue along similar lines.[18]

Transnational capitalist cooperation occurs in institutions (WTO, IMF), governance and international law (UN, ICC), intellectual property (patents, licensing), technology (industrial standards), communication, transport, and firms, particularly in mining, energy, telecoms, and finance.[19]

There are limits to such cooperation. Currency, interest rates, trade policies, sovereign wealth funds are jealously guarded national agendas. Security, logistics, trade routes, strategic resources, energy and metals, sensitive technology, cyber security, and foreign investments are closely watched as well. In 2006, the US Congress resisted Dubai Ports World's bid to buy the British firm P&O and take over the management of major US port facilities. US regulators rejected China's CNOOC's bid to buy Unocal, a US oil company, and Huawei's offer to buy 2wire, an Internet software group and a unit of Motorola. Australia rejected the bid of Chinalco, China's state-owned metals group, to invest $19 billion in Rio Tinto. Western companies complain of restrictions they face in China and China complains about restrictions on technology transfer. As transnational enterprises, migrants, and 'new argonauts' straddle regions and combine technologies and resources, this doesn't rule out differences across countries and zones and may actually reinforce them. Firms practice institutional arbitrage, juggling arrangements among countries (tax laws, labor rights, environmental regulations, special economic zones) so their actions are conditioned by and condition institutional differences.[20]

Thus, processes are layered and include transnational cooperation as well as national, regional, and local agendas and corporate interests. Layered processes produce layered outcomes—with uneven and combined patterns of transnational, regional, national, local, and corporate cooperation and competition, so diverse scenarios intersperse across multiple levels.

Another perspective holds that the most advanced form of capitalism—which is taken to be neoliberalism—dominates. David Harvey, Mike Davis, Patrick Bond, and others tend to equate contemporary capitalism and neoliberalism, and take differences in capitalist organization to be marginal.[21] This is the 'neoliberalism everywhere' thesis (discussed in Chapter 9). Let me note that scholars who in the 1980s argued that the semiperiphery wouldn't fly, such as Samir Amin and James Petras, now typically dismiss EM as neoliberal economies,[22] so theirs is a script in which Western capitalism always wins.

Grim perspectives on the left mirror diehard triumphalism in Western business circles. Scenarios are contingent; they depend on paradigms, ideologies, policies, institutions, data sets, expectations of continuity, and risk. Unbundle general dynamics and in contention are narratives of crisis, frontiers of regulation, and developments in AE and EM.

In American elite views, the crisis is a systemic failure, no one's fault, and Wall Street wizards are needed to unwind the mess.[23] A dominant view is that crisis was brought about by a 'savings glut' in Asia; remedy: cut savings in Asia, borrow less in the US. An additional factor is financial excess and deregulation in the West; remedy: regulate banks. Then, a broad (though not uniform) expectation in Wall Street and London is that rebalancing will converge on dominant institutions and will restore the balance that existed prior to the crisis.

Nigel Lawson, former Chancellor of the Exchequer, asks 'Will capitalism need to change in the future?' He argues:

> The lesson of history is that the answer is 'not really'. The economic cycle is endemic and inescapable, and everyone . . . has always known this. What the current cycle does underline, however, is that a cyclical downturn associated with a collapse of the banking system is by an order of magnitude worse than a normal cyclical downturn.

So we need to re-install the separation between commercial and investment banking that was eliminated under the Clinton administration.[24] Such is the extent of the reform required.

Regulation is on the table and reform is inevitable, but there is ample pushback on the frontiers of regulation. During the noughties, bank lobbyists spent almost $370 million in Washington on lobbying and campaign donations to ward off tighter regulation of their industry.[25] Gary Becker of the Chicago school cautioned that the 'cure' should not destroy capitalism, and a recession isn't the right time to change the rules of the economic game.[26] Wall Street voices claim that derivatives are necessary, insider trading makes markets function more smoothly, speculation is crucial to the functioning of financial markets, robo-trading is functional, and 'government control' is a nightmare that haunts investors.[27] Business fights back 'in defense of free enterprise' by pointing out the problems and cost of government control, the mistaken idea that the recession has been purely a failure of markets and that market failures are readily overcome by government solutions.[28] Tory historians such as Niall Ferguson counsel against creating yet another layer of government regulation.[29]

Reforms, then, should not go too far. The rise of EM takes time and for all their shortcomings Western institutions and financial markets are best placed to manage the transition. Globalization is moving at mach speed, and the crisis is just a small cloud fleeting over the highway of rapid global innovation.[30] Across the world, the tide has turned in favor of regulation but 'the skyscrapers are high and the regulators are far'.[31] Institutions are resilient, paradigms are slow to give way, market forces swing back, herd behavior hasn't ended, the rewards of discipline are unclear, and reforms are likely to be relatively marginal. The new normal anticipated in financial markets, according to El-Erian, is slow growth in the West, more regulation, and rising risk of sovereign debt.[32]

In the United States, the FIRE sector (finance, insurance, real estate) employs 20 percent of the workforce, the largest sector of employment. 'In 1995, the assets of the six largest banks were equivalent to 17 percent of GDP; now they amount to 63 percent of GDP'.[33] In 2002, finance generated 41 percent of US corporate profits, which was down to 30 percent in 2016.[34] The pay rate in the finance sector is 181 percent of median pay. In 2007, American households spent on average 20 percent of their disposable income on finance charges. In the US and UK, it is a story of 'banks gone wild' and 'a financial sector that turned away from the business sector, then caused its self-destruction, and a business sector beset by short-termism'.[35] When during the US Senate hearing of Goldman Sachs, a senator exclaimed 'this is gambling!', it elicited a swift, indignant response from the Las Vegas casino industry: the comparison is insulting for our industry, unlike theirs, ours is highly regulated; here a pit boss knows exactly what is going on, but they have no clue. Susan Strange's 'casino capitalism' was a daring critique when it was published in 1986 but has long been overtaken by (simply citing the business press) toxic finance, death-wish finance, financial weapons of mass destruction, doomsday finance.

Many accounts deal with financial crisis and gloss over economic crisis. They treat crisis as a liquidity crisis, a credit squeeze triggered by external circumstances and overlook the solvency crisis,[36] which in the US may be more serious than in Europe and Japan. The problem in the US is decades of underinvestment in productive capabilities. A trenchant diagnosis is that 'bankruptcy could be good for America' for bankruptcy focuses the mind.[37] On a wider canvas, Luke Johnson explains 'why I fear the west's luck has run out' and offers a dark, mournful evocation of global rebalancing:

> It is clear that as a society we must learn something painful and radical—how to live within our means—because the credit just is not there anymore. The easy money is all gone, and there will be no more for a long time. . . . The growth game is over. . . . So why should industrious Asians earn a tiny fraction of what citizens in the west earn? Especially when they have so much of the cash and productive resources, while we have deficits, high costs and poor demographics. Prepare for a wrenching, unstoppable redistribution of resources—and I am not talking about domestic taxes.[38]

The consensus in Washington has long been what is good for Wall Street (it used to be General Motors) is good for America. The financial sector carries formidable institutional power and soft power in ideology, campaign financing, lobbies, Beltway intel, and political access. Because of the revolving door of corporations-government, many Wall Street insiders are also Treasury and government insiders. (In 2009, 1,537 finance lobbyists spent $344m to press for deregulation; a ratio of 25:1 for the spending of consumer groups and unions.) The 'systemically-important' megabanks (too big to fail, too big to jail) come with excess risk, less competition, and lower borrowing rates, a hidden subsidy that amounts to half their profits.[39]

The banks' reach extends wider still under the umbrella of financialization. Financialization is understood in several ways—as the growing share of corporate profits from financial operations; the influence of financial instruments also on non-financial corporations; the ascendency of the shareholder value orientation; the financialization of everyday life; and the spread of entrepreneurial discourses of risk-taking and self-management.[40]

In sum, the weaknesses of the global plutocracy script are structural. The Anglo-American financial sector is vast, politically embedded, and out of control. Because of decades of deregulation and structural deficits, it is crisis-prone. Since the 2008 crisis its appeal has receded. Anglo-American institutions can possibly co-opt part of emerging markets' elites, but not all, and it will be mostly an instrumental embrace. Economic and financial surplus has shifted and international institutions, too, must adopt a more balanced course.

3 Multipolarity, global restructuring?

In Asia and the global South, global rebalancing holds different meanings than in the G20. According to Ronnie Chan, a banker in Hong Kong it entails:

- a shift in moral authority in which the west no longer holds the moral high ground;
- a shift in decision making in the world economy in which emerging economies carry greater weight (as in the expansion of voting rights in IMF and World Bank);

- a shift in the center of gravity of the world economy from the Atlantic to the Pacific;
- a gradual shift away from the US dollar as world reserve currency in favor of a basket of currencies and bilateral currency deals;
- a shift towards growing East-South or South-South economic cooperation.[41]

Since for Asia the new normal means shrinking demand and rising protectionism in the West, regional cooperation and FTAs in Asia have been expanding rapidly,[42] and trade between Asia, Latin America, Africa, and the Middle East has been growing steadily. Part of this are 'new Silk Roads' between Asia and the Middle East, and China's ambitious OBOR projects.

Measured in financial assets, EM (including the Middle East and Eastern Europe) add up to about $25 trillion, the US about $54 trillion, the EU $42 trillion and Japan $26 trillion, so the total assets of EM are less than those of Japan and of course are more disparate and dispersed. From the viewpoint of Western institutions, EM and their financial markets are too small to absorb major investments. The other side of the equation is that although the large financial markets are in the West, growth and surplus are increasingly in EM, and this is where trends are turning. In mergers and acquisitions and in bankers' 'call sheets' (the list of potential buyers contacted when a company is put up for sale), the trend is clear:

> In 2010, the player at the edge of the frame has now moved to its center: Asia. The change has been building for nearly a decade. It's finally here. From Tokyo, west to Seoul, to Beijing, south to Hong Kong, and west again to Mumbai, Asian companies and governments are asserting themselves as the deal makers who matter. Asian acquirers—not including Australia and Japan—have been behind one of every six deal-making dollars globally in 2010 and are on pace for the biggest year ever . . . much as the United States [after the Second World War] was left to rebuild a devastated world in its own image, so today are hale Asian companies filling a vacuum that the West occupied before the financial crisis.[43]

The idea that Western financial markets can absorb the EM underestimates the hiatus between financial institutions in the West and financial surplus in EM. According to Martin Wolf:

> Go east! That is the advice one would give an ambitious financier. This will change the nature of the financial industry. It will also change the philosophy of finance: for most emerging and developing countries, the financial industry exists to push the economy along a development path broadly determined by the state.[44]

A report notes, 'within 15 years half of capitalization will be in emerging markets and asset allocation will reflect that'.[45]

Asia has overtaken the US as home of the largest number of wealthy individuals since 2015. 'Asia is home to 4.7m of the world's rich people who hold $15.8tn that should be in search of management'. Western banks queue up to provide services, but find it difficult to gain entry because of regional competition (notably in Singapore and Hong Kong), compliance issues, and the expectations of clients who favor long-term relationships, hold more cash than the rich elsewhere, and expect their bank to extend more credit than elsewhere, all of which eats into profitability.[46]

In portraying the 2008 crisis as a global system crisis, US and UK governments have sought a tripling of IMF funds while the IMF agreed to expand emerging economies' vote quota by 6 percent.[47] The call was to China, Saudi Arabia, and other surplus countries to contribute funds to enable the IMF to act as crisis manager. EM stepped into the breach with provisional arrangements such as the IMF issuing bonds, rather than their granting loans. Additional Special Drawing Rights may function as a channel through which surplus economies can offload unwanted US dollars without upsetting the applecart. Such arrangements signal an unstable interregnum. Surplus countries are underrepresented in international institutions and are yet supposed to carry a major burden of global economic recovery, while the benefits accrue to hegemonic countries whose institutions have been the agents of financial shipwreck. It stands to reason that significant adjustments in the global power structure are in the cards.

If economic and financial multipolarity is not in question, let's consider its potential for global restructuring. A key question EM pose is whether their rise is mainly a matter of their 'joining the club' or holds democratizing or emancipatory potential. Will the rise of EM be on balance emancipatory in the sense of benefiting domestic majorities and the world majority? There are general, domestic, and transnational components to this question.

General considerations are, first, the threshold is low. Two hundred years of North-South domination have been framed by the succession of the British Empire and American hegemony and imperial rivalries, the Cold War, and vanity wars in Afghanistan and Iraq.[48] Second, in the big picture development aid has had little effect. It has often been a disciplinary exercise (as in IMF conditionalities and World Bank structural adjustment), a matter of 'aid-in-reverse', or rhetorical grandstanding with targets that have been habitually unmet such as the Millennium Development Goals (or when they were met it was due to countries outside the orbit of Washington institutions, such as China and India). Far more important has been the interdependence of new industrializing societies and developing countries, far more than the intricacies of international development cooperation that are discussed at length in development studies. Third, the East-South turn represents a comeback of oriental globalization and global history returning to its 'normal' mode (Chapter 2), and Asia is far larger and more diverse than any other region (Chapter 3).

Turning to domestic considerations, because EM are also developing countries for economic reasons (skills, domestic market), political (stability) and social reasons (cohesion), some degree of broad-based development policies is likely over time. On these grounds, apartheid came to an end in South Africa. It isn't possible to boost development with the majority of the population dispossessed and excluded (which is not to say that post-1994 South Africa is a model of balanced development).

Due to stagnation in advanced economies, EM exports will increasingly go to regional markets and the global South. When export-led growth makes place for domestic demand-led investment and consumption, it requires broad-based social development rather than fast-lane growth, which is a complex path. Since economic development involves tech changes, strategic groups, multinationals, and global value chains, it involves inequality as a variable in competition and generates new inequalities. Besides, in most societies, inequality is deeply embedded and culturally encoded, so this needs to be examined empirically (Chapter 5).

The key contradiction is that export-led growth requires low wages while domestic demand requires purchasing power. In between lies the middle-income trap. Yet, on balance the East-South turn holds greater emancipatory potential than North-South relations. There are structural, political, and cultural elements to this argument.

When during the postwar boom industrial countries in the West and Japan were drivers of world economic growth, commodity prices were high, commodity exporting countries prospered, and it was a period of relatively equalizing growth globally. The period 1980–2000, when postindustrial consumer societies propelled the world economy, was marked by unequal, polarizing growth in and between countries. With industrializing economies again driving the world economy, rising commodity prices enabled relatively equalizing growth globally. Thus, the East-South turn redirected the overall pattern towards global redistributive growth.

Zoellick notes:

> The developing world's share of global GDP in purchasing power parity terms has increased from 33.7 percent in 1980 to 43.4 percent in 2010. Developing countries are likely to show robust growth rates over the next five years and beyond. Sub-Saharan Africa could grow by an average of over 6 percent to 2015 while South Asia, where half the world's poor live, could grow by as much as 7 percent a year over the same period.[49]

Such figures were inconceivable in the eighties and nineties; a different pattern has set in.

Because EM are developing countries and share colonial experiences and frictions with institutions of the North, EM have greater affinity with other developing countries and are less burdened by stereotypes. An example is the role Brazil, South Africa, India, and China played in the WTO negotiations of the Doha round in Cancún, taking the position that 'no deal is better than a bad deal' and acting on behalf of the G77 of developing countries.

EM also compete with one another and with light industries in developing countries. Chinese garment exports have had a devastating impact on textile industries in Bangladesh, Kenya, South Africa, and other developing countries; China's shoe exports have eliminated Pakistan's shoe industry. East-South relations are not exempt from unequal exchange, reproducing an old type of international division of labor, big power aspirations, and regional hegemony. As semiperipheries, they play core roles vis-à-vis peripheral countries. Manoranjan Mohanty reviews social movement debates in India and China and finds:

> [t]he probable scenario is the simultaneous unfolding of both these trends—the rise of India, China and some other countries and their entry to the big power club and those policies being increasingly challenged at various levels and the demand for democratization growing in strength . . . The ideology of domination is under attack everywhere . . . Today not only global hegemons are under challenge; regional hegemons are under even greater challenge. In South Asia, for example, not only Pakistan but even smaller countries like Nepal, Bangladesh would not accept any form of domination by India.[50]

Mohanty contrasts global rebalancing and global restructuring and puts the bar high. Global restructuring:

> [r]efers to a fundamental restructuring of the world political economy to fulfil the demands for equity, justice and autonomy at every level in all regions of the world from local to global realms in all spheres, economic, political, cultural, science and technology, information and knowledge spheres.[51]

This sets the bar so high that global restructuring lands outside politics. I opt for an incremental approach of counterpoints that gradually tilt the overall balance to emerging economies and developing countries and achieve a tipping point, an East-South turn, and a reorganization of globalization (Chapter 10).

4 After crisis

> 'The world has turned into Japan', according to the head of a Hong Kong-based hedge fund. 'When rates are this low, returns are low. There is too much money and too few opportunities'.[52]
> 'Let them eat chaos', Kate Tempest

Advanced economies are in a rut of slow growth, the new normal (El-Erian), or is it the end of normal (Galbraith)?[53] Growth was slim before the 2008 crisis and recovery after crisis has been sluggish as well with growth around 2 percent in the US (2.2 percent in 2017, by IMF estimates), 0.6 percent in the EU, 0.7 percent in Japan (2016). An ordinary period headline is, 'U.S. in weakest recovery since '49'.[54] EMDC face a 'middle-income trap' and 'premature deindustrialization'; energy exporters see oil prices collapse from above $100 per barrel to below $50 (2014), and advanced economies are in a 'stagnation trap'.

Explanations of the conundrum are perplexingly meager. Many accounts are largely descriptive, such as secular stagnation and the 'new mediocre' (IMF, 2016)[55]—noted, but why? (Secular stagnation derives from Alvin Hansen's 1938 adaptation of Marx's tendency of the rate of profit to decline, hence real interest rates decline, therefore policy interest must decline.[56]) Or, uncertainty—which is odd because policies haven't changed for years. Or, corporate hoarding—corporations, particularly in the US, are sitting on mounds of cash, buy back their stock, buy other companies, and reshuffle, but are not investing—noted, but why? A general account is that advanced economies have been on a technological plateau since the 1970s.[57] Which is odd because this is the era of the 'fourth industrial revolution', the knowledge economy, the digital economy (and the gig economy of Uber, Airbnb, and freelance telework), innovations of Silicon Valley (Apple, Google, etc.), pharma and military industries, also in EM, so innovations abound. Yes, contemporary innovations are more capital-intensive and narrower in effect than those of the past. Besides, notes Martin Wolf, the shift to services in postindustrial societies means a shift towards sectors (such as healthcare, education, personal care) where it is hard to raise productivity.[58]

Neo-Keynesian economists view slowdown in developed countries as a consequence of widening income and wealth inequality, limiting final demand (Stiglitz, Krugman, Reich, Baker). Other diagnoses are aging (according to Pope Francis, the EU behaves like a grandmother), and clinical depression.[59]

If we consider policies, the picture gets worse because implemented year after year, they clearly don't work and indications are they make things worse. Fiscal policy is generally ruled out because of fear of deficits. The policy instrument that remains is monetary—low interest rates and QE in the US, UK, EU, and Japan. Other standard policies are austerity in the EU—which may cut deficits but obviously doesn't generate growth (and by depressing tax revenues over time worsens deficits)—and structural reform. Besides privatization, the main component of reform is labor market flexibilization, in other words depressing wages and incomes. 'Labor market restructuring' in France, Italy, and Spain (2016) makes hiring and firing easier, which is in effect wage repression. In the US, this has been implemented since the 1980s, in the UK in the 1990s, in Germany and South Korea in the 2000s, and in Japan in the 2010s (the 'third arrow' of Abenomics). 'Rigidities of the labor market', all along the American criticism of European social market capitalism and its explanation for slower (but also higher quality and more sustainable) growth in Europe, are now on the table. The objective is to boost international competitiveness by depressing wages and benefits which (a) ceases to have effect when every country is doing the same, (b) assumes the key problem is cheap supply, whereas supply is actually abundant and what is lacking is demand, (c) by depressing wage incomes, further reduces domestic demand. No wonder these policies make matters worse. Thus, explanations of slow growth fall short and policies have been counterproductive.

Jack Rasmus's (2016) book, *Systemic Fragility in the Global Economy* offers a far more pertinent analysis of the stagnation trap. The main points of his approach are (1) taking finance seriously, not just as an intermediary between stations of the 'real economy' (as in most mainstream economics) but with feedback loops and transmission mechanisms that affect the real economy of goods directly and indirectly; (2) a three-price analysis—beyond the single price of neoclassical economics (the price of goods), the two-price theory of Keynes and Minsky (goods prices and capital assets prices), Rasmus adds financial assets and securities prices; (3) a focus on the long-term slowdown of investment in the real economy and the shift to investment in financial assets, which has been occurring because financial asset prices rise faster than the prices of goods, their production cost is lower, their supply can be increased at will, the markets are highly liquid so entry and exit are rapid, new institutional and agent structures are available, financial securities are taxed lower than goods; in sum, they yield easier and higher profits. Financial asset investment has been increasing for decades, and has expanded rapidly since 2000 and 'from less than $100 trillion in 2007 to more than $200 trillion in just the past 8 years'.[60]

Government policy has shifted from fiscal policy to monetary policy. 'Central banks in the advanced economies have kept interest rates at near zero for more than five years, providing tens of trillions of dollars to traditional banks almost cost free'. Low interest or zero interest rate policies benefit governments (it lowers their debt and interest payments) and banks (affords easy money) while they lower household income (lower return on savings and lower value of pensions), so in effect households subsidize banks.[61]

QE has released massive injections of money capital in the US ($4 trillion), UK ($1 trillion), EU ($1.4 trillion), and Japan ($1.7 trillion) since 2008, or 'about $9 trillion in just five years'. Add China ($1–4 trillion) and bank bailouts over time and, according to Rasmus, the total global liquidity injected by states and central banks is in the order of $25 trillion.[62] The injections of liquidity into the system allegedly aimed to stimulate investment in the real economy (by raising stock and bond prices), which raises several problems:

- Investment in the real economy isn't determined by liquidity but by expectations of profit.
- Funds that are supposed to be invested in the goods economy leak overseas via financial institutions investing in EMDC, where returns are higher (and more volatile).
- Most additional liquidity goes into financial assets, boosting commodities, stocks, real estate, and leads to price bubbles:

The sea of liquid capital awash in the global economy sloshes around from one highly liquid financial market to another, driving up asset prices as a tsunami of investor demand rushes in, taking profit as the price surge is about to ebb, leaving a field of economic destruction of the real economy in its wake.[63]

The post-crisis attempts at bank regulation overlook the shadow banks, even though the 2007–08 crisis originated in the shadow banks rather than the banks. (Shadow banks include hedge funds, private equity firms, investment banks, broker-dealers, pension funds, insurance companies, mortgage companies, venture capitalists, mutual funds, sovereign wealth funds, peer-to-peer lending groups, the financial departments of corporations, etc.) The integration of commercial and shadow banks is another variable. Shadow banks control in the order of $100 trillion in liquid or near liquid investible assets (2016). Add up these trends and policies and they produce several forms of fragility, which is the culmination of Rasmus's argument.

Rasmus distinguishes fundamental, enabling, and precipitating trends that contribute to fragility. The explosion of excess liquidity goes back to the 1970s and has taken many forms since then. QE policies amplify this liquidity and have led to financial sector fragility, which has been passed on to government balance sheet fragility (via bank bailouts, low interest rates, and QE), which have been passed on to household debt and fragility (via austerity policies). 'Austerity tax policy amounts to a transfer of debt/income and fragility from banks and nonbanks to households and consumers, through the medium of government'.[64] This in turn leads to growing overall system fragility.

Several elements of Rasmus's theory of system fragility aren't new, such as work on austerity and finance.[65] But by providing an organized and systemic focus on finance and liquidity, Rasmus makes clear that the policies that aim to remedy stagnation (low interest rates, QE, competitive devaluation, bank bailouts) and provide stability are destabilizing, act as a break on growth, and aggravate the problem. According to Karl Kraus, psychoanalysis is a symptom of the disease that it claims to be the remedy of, and the same holds for the central bank policies of crisis management.

This doesn't mean the usual arguments for stimulating growth (spend on infrastructure, green innovation, etc.) are wrong, but they look in the wrong direction. For one thing, the money isn't there. Courtesy of central banks, the money has gone by billions and trillions to banks, shadow banks, and thus to financial elites. Surprise at corporations not investing is also beside the point when government policies are at the same time undercutting household income and consumer demand, reproducing an environment of low expectations.

Criticism of QE has been mounting, even in bank circles (it's the *real* economy, stupid). Yet the role of finance remains generally underestimated. Rasmus's analysis of central bank policies overlaps with El-Erian's book on central banks,[66] but his critique of economics is more fundamental and the implications of his analysis are more radical. A turnaround would require different economic analytics and profoundly different policies.

Asian countries have been less dependent on Western finance than Latin America and Africa and having learned from the Asian crisis of 1997, have built buffer funds against financial turbulence, stand apart from general financial fragility, and tend to ring-fence their economies from Wall Street operations. Of course, this remains work in progress.

After-crisis policies of EMDC vary according to their growth model—commodities, oil, industrial, or agricultural exports. Recession among energy exporters triggered going to the IMF for loans (Angola, Azerbaijan, Ghana, Nigeria, Mongolia, Suriname), governance crisis (Venezuela, Brazil), austerity (Emirates, Saudi Arabia, Kazakhstan), and currency depreciation (Russia, Brazil, Nigeria, Malaysia). Saudi Arabia borrowed on the external market, issued bonds on a major scale ($17.5 billion), and set in motion a reform program to diversify the economy away from fossil fuels. Other commodity exporters, such as metals exporters in Africa, Latin America, and Australia experienced steep recessions. General responses have been cuts in public spending, currency devaluation to regain growth, and competitiveness and labor market reforms (in Argentina and Brazil).

5 One Belt, One Road

China follows a very different path. In response to the 2009 slowdown, it embarked on a massive stimulus of RMB 4 trillion (15 percent of GDP) that amplified its shift from export-led to investment-led growth and led to overinvestment and overcapacity. From 2013, China embarked on new Silk Road projects, OBOR, part of which is the Maritime Silk Road (MSR), a large-scale program of infrastructure investments in Southeast Asia, Central and West Asia, towards Europe and Africa (Chapter 2.4). OBOR involves high-speed rail links between Kunming and Singapore, between Xinjiang and Gwadar port in Pakistan, between Chongqing and Duisburg and beyond. The MSR involves links between ports of Guangzhou (former Canton) and Fujian, Southeast Asia, Sri Lanka and the Indian Ocean towards East Africa and the Persian Gulf. The infrastructure investments involve new tech, Information Silk Roads, and regional finance hubs. It is backed by the Silk Road Fund and the Asian Infrastructure Investment Bank (AIIB, 2015) for the wider region. In June 2016, the China Development Bank announced an investment of $890 billion in over 900 OBOR projects across 60 countries (Figure 6.2 is an overview).[67]

Let's consider the upsides and downsides of these major undertakings. In stark contrast to the liquidity injections of central banks in US and EU, China's stimulus spending is being invested in the real economy of infrastructure, productive assets, and urbanization. Yanis Varoufakis discusses the American postwar rise to hegemony as a Global Surplus Recycling Mechanism (GSRM).[68] The Marshall Plan for Europe and the Alliance for Progress in

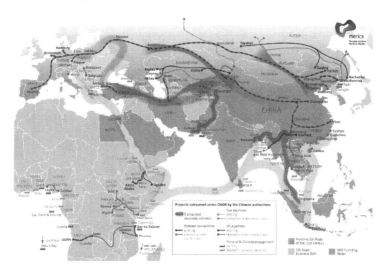

Figure 6.2 China's One Belt, One Road initiatives 2015
Source: Merics China Mapping, 2015.

Latin America intertwined economic, political, and geopolitical objectives and aimed to build the architecture of the 'Free World'. Like the US in the 20th century, China is the driving force in the 21st-century world economy, and China's interest likewise is in contributing to a wider architecture. Differences with the American GSRM are several. China's investments aim at regions that are geographically adjacent with which China has deep historical connections, the Silk Roads. In OBOR, China resumes the Ming era of Zheng He's voyages, the era before China's withdrawal from the world stage. OBOR comes with historical memory, financial depth, patience, and a long time horizon—all of which the US lacks. Proportionally, the financial outlays and investments of OBOR are far larger than the Marshall Plan ($130 billion in today's dollars). Another difference is that now there is no Cold War setting. China's approach is non-ideological; the heading is mutual benefit. Military industries and arms trade come in but don't play a major role.

The British geographer Mackinder's thesis, 'He who controls the heartland controls the world' (in which the heartland is the central zone of Eurasia) has influenced American security policy. Zbigniew Brzezinski, national security adviser of President Carter, shared this view,[69] and it may have played a part in the Carter doctrine (according to which the Persian Gulf is in the US's vital national security interest). Later it was a subtext of neoconservatives' objectives in Afghanistan and Iraq. Through OBOR, China may be able to achieve what the US could not. China would achieve it not through geopolitics, military intervention, and regime change, but rather through rail, roads, ports, pipelines, trade, and aid.

Stepping stones of OBOR include the Shanghai Cooperation Organization, loans to Kazakhstan and Turkmenistan, and rapport with Russia and Iran. China has concluded an agreement with Russia on harmonizing the rail gauge so OBOR will merge with Russia's Eurasian Economic Union. OBOR is part of wider institution building such as the FTA with ASEAN, the AIIB (57 countries, 2015) and the BRICS' NDB and CRA (2015).

Compare China and Germany, two major manufacturing surplus economies. Germany upholds EU austerity policies, squeezes Greece, and questions making a contribution to the meager EU investment plan of €21 billion (2015). In contrast, China demonstrates a profound commitment to the regional and global economy.

Differences with China's previous investments are several. China buying US Treasuries contributed to American ballooning debt (then came 2008). Unlike investments and loans in Latin America and Africa, OBOR represents a *regional turn*. Projects in adjacent regions build on historical depth and cultural affinities. Chinese diasporas, especially in Southeast Asia, can serve as interlocutors and interconnect SMEs. Parallels to China's infrastructure investments are Dubai with major port and airport investments in a geostrategic location amid time zones and rising regions, and Singapore's port and airport investments.

Benefits for China are several. OBOR projects *externalize* investment-led growth, redeploy steel, cement, construction, rail companies, and banks, and thus lower the resistance of powerful interests (especially SOEs) to cutting investment-led growth within China. They will boost the development of West China, China's poorest region, with Xinjiang as the hub of rail links to Central and West Asia; and of southwest China with Yunnan as the hub of rail links to Southeast Asia. The projects will likely contribute to regional stability. They will boost trade with Central Asia and the Mediterranean. By providing markets for manufactured goods they will enable China to prolong export growth. China may achieve what Germany did in the EU and the Eurozone in relation to southern and eastern Europe—secure markets for exports of durable manufactured goods. Perhaps in this way China may be able to achieve the transition from middle- to high-income level.

Table 6.2 lists China's financial disbursements and commitments in OBOR, regional, and international initiatives, which add up to over $1 trillion. Further add China's investments and loans in Latin America and Africa and the grand total is in the order of $2 trillion. This is a formidable commitment to the regional and global economy, a commitment and perspective that is profoundly different from the advanced economies and their after-crisis policies. A report on OBOR in the *South China Morning Post* is titled 'Bringing half the world together'.[70]

China's effective state has a record of large-scale infrastructure projects such as the Three Gorges Dam and is capable of swift decision making. On the downside, OBOR is the mother of all megaprojects. It follows a modernist engineering perspective that has a poor or uneven record in terms of environmental damage and the displacement of people. Thus, regionally and in each country, its implementation must be negotiated.

Table 6.2 China, OBOR, regional, and international institutions—financial commitments[71]

	Institutions	China	Others	Total
OBOR	Silk Road Fund	$40bn		
	OBOR	$890bn		
Regional	AIIB	$30bn	$20bn (will rise to $70bn)	$100bn
	Chiang Mai Initiative	$77bn	$163bn	$240bn (2012)
	Asian Bond Fund	$250m	$2.75bn	$3bn
International	NDB	$10bn	$10bn each of BRICS	$50bn
	CRA	$41bn	Brazil Russia India each $18bn, South Africa $5bn	$100bn
Total		$108.9tn		$493bn

In China, many economists are skeptical about OBOR.[72] Infrastructure investments in China are in question[73] and investments outside China may be more vulnerable still. Crossborder investments are subject to unpredictable political risks. They run into security problems and the viability of some projects and loans (such as in Venezuela and Zimbabwe) is in question as well. Among OBOR projects, Gwadar port in Pakistan is ready for operation but stands still because an insurgency in Baluchistan blocks the supply routes.[74] High-speed rail from Kunming, Yunnan to Singapore runs into hurdles in Laos, Cambodia, and Thailand.[75] Japan is a competitor in the region in rail, port, and power (in India, Indonesia, Bangladesh).

Conventional 'return on investment' doesn't apply in a narrow sense because return isn't measured simply in economic terms. China has financial depth, the world's largest current account surplus, $3.5 trillion. Further noteworthy points are:

- Scale and size—for instance, 'in just two years—2011 and 2012—China produced more cement than the US did in the whole of the 20th century'.[76]
- Efficient—China's high-speed trains are as efficient and 50 percent cheaper than those of Kawasaki, Alstom, Siemens.
- Effective—for instance, in infrastructure in Afghanistan (pipelines, roads) China succeeds where American plans for roads and an electricity grid have foundered (because of subcontracting to private enterprises and lack of long-term support).[77]
- Inclusive—China invites Russia to join OBOR in Central Asia; invites the US to join the AIIB and infrastructure investments in Africa; invites ASEAN and others to join the MSR; and cooperates with the Asian Development Bank in AIIB. In contrast, the US excluded China from TPP and warned countries against participating in the AIIB. On both scores, the American exclusionary stance has failed.

Perhaps most distinctive is China's long-term approach—China's expansion, infrastructure investments, and loans indicate a long time horizon. Investments in and loans to countries that are weak (Greece), are spurned by the West (Venezuela, Sudan, Russia), or are dictatorships (Myanmar, Thailand, Egypt) suggest a distinctive perspective. Governments come and go but ports and roads remain. Most commentary is short term while China's transformations are long term. The time frame of finance is in the order of 1 to 5 years, of economics 20 years, sociology 50 to 100 years, and history reckons with the *longue durée* of hundreds of years or more. OBOR is a long game that is without precedent in modern history.

Notes

1 Gamble 2014.
2 Taleb 2007; Roubini and Mihm 2010; Helleiner *et al.* 2010; Rajan 2010.
3 See Baker 2009.
4 See Palan *et al.* 2010.
5 E.g., Roubini 2006; Feldstein 2008.
6 El-Erian 2008; Bagnai 2009; Okimoto 2009.
7 P. Stephens, Co-ordination falls away as the global crisis abates, *Financial Times* 6/26/2009: 9.
8 K. Guha, Imbalances imply a trouble well beyond risky banking, *Financial Times* 3/10/2009: 9.
9 Baker 2009; Phillips 2009; Nederveen Pieterse 2008; Taibbi 2010.
10 E.g., Wolf 2010.
11 Zachary Karabell, The 'global imbalances' myth, *Wall Street Journal* 12/21/2009: A21.
12 Nederveen Pieterse 2008; Reich 2010.
13 Gong 2012.
14 Editorial, Currency confusion, *China Daily* 6/26-27/2010: 5.
15 Daniel Yergin, A crisis in search of a narrative, *Financial Times* 10/21/2009.
16 'Just as the crash was inevitable, so will be the pendulum swinging the other way. The teeth and claws of capitalism will be blunted, and we will see the return of forms of state corporatism familiar to those of us who lived and worked in the 1970s. We in business need to be philosophical: if taxpayers are required to bail out banks or other businesses, they should expect a say. The devolved Wales and Scotland were already operating on a Scandinavian model; we should expect more of the same. It is part of the hangover from the party, but probably not the cure for a punishing headache. . . . Just as business is poor at government, so government is feeble at running business. . . . At some point, the cycle will begin afresh. Henry Kravis of the private equity house KKR recently said that at least $300bn–$400bn of private equity money is waiting for deals. Eventually, low stock market valuations will become irresistible, and the gears of mergers and acquisitions will again crunch into action—albeit with considerably less leverage than before. Then the pendulum will begin to swing back. At the same time, another change is playing out. The geographic balance of power is reversing—returning to the east and south, from where it came two centuries ago. The new capitalism will have an Asian-Pacific, Latin American flavour—more orderly, more pragmatic and more flexible. . . . Despite the rise of other regional economies, US innovation and ability to raise capital will be

undiminished. The City can flourish again, too, if it is not hobbled by modern-day Keynesians and regulators', M. Sorrell, The pendulum will swing back, *Financial Times* 4/8/2009: 9.

17 Rothkopf 2008.

18 Sklair 2001.

19 Hertie 2013.

20 Ong 2006.

21 E.g., Harvey 2005; Petras 2009; Westra 2010.

22 Amin 1997.

23 US Congressman Barney Frank, quoted in C. Freeland, Top dogs remain in denial over public anger, *Financial Times* 3/27/2009: 2.

24 Nigel Lawson, Capitalism needs a revived Glass-Steagall, *Financial Times* 3/16/2009: 9.

25 'The top 25 US originators of subprime mortgages—the risky assets that sparked the global financial crisis—spent almost $370m in Washington over the past decade on lobbying and campaign donations as they tried to ward off tighter regulation of their industry', E. Luce, Subprime groups spent $370m to fight regulation, *Financial Times* 5/6/2009: 1. See *Wall Street Journal* Report on The Future of Finance: Fixing Global Finance, 12/14/2009: R1–9.

26 G. Becker and K. Murphy, Do not let the 'cure' destroy capitalism, *Financial Times* 3/20/2009: 9; G. S. Becker, S. J. Davis and K. M. Murphy, Uncertainty and the slow recovery, *Wall Street Journal* 1/4/2010: A17; P. Robinson, Interview with Gary Becker, *Wall Street Journal* 3/27–28/2010: A13. He also argues that the Obama administration's healthcare bill is flawed and voters will go back to limiting government.

27 J. Quinlan, The nightmare of government control that haunts investors, *Financial Times* 10/21/2009: 22; D. Boudreaux, Learning to love inside trading, *Wall Street Journal* 10/24–25/2009: W1-2; P. Murphy, The truth about speculators: They are doing God's work, *Financial Times* 3/13–14/2010: 9.

28 Particularly on the editorial pages of the *Wall Street Journal*. K. A. Strassel, The weekend interview with Tom Donohue (president of the Chamber of Commerce), *Wall Street Journal* 10/24–25/2009: A13.

29 N. Ferguson and T. Forstmann, Back to basics on financial reform, *Wall Street Journal* 4/23/2010: A19.

30 According to Easterbrook 2009.

31 F. Guerrera, The skyscrapers are high and the regulators are far away, *Financial Times* 3/27–28/2010.

32 Mohamed A. El-Erian, The new normal, *Businessweek* 6/1/2009: 73–4.

33 *New York Times* 4/21/2010.

34 'The financial sector in 2013 produced approximately 30% of corporate profits, dropping from a high of 41% in 2002.' J. Weissmann, How Wall Street devoured corporate America, *The Atlantic* 3/5/2013.

35 E. Phelps, Uncertainty bedevils the best system, *Financial Times* 4/15/2009: 9.

36 Morris 2008.

37 G. Rachman, Bankruptcy could be good for America, *Financial Times* 1/12/2010: 9.

38 Luke Johnson, Why I fear the west's luck has run out, *Financial Times* 1/28/2009.

39 Johnson and Kwak 2011; Taibbi 2010.

40 Zwan 2014. Rasmus 2016: 233.

41 R. Chan, The west's preaching to the east must stop, *Financial Times* 1/4/2010: 11.

42 P. Stein, West is wary, so Asia seeks free trade within, *Wall Street Journal* 3/22/2010: C7.

43 D. K. Berman, The deal makers who matter are rising in the East, *Wall Street Journal* 9/21/2010: C1.

44 M. Wolf, New dynamics, *Financial Times* report on The Future of Finance, 11/9/2009: 3.

45 B. Bollen, A new economic leadership stirs, *Financial Times* 4/7/2008: 14.

46 J. Hughes, It'll be no easy ride for banks as they try to court Asia's wealthy, *Financial Times* 4/20/2016: 14.

47 G20 2009.

48 Harbaugh 2013.

49 Zoellick 2010.

50 'There are big debates within both the countries today as to whether they just travel on the western path of industrial revolution or on paths that make their economic development consistent with their cherished values. The debates are reflected in the many social movements going on in India—ranging from the movements against mega projects that cause large scale displacement to tribal people's movements for forest rights and dignity. In China it may have taken different forms, but the questioning of the current strategy of rapid economic growth was as pronounced. That is why the Hu Jintao leadership propounded "scientific outlook on development"— a balanced development that was socially just and environmentally sustainable in order to build a "harmonious society"', Mohanty 2009.

51 Mohanty 2015: 166.

52 H. Sender, Short-term relief for hedge funds belies tough search for yield, *Financial Times* 7/12/16: 22.

53 Galbraith 2012.

54 E. Morath, U.S. in weakest recovery since '49, *Wall Street Journal* 7/30-31/2016: A1-2.

55 L. Summers, Why stagnation might prove to be the new normal, *Financial Times* 12/15/2013.

56 Hans-Werner Sinn, Secular stagnation or self-inflicted malaise? *Project Syndicate* 9/27/2016.

57 Cowen 2011; Gordon 2016.

58 M. Wolf, An end to facile optimism about the future, *Financial Times* 7/13/2016: 9.

59 E. Luce, Is the west clinically depressed? *Financial Times* 12/21/2014.

60 Rasmus 2016: 212.

61 Rasmus 2016: 220, 471.

62 Rasmus 2016: 185, 262, 263.

63 Rasmus 2016: 473.

64 Rasmus 2016: 472.

65 E.g., Blyth 2013; Goetzmann 2016.

66 El-Erian 2016.

67 V. Mansharaman, China is spending nearly $1 trillion to rebuild the Silk Road, PBS News hour 3/2/2016. www.pbs.org/newshour/making-sense/china-is-spending-nearly-1-trillion-to-rebuild-the-silk-road/. Accessed 10/31/2016.

68 Varoufakis 2015.

69 Brzezinski 1997 quotes Mackinder.

70 F. Cang and C. Wong, *South China Morning Post* 12/2/2016.

71 Sources Asian Bond Fund Initiative: Sohn 2007; Kawai 2015.

72 According to a workshop of economists I attended in June 2016 at Fudan University, Shanghai. On OBOR see e.g., Yunling 2015, Chung 2015, Overholt 2015, Nederveen Pieterse 2015b, Engdahl 2016. The new trade routes: Silk Road corridor, *Financial Times* 5/10/2016 (www.ft.com/reports | @ftreports). J. Farchy,

China revives old paths to profit, *Financial Times* 5/10/2016. W. Engdahl, The Eurasian century is now unstoppable, *Global Research* 10/7/2016.

73 G. Wildau, Beijing's infrastructure investments criticized, *Financial Times* 9/12/2016: 6.

74 A. Kazmin *et al.*, China and Pakistan pin hopes on Arabian sea port: Separatist insurgency in Baluchistan threatens to disrupt ambitious plan for hub, *Financial Times* 10/3/2016: 4.

75 M. Peel, L. Hornby, China regional rail link struggles to gather speed, *Financial Times* 9/26/2016: 4

76 J. Anderlini, Property bubble is 'major risk to China', *Financial Times* 8/25/2014.

77 Cf. Bijlert 2009.

7 Media and hegemonic populism

Representing the rise of the rest

For Jan Ekecrantz

1   Free market paradox
2   Goldilocks globalization
3   Recycling 9/11, representing war
4   Overusing celebrity narratives
5   BC/AC

In the buildup to the Iraq war, mainstream media were asleep at the wheel. Mesmerized by the 9/11 attacks and machinations of power, mainstream media, particularly in the US and UK, allowed the Iraq war to unfold and placed no obstacles in its course. This has been widely discussed; here let us consider other media contributions to creating or sustaining global divides. I focus on the following: echoing free market ideology, representing the rise of the rest as threat, recycling the 9/11 complex, and overusing celebrity as narrative.

We are in a dramatic vortex. Like a giant oil tanker, the world is slowly turning. The emerging centers of the world economy are in the East and South. Globalization once seemed to belong to the West and now the tables are turning. We have entered the era of the rise of the rest (as discussed in Chapter 1). Western media and representations have celebrated the rise of the West for some 200 years, how then do they treat the rise of the rest?

Main trends are that the rise of the rest is ignored because it doesn't fit national narratives in the West, is represented as a threat because it fits existing enemy images, is blamed for the stagnation of the West, or is celebrated in business media as triumphs of market forces. A summary headline version might run: 'Western media complacent, display West-bias'. In frequently representing contemporary globalization as a source of risk, Western media showcase Western privilege and conservatism. As mainstream media ignore the rise of the rest, in effect they reinforce the relations between the rest and the rest, rather than between the rest and the West, and may thus contribute to the creeping irrelevance of the West. Table 7.1 gives a précis of the main arguments.

Table 7.1 Media and global divides

Media	Global divides
Promoting free market ideology	Wealth polarization
Representing the rise of the rest as threat	Economic and political polarization
Recycling the 9/11 complex	Political and cultural polarization
Overusing celebrity narratives	Existential polarization between celebrities and common masses

The treatment follows the sequence of these arguments. Recycling 9/11 is part of a wider problematic of representing war to which I also devote a section. The emphasis in this discussion is on international reporting in Western mainstream media; closing sections make brief observations on how media in the global South represent global trends. I close with a reflection on representations before and after the 2008 crisis with a focus on sovereign wealth funds.

Part of the wider setting is the gradual decline of hegemony. From the point of view of the hegemon, the world looks like a lineup of security problems and threats, a world of rivals and potential rivals. Americans have been socialized into viewing the United Nations as ineffective, bureaucratic, and corrupt, quite unlike in Europe; but then from the American viewpoint, the UN is a rival to its leadership. In the American bubble, international reporting routinely focuses on threats or potential threats. Scathing views of the world outside America are common. Magazines publish issues devoted to 'pick your worst dictator'. In the worldview of hegemonic provincialism, the wider world appears as either irrelevant or as a theater of paranoia. Hegemonic populism is part of this culture and includes, besides UN bashing, China bashing, Russia bashing, Islam bashing, applause for Israel (Cuba bashing and Iran bashing have finally wound down, at least temporarily). Guiding principles include neutralize competitors, keep rising forces down.

Late 19th-century popular imperialism was expansive and served as a calculated palliative for class struggles in metropolitan countries. In contrast, contemporary hegemonic populism is defensive, blames metropolitan woes on rising forces such as China, on trade liberalization and globalization, while it also suggests a populist fix for metropolitan strife. Can China, Russia, and Islam bashing remedy stagnation and growing inequality in advanced economies?

1 Free market paradox

In his last published article, Jan Ekecrantz urges media studies to pay more attention to economic inequality and the role of media in sustaining and representing inequality.[1] A pressing question is, after decades of echoing and worshiping market forces, when the 'free market' goes kaput, now what? For years, Western media passed on the admonitions of the free market gospel, the Nobel Prize winning economists of the Chicago school, the stipulations of the IMF and World Bank, and the tropes of the Washington consensus—don't intervene in the market, cut taxes, roll back government, liberalize, privatize, lift capital controls, the free market and democracy go together. When crisis hit developing countries, IMF conditions invariably stipulated cutting government spending.

Since 2008 everything has been topsy-turvy. Crises are supposed to take place in developing countries and to serve as instruments to discipline and punish the periphery and its unruly elites. When financial crisis hit the United States and Europe in the most serious crisis since the Depression, by mid 2008 the same economists who had counseled liberalization and market shock therapy for developing and post-socialist countries—such as Larry Summers and Jeffrey Sachs—pleaded for government spending and infrastructure programs to stimulate the economy.

For decades, people were told that the free market is superior, is the only viable economic model, there is no alternative—but now that the 'free market' goes bust, sovereign wealth funds rescue Wall Street power houses. State capitalism—declared old fashioned and ineffective by the Anglo-American power/knowledge grid—came to the rescue when the free market went down the toilet. According to Martin Wolf, the day the US government bailed out Bear Stearns with $30 billion, was 'the day the dream of global free market-capitalism died':

> Remember Friday March 14 2008: it was the day the dream of global free market-capitalism died. For three decades we have moved towards market-driven financial systems. By its decision to rescue Bear Stearns, the Federal Reserve, the institution responsible for monetary policy in the US, chief protagonist of free-market capitalism, declared this era over. It showed in deeds its agreement with the remark by Joseph Ackermann, chief executive of Deutsche Bank, that 'I no longer believe in the market's self-healing power'. Deregulation has reached its limits. . . . The US is showing the limits of deregulation . . . we must start in the right place, by recognising that even the recent past is a foreign country.[2]

Since then, there have been many days like that. In the course of 2008, with bailouts climbing to $700 billion on to trillions, those seem days of innocence. There go the banks, the hedge funds, the rating agencies, the boards, and for that matter, the business pages—each with the smartest people in the room, now queuing at the exit. One may cherish the irony of this historical twist, but it is do-it-yourself irony because media rarely concede the U-turn and appear oblivious to the gaping contradiction between 30 years of propagating the 'free market' and the volte-face of 2008. If you like world history, 2008 and 2009 are good years.

By echoing free market rhetoric unhindered, media have contributed to unprecedented transfers of wealth, producing a vast concentration of wealth. According to UNDP, 350 billionaires own as much as half the world population (1994), which shrank to 65 billionaires (Chapter 5). Through 30 years of free market propaganda, media have been dozing at the wheel and under the happy-end narrative of trickle down have enabled the steep growth of inequality within and between societies.

However, should we not concede that social inequality is nowadays mostly caused by technological change, which brings about skills differentials, and by the effects of globalization? Not per se. It *is* possible to combine innovation and economic dynamism and equity. Contrast Nordic Europe and Northeast Asia with the US, UK, and the developing countries that underwent structural adjustment. Technological change does not cause inequality; political change does. One might wonder, too, when banks, boards, rating agencies, hedge funds, and analysts all lost their marbles because they miscalculated risk, how could media have done better? The point is, however, that by joining the free market bandwagon and falling in line with propaganda and by failing to inculcate civic vigilance, media contributed to a climate of lax regulation and permissive capitalism which, in turn, fostered creative accounting and corporations producing quarterly numbers by cooking the books. In time, these dynamics produced the Enron and Anderson series of corporate scandals (2001), the crisis of 2007–10, and bank frauds such as Libor, Goldman Sachs (2010), and Wells Fargo cross-selling phony accounts (2016).

To the extent that business media are an exception in representing the rise of the rest in a positive light, they tend to display a different bias: 'what is good for market forces is good for society'. When the West was winning, when it drove and 'owned' globalization, free market stories sounded attractive. The world is flat and outsourcing is beneficial in the end. Now it appears it has all been bubbles all along—the high-tech bubble, dotcom bubble, easy money bubble, real estate bubble, consumer credit bubble, mergers and acquisitions bubble, petrol and commodities bubbles, bailout, stimulus, low interest, and QE bubbles. Media duly followed and fed each of these bubbles.

This includes the role of media *as* market forces. Media play a major role in market growth. Carlos Slim, the world's wealthiest man, made his fortune in Mexico's telecoms. Thaksin Shinawatra made his fortune by selling computers to Thailand's police force and became a telecom magnate. Berlusconi was Italy's media tycoon. Bill Gates' wealth is well known. Dan Schiller has discussed the role of media and telecoms in the era of digital capitalism, as did Susan Strange.[3] The deregulation of telecoms in the nineties was a major contributor to the financialization of the American economy[4] and to the Wall Street frenzy that, in time, produced the Enron and WorldCom scandals. American media and Hollywood are deeply wired into the military-industrial-media complex.[5] Media, of course, are major political forces as well. Conrad Black maintained links with rightwing think tanks. Rupert Murdoch's media contribute to pro-market propaganda and rightwing politics. A 'Murdoch-Trump alliance' shaped the 2016 American election campaign. Keen on ratings during an 18-month election cycle, media gave Donald Trump $4 billion worth of free airtime and enabled the rise of alt-right discourse in the public sphere.[6]

The paradox of liberalization is that under the banner of the free market, market forces have been cast as panacea. Business media and accounts such as Thomas Friedman's attributed the rise of East Asia, China, and India to liberalization; to Deng's modernization in China in 1981; and to India's financial liberalization in 1991.[7] Likewise, the World Bank attributed the 'East Asian miracle' to economic liberalization and export orientation. This narrative completely overlooks the role of the public sector (Chapters 3 and 8). In each of these cases, developmental states played a fundamental role in establishing the conditions that made market growth possible, from infrastructure, land reform, fiscal reform, and broad-based education in Northeast Asia, to Mao's reforms in China and Nehru's industrial policies in India. This is typically ignored in Anglo-American free enterprise accounts of economic success.

'Freedom' has historically been a language of power and a doctrine of hegemons, so the free market is a doctrine of winners.[8] But when winners become losers, discourse and policies shift gear to protectionism.

As new industrialization in the global South produced a commodities boom, including high energy prices, high commodity prices had a relatively equalizing impact in the world economy, as during the postwar economic boom. Western representations zeroed in on the downside of these trends. According to Thomas Friedman, the 'first law of petro politics' is 'that the price of oil and the pace of freedom always move in opposite directions'.[9] Cases in point are Iran, Venezuela, Nigeria, and Russia. The message between the lines is that Friedman treasures the American way and bemoans the growth of state capitalism. The selection of cases is biased. In states that support American policies such as Saudi Arabia, petro politics poses no problem.[10] The problem, rather, is unruly petro politics. Besides, in hindsight, freedom and the American way take on different meanings.

2 Goldilocks globalization

According to opinion surveys in the nineties, people in the West generally felt that the pace of globalization was just right—not too fast, not too slow. However, according to a Pew survey in 2007, 57 percent in G7 countries felt that the pace of globalization was 'too fast', whereas the majority in the global South deemed its pace just right.[11] Goldilocks globalization has changed place.

In the nineties, the global South felt threatened and overwhelmed by globalization. The risks of liberalization and financial crisis were real enough and culminated in the 1997 Asian crisis. In the 21st century, advanced countries feel threatened by job losses and in the US, by mounting trade and external deficits. According to populist views, competition from the South ('China') threatens job loss and undermines prosperity in the West. What mainstream media do *not* discuss, however, is the difference *among* Western countries: why are Scandinavia, Germany, and Nordic Europe able to combine innovation, economic dynamism, and a welfare state, and the US and UK are not? What is also not discussed is the other side of the story: decades of private sector offshoring combined with underinvestment in American plants, technologies, and innovation, and a shift of investment to financial assets (Chapter 6.3).

In American media, the problem is rather, China and its undervalued renminbi, cheap exports, excessive savings, and a thirst for resources. Complaints about China's currency run from media through congress and the Treasury and make a policy point: forcing upon China a similar currency devaluation as Japan accepted in the 1985 Plaza Accord, which made Japan's exports to the US much less competitive. China learned Japan's lesson. By the end of 2010, US pressure on China to devalue its currency had still come to naught. In 2016, the IMF granted the RMB reserve currency status.

China bashing shifts over time: in the nineties, China's vast growing consumer market was a dream come true for Western multinationals; in the 2000s, it is treated as a threat. China is criticized for its human rights record ('the butchers of Beijing', according to Bill Clinton), for increasing military spending and expansion in the South China Sea. After the 2008 crisis, the discourse shifted again (discussed later in this chapter). The underlying script change is that drivers and winners of globalization, particularly during the last decades of the 20th century, are becoming losers in the 21st century. At issue, of course, are not merely representations but also policies. Not just attitudes and media but also policies change—advanced countries that used to push free trade now opt for protectionism, not just in agriculture but also in manufactured goods and technology. Meanwhile the global South is often blamed for the failure of international negotiations, such as the Doha round of the WTO.[12]

A further twist is that the rise of the rest threatens the global environment. Rising middle-class consumption in China, India, Brazil, and other EM competes with resource use and consumption in the West. Indulge for a few hundred years in uncontrolled modernization and then cast the rise of the rest as a threat to planetary survival. Four percent of the world population in the US has been absorbing 40 percent of the world's resources, and now the consumption of rising middle classes in EM threatens the global environment.

3 Recycling 9/11, representing war

In social science, Eurocentrism has been taken to the cleaners by Edward Said, postcolonial studies, and media studies,[13] but it made a comeback in media and politics, particularly in relation to Islam. In history and art, the contributions of Islam to science and civilization as a wide and early cosmopolitanism are widely recognized; but in Western political discourse the 'clash of civilizations' prevails.

The 9/11 complex has turned into a Western cul de sac. Go to Brazil, South Africa, South Korea, to most of the world and the American and European obsession with the Middle East and Islam barely exists. This is the West's front seat in the gallery of paranoia. Everything to do with Islam and the Middle East is tainted with threat. In 2008, the number of terrorism suspects on American security lists exceeded a million.

War-on-terror tunnel vision homogenizes Islam and treats Islam as a threat. This is a boon for security experts, for terrorism is the successor to the Cold War; for rightwing parties who also had to make do without a communist enemy; and for Western media, for media love a ready-made narrative. As Abrahamanian points out, American media interpreted 9/11 without fail through the lens of Samuel Huntington's clash of civilizations.[14] There have been many sequels to the 9/11 episode (such as the furor surrounding the 'Ground Zero mosque' in New York).

Media such as Copenhagen's *Yillands-Posten* and *Charlie Hebdo* in Paris volunteered to serve as frontiers in this clash of civilizations. Mainstream media follow or allow rightwing populist trends in the West (in Denmark, Sweden, the Netherlands, Belgium, France, Austria, Poland, Hungary, Macedonia, the US). These trends merge anti-immigrant sentiment, denigration of Islam, and ignorant or hostile images of the global South. Pim Fortuyn ('the Netherlands is full'), Ayaan Hirsi Ali, and Geert Wilders recycle Orientalism.[15] When Ayaan Hirsi Ali counsels 'How to win the clash of civilizations', it consists mainly of nagging about Middle East governments that are not pro-Western enough (such as Turkey, Iran, and Syria).[16] Paul Berman criticizes Muslim intellectuals for not upholding the values of universalism. Thinkers and policy makers across the West think that by condemning expressions of religion in the global South, especially Islam, they are defending the ramparts of civilization.[17] Italian media in 2008 targeted and scapegoated Roma people, as did French media and politics in 2010. At times, cultivating these cultural frictions serves to divert attention from political and economic transformations or geopolitical objectives. Some argue that attacks on Islam such as the Danish cartoons serve to deflect attention from Israel-Palestine tensions.[18]

Anti-immigrant sentiment in the US and Europe is another expression of globalization worries. Immigration has been a flashpoint of global inequality for some time, located at the intersection of Western labor demand, border controls, global inequality, and conflict.

The clash of civilizations is an imagined clash, a political narrative masquerading as cultural friction. Apply double standards to the Middle East for decades (the official terminology is the 'Roadmap to Peace') and eventually it boomerangs, especially since the region is also the recipient of major petrol revenues so social forces have the motivation *and* the resources to strike back. The clash of civilizations is a self-fulfilling prophecy. View the world through the lenses of perverse Orientalism and the Middle East hits back.

This is a good moment to turn to representations of war. Media reflect—and at times, stage manage and produce—the different sides to war. Over time, media representations of war, at any rate on the part of war parties, have become more, not less biased because war is increasingly conducted via airwaves and cyberspace with media as major arenas of psychological operations and black information ('black ops') on the frontlines of public opinion.

Media representations in the US, particularly of conflicts in the Middle East and adjacent regions and of Israel's policies, often diverge from those in the region, clearly so during the neoconservative project of 'transforming the Middle East', as a glance at CNN and, in contrast, *Al Jazeera*, *Al Arabiya*, and other Mideast media shows. Secretary of state Madeline Albright declaring in 1996 on the death of half a million Iraqi children under five because of US sanctions, 'we think the price is worth it', exemplifies the divide. Secretary of state Condoleezza Rice's statement, as Israel's devastation of Lebanon was underway in August 2006, that 'a new Middle East is being born' was oblivious to sentiments in the region.

For years Afghan President Hamid Karzai protested at regular intervals that American air raids and drones killing Afghan civilians are intolerable, without noticeable effect on operations. American air raids and drones spread to Pakistan's border areas and to nontribal areas such as Baaur. Pakistan's prime minister voiced similar concerns. Public perceptions in both countries are that drone operations are part of a tacit arrangement with the Pentagon, and political leaders go through the motions of protesting for domestic legitimacy's sake, which documents released later by WikiLeaks have confirmed.[19]

Reporting of the clash between Georgia and Russia in summer 2008 was one-sided; for critical treatments one had to wander far off the beaten track. Also, according to otherwise reasonably independent sources, Russia's intervention in Georgia signaled the re-emergence of a totalitarian regime. In the *Financial Times* Philip Stephens compared Russia's actions to those of Nazi Germany and the Soviet Union.[20] In a *New York Times* op-ed column, citing Georgia's then president Saakashvili's view of Putin ('today we are looking evil directly in the eye'), Maureen Dowd casually used the language of 'evil'.[21] The American battlefield language of 'good guys' and 'bad guys' permeates American media and movies. It is a small step from rehearsing unexamined assumptions to war mongering. Months later, reports emerged in the BBC and other sources that Georgian forces had used indiscriminate violence against civilians and homes in South Ossetia, which Russia responded to with proportional restraint—the complete opposite of the account that had been circulating for months. By the time these reports emerged, the story was long off the front pages and the rites of indignation had come and gone. It takes little for mainstream media to echo government narratives, but it takes a lot to self-correct and to break narratives.

Reporting on Iraq, Afghanistan, Pakistan, Ukraine, Yemen has been extensive and biased. Regarding Darfur, the public knew about the 'Janjaweed' and images of parched stretches of land, but received no information about problems of water that underlie ethnic strife and conflicts with Chad. The International Criminal Court indicted Sudan's head of state for genocides of three tribes that the general public had never heard of. The hiatus between these charges and public knowledge shows the gap in reporting. Reporting on the Gaza war and blockade and on Israel's attacks on flotillas that seek to bring supplies to Gaza has likewise been biased and inadequate.

It is a cliché that media don't function well in war and the frontiers of patriotism are messy. Developing a cultural conversation and coming to terms with the First and Second World Wars and the Vietnam War took decades. Michael

Ware, former war correspondent in Iraq, notes, 'In film and TV, we can't do it while the conflicts are still underway'.[22] This delayed reaction applies to the Iraq and Afghan wars and to the Syrian crisis, the backdrop to the Syrian refugees in Europe.

The Syrian crisis involves strands that stretch back in time. Sixty years of American hegemony in the Middle East, since the Suez crisis of 1956 placed the region outside the currents of globalization. The Cold War involved cultivating Muslims as countervailing forces against communism, such as the Mujahedeen in Afghanistan and Hamas in Palestine. Part of this is the American alliance with Israel and Saudi Arabia. The alliance with Saudi Arabia goes back to the founding of Aramco (1944) and the oil-dollar system involves what Tim Mitchell calls 'McJihad', American oil money funding reactionary Wahhabi Islam throughout the region and the world.[23] Playing off Sunnis and Shia for decades (with American support for Iraq in two Iran-Iraq wars, isolating Iran and Shia) cemented the alignment of Iran, Syria, Hezbollah, and Russia. Neoliberalism in the Middle East, the opening up of economies (infitah), and retreat of the state, amplified Saudi conservative influence. These entanglements have been decades in the making and all come with blowback and payback, so now there is no quick fix for the Syrian crisis. Media, devoid of historical awareness (presentism) and critical awareness are unable to address these crises in a remotely meaningful way.

4 Overusing celebrity narratives

By following Bob Geldof and Bono, Angelina Jolie and Madonna as tour guides to world problems, media offer comic book versions of world problems and relief and adopt tabloid views of globalization. This to the dismay of social movements and NGOs who for decades have sought to present images of Africa emancipated and empowered and not as an object of charity.

That media create and use celebrity is ordinary; stardust and glamor serve as emotional glue and media offer emoticons with celebrities as props. Locales, regions, and nations are extended families of sorts and media provide their narratives. Through incessant repetition, national narratives attain 'truthiness' in the sense of generating a common sense. That celebrities and movie actors take up global engagement and articulate social responsibility is welcome and sometimes their ideas are smarter and more grounded than their media representations.[24] What is problematic, however, is media overusing celebrity to the point of distorting global relations. Thus, Western discussions were dominated by Gleneagles' promises of debt relief for Africa, which years later turned out to be largely unmet. Discussions of international development have long been dominated by the Millennium Development Goals (Sustainable Development Goals since 2015). The declaration of new targets and goals diverts attention away from the circumstance that past targets have not been met. In response to Geldof and Bono escapades, entrepreneurs and investors note that by making Africa look like an object of charity they reduce the actual interest in investing in Africa.

This is not where the energy is and this is not how the ship has been turning. Asian investment in Africa has been rising significantly. While the main driver has been rising demand for commodities, an additional factor is that, unlike the West, China and India have not been burdened by the mortgage of denigrating representations. Growth in several African countries rose to 6 percent—after 'lost decades' of feeble or negative growth—largely due to demand and investments from EM. The World Bank reported that 'for the first time in three decades African economies are growing with the rest of the world', which fuels 'hopes of new business era in Africa'.[25] Africa 'is at the heart of the latest surge of enthusiasm to hit emerging markets. Factors: commodities boom, debt relief, improvements in economic policy. Private capital flows have tripled since 2003 (45 billion in 2006)'.[26]

If we compare media North and South, the general tenor in media in the global South is more positive about the growing role of the South, more concerned with South-South cooperation, more impatient with the postwar power structure and more critical of Western bias, as glancing at *Al Jazeera* or *Al Arabiya* programs or leafing through *Frontline, Dawn, Al Ahram, Daily Star, Uno Mas Uno, La Jornada, China Daily, South China Morning Post, Times of India* or *New Straits Times* shows. The common experience of Western colonialism and neocolonialism obviously plays a role. Media in the South are also more aware of the ironies of Western bias. Thus, the *Times of India* reported the story of a US Senator outsourcing a speech critical of the globalization of Oregon to a firm in Bangalore, India.[27] Another trend in media in the global South is growing assertiveness. According to Chandra Nair, 'Speak up, Asia, or the west will drown you out': 'What is needed is the emergence of a confident body of Asian intellectual leaders'.[28] A Reuters story in the *Hindustan Times* is headlined 'Stop lecturing us, India tells rich nations':

> The time has come for the developed world to attend to its own problems, and stop lecturing emerging economies about what is right and what is wrong, Finance Minister Palaniappan Chidambaram said on Monday. As growth looks sure to slow in much of the rich world, partly due to the fallout from reckless lending in the United States, new economic power-houses like India say they are tired of being told what to do. 'For too long the advanced economies have told the developing economies that this is right and this is wrong', Chidambaram told Reuters on the sidelines of the annual meetings of the International Monetary Fund and World Bank. But his biggest criticism was of financial authorities in developed countries for not keeping up with the new and complex financial market instruments that lay behind recent credit market turmoil. 'Their regulators have fallen behind. They are beginning to rethink their regulatory structure', he said. . . . 'In the name of innovation, regulators or governments in the advanced economies have fallen behind the curve', he said. 'The lesson is that the model we have adopted, cautious calibrated opening of the economy, is perhaps the right model'.[29]

Another instance of the South talking back is China's human rights report on the United States. Drawing on Human Rights Watch, FBI reports, etc., the report criticized American violent crime, its large prison population, police brutality, restrictions on workers' rights to unionize, and the wars in Iraq and Afghanistan.[30]

Meanwhile, in some areas, mainstream media North and South tend to converge. 'Blessed are the poor' according to one of the prophets, but not according to the world's media. In the North, refugees and economic migrants from the South are easy targets for discrimination and allegations of crime. In the South, poverty is often associated with crime and disease.[31] Middle-class sensibilities and glitzy marketing aesthetics prevail in most media, also in the South.[32] The paradox of poverty is that while it ranks high in official rhetoric and development policy since the late 1990s, media display middle-class bias and mostly take a condescending approach to the poor, if they are in the picture at all.[33] Hence the meager status of anti-poverty policies.

5 BC/AC

Discussed above are global divides that media uphold in the early 21st century. Whether media merely reflect and follow or create divides is a question that cannot be addressed here. Mainstream media under-represent the rise of the rest. In this respect, they differ from business media that are keen to identify 'new champions' and in whose interest it is to do so, whether from the point of view of markets, competition, or investment. They differ also from intelligence agencies—CIA and American security intelligence reports have long identified the major economic and power realignments to come,[34] but don't make popular reading. In representing the rise of the rest as a threat, mainstream media send the message that if globalization isn't ours, then it isn't. As long as this is the common sense in the West, it suggests the diagnosis 'does not play well with others'.

Their representation of new emerging globalization meets the needs of conservative, complacent societies, a bourgeois response that enables bourgeois repose. It keeps horizons near and flat. How would conventional wisdom come to terms with the ironies of history? How would media represent self-criticism and reflexivity? Media are mostly windows of clichés, air vents of knowledge without depth, with occasional smart op-ed comments and probing investigative reports. The American and European bubbles vent regional narratives of power. To the extent that media are bubble media—display windows of collective narcissism in which world events figure as sidebars to national narratives—they institutionalize national and regional comfort zones. The crisis of 2008, however, has been a game breaker and wakeup call for the 'masters of the universe'. There have been marked differences in public discourses Before and After Crisis, BC and AC (or Before Lehman and After Lehman, as it is known in financial circles). The discussion above mostly portrays BC views.

Twenty-first-century shifts manifest to a large extent as economic shifts with finance as a salient dimension and sovereign wealth funds (SWF) (government owned investment corporations) as key players. SWF mainly come from two sources, surplus accumulated through exports of manufactures, as in China and South Korea, and fossil fuel exports, with Norway and the United Arab Emirates in the lead, followed by other oil exporters. Before the crisis, perspectives on SWF followed the general American pattern of distrust of state institutions. In 2005, the US Congress vetoed China's CNOOC's bid to acquire the oil company Unocal. In 2006, Congress overruled the Dubai Ports World holding company taking over the management of six US ports. Larry Summers voiced the philosophy underlying this distrust. According to Larry Summers, SWFs 'shake the logic of capitalism': 'governments as shareholders . . . may want to see their national companies compete effectively, or to extract technology or to achieve influence'.[35]

Actually, what is wrong with governments seeking to build the national economy? In Europe, industrial policy has been the norm; in East Asia the developmental state has been the path to success. But in the US, the default ideology is 'free enterprise', and government 'picking winners' is taboo. Summers upholds a singular, American notion of capitalism and implicitly condemns forms of mixed economy. Obviously, this position is no longer tenable with banks, insurance companies such as AIG, and Detroit automakers leaning on government for support. The criticism that SWF follow political rather than economic objectives no longer holds when politics and economics are no longer clearly distinguishable. In the words of Philip Stephens, 'Broken banks put the state back in the driving seat', and 'government is no longer a term of abuse'.[36]

After crisis, the story lines changed. The story is essentially simple: 'Sovereign funds put cash in the banks'.[37] Funds from China to the Gulf Emirates bought stakes in Wall Street banks. As the China Investment Corporation bought a 10 percent stake in Morgan Stanley for $5 billion and a 10 percent share of Blackstone, 'the fund sees a unique opportunity in the credit crisis of developed markets'.[38] It is not just the Abu Dhabi Investment Authority buying Manhattan's Chrysler building or SWF from China and Singapore buying into Wall Street power houses; it is that accumulation patterns have changed. The portée of the intervention of SWF is that the 2008 crisis ushered in the comeback of state capitalism in liberal market economies.

Reviewing the cycle, at one stage SWF were shunned, next they were reluctantly allowed in, then they were embraced, next they were actively sought after, expected to take part and drawn into institutions, or reprimanded for not taking part—much of this in the course of a year. Daniel Gross summed up the unfolding plot:

> With U.S. banks and financial institutions retrenching in the wake of the subprime debacle, cash-seeking American hedge funds, private-equity firms and corporations will be booking passage for Beijing and Bahrain.

'They [SWFs] have almost replaced U.S. pension funds as the principal source of capital for alternative investments', says Michael Klein, chairman of Citigroup's investment-banking unit.

The rising pace of SWF investment in blue-chip American companies will provoke plenty of angst. SWFs operate with a Cheneyesque opacity. Americans tend to imagine free trade and globalization as McDonald's in Riyadh and shoe factories in Vietnam producing cheap goods. But governments of nondemocratic countries in the Persian Gulf and Asia owning big chunks of America's financial infrastructure? Not so much.[39]

Consider the shifting nuances in headlines and story lines in the Western business press from 2007 through 2008, in chronological sequence, at times with contradictory signals even on the same page or in the same article.

Big spenders: how sovereign funds are stirring up protectionism (J. Willman) and Markets eye the new rich kids on the block (J. Chung, *Financial Times* 7/30/2007).

A passage to the west for sovereign wealth funds (J.F. Vail, *Financial Times* 10/31/2007)

Officialdom finds a new, unprincipled bogeyman (J. Dizard, *Financial Times* 11/27/2007)

Sovereign funds should lend support to equities (*FT* 12/13/2007)

Why SWFs will not fix the western financial mess (T. Jackson, *FT* 12/17/2007)

Credit crunch led to rapid rise of sovereign wealth fund investment in US and European banks: since January 2007 Singapore's Temasek spent $41.7 billion (for stakes in Merrill Lynch and Barclays), the UAE $10.7 billion and China $8 billion (*FT* 3/24/2008).

IMF clears way for development of sovereign wealth funds code (*Wall Street Journal* 3/24/2008)

The wealth of nations is reflected in the stellar rise of sovereign wealth funds (*FT* 3/31/2008)

The new global wealth machine (*New York Times* 4/2/2008)

Do not panic over foreign wealth (G. Rachman, *FT* 4/29/2008).

Sovereign wealth funds to the rescue: are they saviours, predators or dupes? (I. Warde, *Le Monde diplomatique* 5/2008)

Reject sovereign wealth funds at your peril (*FT* 6/6/2008)

SWFs attract controversy but are part of the global solution (Arnab Das, *FT* 7/23/2008)

Managers eye Asian SWF billions (*FT* 8/4/2008)

Fifth of SWFs 'unaccountable' (*FT* 9/15/2008)

Global Investment: Exec desperately seeks SWF. Must be rich. No green card or English required. Send photos and balance sheets to Wall Street (Gross 2007–2008)

A parallel to these changes in representation is the charm of Islamic finance, with London, Amsterdam, and other financial centers queuing up to cater to the new assets.[40] This echoes the recycling of Eurodollars in the 1970s with a twist: Western institutions seeking to retrieve money that went into paying for the West's energy habits.

Initially EM appeared to be safe from the impact of crisis, but gradually letup of demand not only in the US but also in Europe began to impact emerging economies exports. Nandan Nilekani, the head of India's Infosys, adds a further twist: 'we were riding on a global liquidity boom'. 'Remove the "steroid", as is happening now, and 2–3 percent of growth will go'. So the crisis also comes as a corrective in EM: 'After a few years of 8 percent plus growth, we felt that we were already a superpower. We took credit for global factors, and took the foot off reforms'.[41]

The crisis accelerated the transition from the G7 to the G20. The G20 summit of November 2008 edged towards a global rebalancing act with a greater role for EM. A Dutch newspaper headline during the summit read, matter-of-factly, 'G20 waits for new leader, preferably one with money'.[42] Awareness that the American hegemon is bankrupt has spread.

The declining value of American assets through 2008—such as Citigroup, Merrill Lynch, Morgan Stanley, Washington Mutual—cost the SWFs that went in early dearly. A November 2008 headline read, 'Sovereign funds go cold on rescue finance'.[43] Given continued uncertainty, SWF became more cautious, which, in turn, increased the political pressure for their involvement. As 2008 drew to a close, the China Investment Corporation announced its withdrawal from investing in Western financial houses and Chinese officials lectured the US Treasury on the importance of economic stability.[44]

Ambivalent reporting on the rise of SWF in Western media—oscillating between anxiety and greed—is paralleled by changing representations of the rise of Asia. After the crisis, the rise of the rest is gradually being represented in a more positive light. We can anticipate more such changes. After all, one day the new champions may be called to the rescue. A cover headline of *The Economist* asks 'Can China save the world?'[45] The answer is skeptical, but the question signals that the global landscape has changed radically. As the IMF resumes its role of stabilizing international finance, it does so with new funds, in particular from Saudi Arabia and China. At the time a headline read 'UK confident Saudis will help IMF'.[46]

Saudi Arabia embarked on austerity measures, like the Gulf Emirates, borrowed on external markets, is undertaking an overhaul to diversify its economy away from dependence on fossil fuels, and has issued a record bond sale ($17.5 billion, 2016).

Many emerging economies' SWFs have invested most in advanced economies where slow growth makes for low yield and the earlier expectation of their disruptive impact has tapered off. The conversation about SWF has broadened and moved on. How SWFs are governed has become a major issue—is it citizens' money or the state's kitty?[47] Norway's SWF, the world's largest at $870 billion, has adopted principles of investing in green innovation and cracks down on high executive pay—which is 'significant for almost every listed company in the world as Norway's oil fund owns on average 1.3 per cent of each one'.[48]

Financialization leads not only in the corporate world but also permeates the public sphere and, as the main driver of information, shapes the frames of perception of emerging economies and world affairs. In the West, EME are generally perceived through the lenses of the investor class. Analysis of EM is provided by investor class analysts such as Jim O'Neill (Goldman Sachs), Ruchir Sharma (Morgan Stanley), Mohamed El-Erian (Pimco, Allianz), Stephen Roach (Morgan Stanley Asia), Mark Mobius (Templeton EM), consultancies such as McKinsey, PwC, BCG, Ernst and Young, and banks and insurance companies such as Allianz. The information and analyses are often incisive, but they are from Western investor class angles, the world viewed from Davos, short-term with a view to return on investment (in *The Economist*, *Financial Times*, *Wall Street Journal*, *Bloomberg Businessweek*, *Fortune*, etc., with different levels of quality).

If the Washington institutions have lost influence, the knowledge grid of financial markets remains intact with ratings such as the Economic Freedom Index and Competitiveness Index. Business media and the media big six (such as Time Warner and Rupert Murdoch's conglomerate) echo the impression management of conservative think tanks and corporations. Reporting often blames social unrest in EM on state authoritarianism (fix: human rights), pro-market economists blame government corruption and inefficiency (fix: liberalization), while state and social forces focus on capitalist excesses (and local government incompetence). International institutions, multinationals, financial analysts, and World Bank economists weigh in on debates. Banks such as HSBC, Goldman Sachs, and JP Morgan tune in to local networks; consultancies such as McKinsey, BCG, and Bain collect and transmit information. Thus, middleman institutions buffer or alternatively, dramatize frictions between capitalisms (Chapter 3.3). A second stream is political risk analysis and consultancies such as the Eurasia Group, Teneo, and Kissinger Associates. A third stream is geopolitics from American points of view with emphasis on security and intelligence, such as Robert Kaplan, former heads of intelligence, and armed forces.

Media and discussions in EME and the global South are more up-close, more influenced by government sources and perspectives, often uncritical but also often more socially and culturally aware. The spread of reporting is wider, the time horizon is longer, and the approach more engaged. Thus, OBOR is extensively discussed in the *China Daily*, *South China Morning Post*, and media in Asia but hardly figures in Western media and if it does, reporting is often snide (as in *The Economist*, 'Our bulldozers, our rules').[49] On such issues, media and representations are still worlds apart. Neoliberalism has flunked in the eyes of majorities in the North and South, yet it remains a prevailing adapt-or-die logic whose influence is transmitted via financial markets, international institutions, FTAs, and mainstream media.

Notes

1 Ekecrantz 2007.
2 M. Wolf, The rescue of Bear Stearns marks liberalisation's limit, *Financial Times* 3/26/2008: 15.
3 Schiller 1999; Strange 1996.
4 Phillips 2006.
5 A retired four-star Army general and military analyst of NBC News, Barry McCaffrey, made hundreds of appearances on MSNBC and other networks and had direct access to top US commanders, all the while being under lucrative contracts with major military equipment suppliers. D. Barstow, One man's military-industrial media complex, *New York Times* 11/30/2008: 1, 26–27.
6 E. Alterman, Bromance news, *The Nation* 11/14/2016: 6–8.
7 Friedman 2005.
8 Wallerstein 1984.
9 Friedman 2006; cf. Bremmer 2011.
10 See Vitalis 2006.
11 Poll reveals backlash in wealthy countries against globalisation, *Financial Times* 7/23/2007: 1.
12 E.g., a headline of *Il Messagiero* on the failure of the Doha round talks in Geneva 2008, 'Guerra Asia-USA, fallisce il WTO', 7/30/2008: 1.
13 In media studies, see Curran and Park 2000.
14 Abrahamanian 2003.
15 Extensive discussion in Nederveen Pieterse 2007.
16 A. Hirsi Ali, *Wall Street Journal* 8/18/2010: A17.
17 Berman 2003.
18 Petras 2006.
19 See Nederveen Pieterse 2012b.
20 Ph. Stephens, The vulnerabilities that lie behind Putin's belligerence, *Financial Times* 8/15/2008.
21 M. Dowd, Russia is not Jamaica, *New York Times* 8/17/2008: WK11.
22 R. Weideman, A reporter's Iraqi hell, *Rolling Stone* 4/7/2016: 24–25.
23 Mitchell 2002.
24 Cf. Richey and Ponte 2008 on Product RED campaign.
25 World Bank 2007; A. Russell, Growth data fuel hopes of new business era in Africa, *Financial Times* 11/15/2007.
26 J. Chung, *Financial Times* 7/30/2007.
27 'US Senator outsources speech to India', *Times of India* 11/13/2006.
28 C. Nair, Speak up, Asia, or the west will drown you out, *Financial Times* 1/4/2007: 13.
29 *Hindustan Times* 10/23/2007.
30 AP, China calls U.S. record on rights 'shocking', *International Herald Tribune* 3/14/2008: 3.
31 E.g., Davis 2006.
32 Berger 2008.
33 The way media treat poverty is 'a very poor show'. Simon Kuper, Poverty: a very poor show, *Financial Times* 3/30–31/2013: 2.
34 According to the US National Intelligence Council's report *Global Trends* 2005, released in 2008, 'India and China could rise to join the US on top of a multipolar world in 2025', reports *The Times of India* 11/22/2008: 1. India will become the world's fourth largest economy.

35 L. Summers, Sovereign funds shake the logic of capitalism, *Financial Times* 7/30/2008.
36 P. Stephens, Broken banks put the state back in the driving seat, *Financial Times* 11/28/2008: 9.
37 *Financial Times* 11/28/2007.
38 J. Anderlini, China wealth fund's early coming of age, *Financial Times* 12/21/2007: 18.
39 D. Gross, Global investment: Exec desperately seeks SWF, *Newsweek* 12/31/2007–1/7/2008.
40 R. Sullivan, Islamic investment products offer boost to global exposure, *Financial Times* 11/3/2008.
41 N. Nilekani, Imagining a better India: lunch with BS, *Business Standard* (Kolkata) 11/25/2008: 8.
42 *De Volkskrant* 11/15/2008: 15.
43 H. Sender, *Financial Times* 11/10/2008: 15.
44 China sovereign wealth group to stop investing in western banks, *Financial Times* 12/4/2008: 1. G. Dyer, Chinese officials lecture Paulson, *Financial Times* 12/5/2008: 2.
45 *The Economist* 7/30/2009; cf. Tim Harcourt, Can China save the world? What role will China play in helping solve the financial crisis? *The Globalist* 10/30/2008.
46 *Financial Times* 11/3/2008.
47 Cummine 2016.
48 R. Milne, Norway wealth fund set to launch crackdown on high executive pay, *Financial Times* 2/5/2016: 1.
49 Our bulldozers, our rules, *The Economist* 7/2/2016: 37–38. *Financial Times* reporting is less biased.

8   Governance and protest

A weak state has never been synonymous with a strong private sector.
President Lula da Silva, 2010

How do societies and states navigate 21st-century multipolarity? Dynamics
that EMDC face include the end of the export-led growth model, the end of
the commodities boom, and international financial instability (as in the ebb
and flow of QE in the US). Meanwhile the pressures of neoliberal institutions
largely continue in international finance, credit rating agencies, MNCs, and
trade pacts. Now China is on the horizon, which in many ways follows an
updated version of the East Asian developmental state (EADS) with distinct
differences. Its leading companies are going global and China is undertaking
a major new global surplus recycling mechanism in the One Belt, One Road
initiatives (Chapter 6.5).

   Challenges for EMDC are how to deliver growth when export-led growth
is winding down because of rising protectionism and slow demand in AE, and
how to move beyond the middle-income level and achieve inclusive growth
in an increasingly competitive environment. Unless they succeed in industrial
upgrading they risk 'premature deindustrialization', i.e., deindustrialization at
a lower level of per capita income than in the past. Replacing jobs lost in
industry with jobs in services requires a capacious service sector and adequate
domestic demand, but low wages (as a condition of export-led growth) means
domestic demand is low.

   The big three in social science are the *state*, *market*, and *society*. The varieties of capitalism, liberal market economies (LME), coordinated market
economies (CME), and state-led market economies (SME), each refer to a
different balance of the big three. In LME markets come first, in SME the
state leads, and in CME all three are represented. Making globalization work,

according to Stiglitz, depends on the mix of the big three.[1] Global rebalancing after the 2008 crisis was concerned with economic policies and financial trends (Chapter 6.2); the political and governance crises that follow concern rebalancing the big three.

A contention in the clash of capitalisms (Chapter 3.3) concerns the role of the state, which is supposed to be minimal in LME while it plays a central role in CME and SME. In LME the role of the state isn't actually minimal but claiming that it is, is ideologically and politically important. Industrial policy and 'national economic strategy' are not part of American business etiquette. The military-industrial complex, subsidies for agro-industry, big oil, big pharma, the socialization of corporate losses, and impunity of bank fraud, show that the role of the state is in fact large but is bent in particular directions. Mariana Mazzucato's analysis of the 'entrepreneurial state' uncovers part of this bent by showing that American economic success is also due to public and state intervention, in public-private partnerships in innovation and government funding of research in defense labs and universities.[2] The American federal state (36 percent of GDP, $6.6 trillion, 4 million employees) is large in security, law and order, and in support of corporations, and relatively small in many other respects.

In CME the coordinating role of the state is not in question. In development studies, the role of the state is hardly in question either—the role of the developmental state, as in East Asia, is widely acknowledged. The World Bank's 1997 World Development Report focused on 'bringing the state back in'. The significance of the state is not in question; the quality of institutions and policies is.

In EMDC, the public sector plays a key role in mobilizing and steering growth. Its tasks include building a coalition around a growth path, pacing and sequencing growth so job loss in one area is balanced by job creation in another, and growth is inclusive and sustainable. A widely shared understanding in development studies is that market forces generate growth, but it takes the public sector to see to the quality of growth. A further dimension to consider is the importance of institutions. While politics, political mobilization, and media are mostly concerned with policies, in development thinking the emphasis has shifted to institutions.

Many accounts of transformation in developing countries deal with market forces first and government policies second. As manifestations of social agency, the contemporary protests rebalance the big three and show it is not just markets and powers that are emerging but also societies.

Stock answers to governance in EMDC—democracy, the middle class, good governance —are generic and outdated. Is the issue democracy, or rather *what kind* of democracy and with what institutions? The role of democracy is overstated and the role of institutions is understated—institutions as a check on state power and elite power. Democracy is mostly understood as liberal democracy while for developing countries social democracy is more relevant in view of its in-built institutions.

Is the middle class the way forward? Is what is good for the middle class good for society, as some argue? Do middle classes besides an economic and business role, also play a political role, or are they too diverse to play such a role?

In many waves of protest, a common denominator is inequality. The protest of people 'trampled by neoliberalism' is a sequel of protests of the 1990s against NAFTA, the WTO, and trade liberalization because the gains go mostly to corporations and elites. Protest and populism, left and right, point to governance crises which in many AE is as pressing as in EM.

Several concerns come to a head in contemporary governance gaps—gaps of democracy and inequality, financialization, new technologies and regulation, globalization, and global public goods. Now there is a clearer understanding than in the past that history isn't finished. All is work in progress. This chapter critiques approaches and discusses dilemmas of governance on the cutting edge of themes discussed earlier. The first section deals with the middle class; the second with democracy; the third with protest, and the closing section focuses on governance gaps in AE and EE. A theme that runs through the discussion is *institutions*, which I discuss first.

Through the phases of international development thinking, the emphasis fell first on policies. During the postwar era of modernization, the leitmotiv was get the policies right (industrialization and nation building). In the 1980s, the keynote was 'get the prices right' (remove government distortions, release market forces). From the late 1990s, the adage was 'get governance right' (good governance, transparency, weed out corruption). In the 2000s, the leitmotiv is 'get the institutions right'.

According to Rodrik and colleagues, 'institutions rule'; they are the critical factor in predicting income levels across the world—among all causal factors that account for differences in states' economic performance, the quality of institutions 'trumps everything else'.[3] Policies for growth may be in place but with institutions absent or poorly designed, their efficacy is limited, which is known as the 'governance-policy gap'. Institutions are crucial to achieve not just growth but quality and sustainable growth. Institutions serve to counteract what is variously called state capture, political capture, and elite capture (Chapter 5.4). 'Getting institutions right' has become the adage in development circles.[4]

A distinction runs between informal and formal institutions: *informal institutions* are norms and expectations of behavior in everyday and public culture, and *formal institutions* are part of or sanctioned by the state. Formal institutions are differentiated according to domains of state policy—administrative, judicial, political, and security. Administrative institutions deal with the implementation, regulation, and delivery of services (state ministries, bureaucracies). Judicial institutions are concerned with the interpretation and enforcement of laws (courts). Political institutions deal with policy decision making and the selection of public officials (political parties, legislatures, elections). Security institutions are engaged in law enforcement, border control, citizen protection, and defense (military and police). In each domain, there are distinctions between high- and low-quality institutions.

Of course, there is a gap between informal and formal institutions. India has outlawed caste, but in informal public culture caste endures, particularly in rural areas. The US adopted the Emancipation Proclamation (1863), but segregation and Jim Crow laws carried on for decades in the South; the US adopted civil rights legislation (1963), but this had unintended consequences (such as the rise of southern Democrats), and discrimination and racism endure. Sociology of organization distinguishes between formal rules and informal culture. Thus, a corporation may officially endorse gender equity while workplace culture continues to discriminate against women.[5]

Autocratic, military, and technocratic governments may get policies right, but they leave institutions weak or in shambles. This is the record of authoritarian governments (such as Côte d'Ivoire, Ethiopia, Malaysia, Fujimori in Peru, Uribe in Colombia, Mugabe in Zimbabwe, Kabila in DR Congo, Museveni in Uganda, Erdogan in Turkey) and military governments (as in Egypt, Thailand, Pinochet in Chile).

During his 22 years as prime minister of Malaysia, Dr. Mahathir implemented several good policies (infrastructure, a national car industry, capital controls), but he concentrated power in the ruling party and the office of the PM, and consolidated Malay rule as part of economic policy. Dr. Mahathir achieved much but in the process dismantled institutions of accountability and disempowered parliament and the opposition. With institutions weakened, policies were bent to serve ruling party purposes, ensuring its indefinite rule, and institutionalizing cronyism. Sidelining Chinese and Indian minorities resulted in brain drain and capped Chinese enterprises. Fast forward two decades and Malaysia is saddled with unending ruling party hegemony and an unaccountable PM office that monopolizes government power. Malaysia has become an authoritarian theme park that generates monsters of its own (such as the 1MDB scandal that is under investigation in six countries while Malaysia's attorney general has been sacked).[6] Dr. Mahathir now joins opposition demonstrations against the ruling party and wears a T-shirt with the slogan 'Free Anwar', the imprisoned opposition leader and former deputy PM whom he had maneuvered to be tried and jailed.

While there is a growing consensus on the importance of institutions and, to some extent, on the roles they should fulfill, there is no consensus on *which* institutions and on *how* this role should be fulfilled, which is discussed later.

1 Middle classes

Asian consumers lead economic recovery: Cautious optimism as middle-class spending powers surge in growth.
Financial Times editorial, 8/31/2016

While economic growth is the banner achievement of emerging economies, the growing middle class and its consumer appetite is the way through which the world is aware the societies are emerging. As consumers they are potentially drivers of world growth. They are to take up the slack left by waning consumer purchasing power in the United States. They are the centerpiece of the after-crisis global recovery Plan A. According to Gordon Brown, the former UK prime minister:

> Within a decade, a richer Asia will be home to a middle class revolution equivalent to the consumer power of two Americas, becoming the main driver of world growth. This shift can be the most effective exit strategy from the crisis, and help to rebalance the world economy—but only if Europe and America re-equip and are able to export their superior innovations and global brand name goods to Asia's new billion-strong middle class.[7]

A keynote of Goldman Sachs forecasting is the tremendous growth of the middle class, particularly in India and China.

> Their 2009 report predicts a massive rise in the size of the middle class in these nations. In 2025, it is calculated that the number of people in BRIC nations earning over $15,000 may reach over 200 million people. This indicates that a huge increase in demand will not be restricted to basic goods but will include higher-priced goods as well. According to the report, first China, and then a decade later, India, will begin to dominate the world economy.[8]

The future scenarios of McKinsey, PwC and others offer similar assessments.

Since the 19th-century rise of Europe's bourgeoisie, the middle class has been the centerpiece of major economic and social scripts, the bearer of momentous social missions. In *The Communist Manifesto*, Marx and Engels characterize the bourgeoisie as a 'permanently revolutionizing force'. David Landes presents the middle class as the driving force of Europe's economic development.[9] Charles Morazé's history of 19th-century Europe was titled *Les bourgeois conquérants*; the English translation was titled *The Triumph of the Middle Classes*.[10] As an educated class, the middle class is the torch bearer of modernity, the transformation from Gemeinschaft to Gesellschaft, from particularism to universalism, the key force in capitalist transformation, urbanization, individualization, and the spread of the nuclear family.

Postwar American modernization thinking cast the middle class and its values of achievement and deferred gratification as the leading transformative social force. The middle class retains this role in current assessments that cast the middle class in EM as the vanguard of growth, capitalism, and democracy. According to the Asian Development Bank's report on Asia's rising middle class, the middle class promotes development by providing entrepreneurs,

Table 8.1 Perspectives on the middle class in emerging economies

Approaches	*Role of middle class*	*Sources*
Business	New consumers	Goldman Sachs, McKinsey, PwC
Development economics	Modernizers, consumers,	ADB, Easterly, Birdsall
Political science	Bring democracy, human rights	Diamond, Rueschemeyer
Sociology	Diverse and contextual	European and regional sociologies

instilling 'middle-class values' of accumulation of savings and human capital and by driving demand for high-quality consumer goods.[11] Table 8.1 reviews approaches to the middle class in emerging economies.

Nancy Birdsall argues for refocusing inclusive growth on the middle class:

> [t]he concept of inclusive growth should go beyond the traditional emphasis on the poor (and the rest) and take into account changes in the size and economic command of the group conventionally defined as neither poor nor rich, i.e. the middle class. My main rationale is that growth driven by and benefiting a middle class is more likely to be sustained . . . sustained growth is arguably more likely where a politically salient middle class supports in its own economic interests the sound and stable political and economic institutions that encourage investment by ensuring the rule of law and recognition of private property rights.[12]

A large and politically independent middle class demands the rule of law, legal protections, and the greater accountability of government, and through the tax system it finances education, health, and social insurance programs, all of which also benefit the poor.[13] Thus in Birdsall's script, what is good for the middle class is good for society.

William Easterly also advocates a new World Bank emphasis and defines a 'middle-class consensus' as 'a national situation where there are neither strong class differences nor ethnic differences'.[14] The condition of 'relative equality and ethnic homogeneity . . . facilitates economic growth by allowing society to agree on the provision of public goods critical to economic development', such as public education, public health services, and physical infrastructure.[15] According to the ADB,

> [s]ocieties with a small middle class are generally extremely polarized, and find it difficult to reach consensus on economic issues; they are overly focused on the redistribution of resources between the elite and the impoverished masses, each of which alternates in controlling political power. Societies with a larger middle class are much less polarized and

can more easily reach consensus on a broad range of issues and decisions relevant to economic development.[16]

Given these broad claims, we should consider the definition of the middle class. According to the ADB:

> The middle class is not easily defined as it is not necessarily a distinct or unique group in society that has very different attributes or values than other social classes. It may simply represent a range along the income continuum (a group that lies between the poor and the rich) and social class (a group lying between the working class and the 'upper' class). . . . This report uses an absolute approach defining the middle class as those with consumption expenditures of $2–$20 per person per day in 2005 PPP $.[17]

Other definitions of the middle class refer to those in the second, third, and fourth quintile of the distribution of per capita consumption expenditure; to individuals earning between 75 percent and 125 percent of a society's median per capita income; or individuals with daily per capita expenditures of $2–$4 and $6–$10.[18] Birdsall places the yardstick for inclusion in the middle class higher: 'being a member of the middle class in the classic sense implies a reasonable level of economic security', so she opts for a $10 a day minimum income (at 2005 purchasing power parity terms).[19] The $2–$20 range of daily consumption spending defining the middle class yields three groups:

> The lower-middle class—consuming $2–$4 per person per day—is very vulnerable to slipping back into poverty at this level, which is only slightly above the developing world poverty line of $1.25 per person per day. The 'middle middle' class—at $4–$10—is living above subsistence and able to save and consume nonessential goods. The upper-middle class consumes $10–$20 per day.[20]

Most of Asia's middle class is lower-middle class and most newcomers to middle-class status are in this category.

> In the PRC, the daily consumption expenditure of more than half of the middle class is in the lower $2–$4 bracket, while in South Asia's Bangladesh, Nepal, India and Pakistan, the vast majority of the middle class (75% or more) falls into this group.[21]

After citing Easterly, the ADB report continues:

> Sridharan (2004) makes a similar argument for India. The emergence of a 100–250 million-sized middle class during the 1980s and 1990s, he says, has dramatically changed India's class structure—from one of a small elite

and a large impoverished class—to one dominated by a large intermediate class. According to him, 'the elite-mass class cleavage tended to support a broadly socialistic ideology, while the elite-middle-mass differentiation has created a broader base for capitalism—hence the increased support for economic liberalization'. That successive Indian governments since 1991, from across the political spectrum, have continued to support economic reforms and liberalization, supports his thesis.[22]

This reads like a middle-class utopia, an evocation of the middle class as deus ex machina that serves the wish-fulfillment of economists, embodies their values, implements their policies, and delivers desired outcomes. As an account of developments in India, its bent is ideological and in fact it isn't clear whether this is economics or politics. It is also an example of the economic liberalism that some think tanks in Asia advocate.[23]

Let's turn to political perspectives on the middle class. According to a classic scenario, the middle class is the main protagonist of democracy. The third estate has an intrinsic interest in the rule of law, suffrage, and the right of association and, in liberal democracies, individual rights, and property rights.

For developing countries, the standard account in American political science is that as the middle class grows in number and pays taxes, its demands for accountability in how their taxes are spent grow accordingly. Since rising incomes and rising taxation generate a growing demand for government accountability, the middle class acts as the vanguard of democracy.[24] In this scenario the middle class is a progressive social force, a force for stability and economic progress, along similar lines as in business and development economics thinking. Do trends, past and recent bear this out?

In 1927, the French philosopher Julien Benda published *Le Trahison des clercs* (translated as *The Treason of the Intellectuals,* 1928 and 2006). Benda argued that in the 19th and 20th centuries European intellectuals had often lost the ability to reason dispassionately about political and military matters and instead became apologists for crass nationalism, warmongering, and racism. In later years, this became one of the explanations for the support of fascism among some of Europe's intelligentsia. (A similar argument applies to the working class. The working class in European countries was supposed to follow proletarian internationalism, but instead many labor parties succumbed to chauvinist nationalism in the buildup to the First and Second World Wars.)

We can expand and update the notion of the treason of the intelligentsia as the 'treason of the middle class'—treason, that is, if we would buy into the idea of the middle class as vanguard of democracy. The middle class is supposed to support democracy but at times supports undemocratic interventions.

Consider Egypt. In Egypt, the Arab Spring inspired the Tahrir Square movement, which led to the election of a government by the Muslim Brotherhood. This was no surprise because during the long Mubarak years the Muslim Brotherhood had been the main organized political force.

Its support base includes the rural migrants of Cairo's sprawling slums. The fellahin in the countryside support rural forms of Islam. When Mohamed Morsi's administration overreached in its Islamization fervor, it was ousted by a military intervention. The military in Egypt is part of the deep state. When Muslim Brotherhood protesters rallied on the streets against the imprisonment of Morsi and at one stage in front of the main TV station, newscasters began to refer to them as 'terrorists'. Once this language was used it became inevitable that the military would intervene because now the protests had been framed in security terms. Thus, in effect, broadcast media—a key part of the middle class—had begun to call for military government. This is the moment of treason of the middle class. If democracy brings Islamism, better military rule than democracy.

Consider Thailand. In the long-lasting confrontation between Red Shirts and Yellow Shirts, the Yellow Shirts sided with the monarchy and the military. The class dimension of this confrontation is unmistakable. The income levels of the two clearly diverge and they overlap with urban–rural and South-North divides.[25] While Thailand's urban middle class is a mainstay of the Yellow Shirts, the Red Shirts are mostly from the poor rural Northeast and North. Thaksin Shinawatra's political party took up policies in support of the rural Northeast such as a subsidy for rice growers. The party was viewed as corrupt and some policies were questioned as being superficial, but they did make a difference in the Northeast and garnered votes for Thaksin's party. After Thaksin was ousted, his sister Yingluck won a landslide victory with a successor party that supported similar policies in favor of the Northeast, including a commitment to buy rice at above-market prices. Her party was ousted by a military coup that received wide support from Thailand's urban middle class. Thus, if democracy unlocks the vote of the rural poor and comes with populist pro-poor policies, a significant segment (or a majority) of the middle class opts for military rule over democracy.

Consider China. China's middle class is part of the grand bargain that keeps the Communist Party in power. As long as living standards improve, people continue to support the ruling party. It is 'a middle class without democracy'.[26] Another feature of China's middle class is the secession of the rich. According to a headline in the *Shanghai Daily*, 'Half of China's rich plan to emigrate'. A 'global survey of 2,000 high net-worth individuals by Barclays Wealth Fund found that 47 percent of the wealthy Chinese who were questioned plan to move overseas within the next five years'. Preferred destinations are Hong Kong and Canada and key reasons are better education and employment opportunities for their children and environmental problems.[27] If firms can go multinational, so can families if they have the means. If MNCs can be footloose and practice institutional arbitrage, so can families. Wealthy immigrants can 'buy citizenship' in the UK, Canada, and Australia. Capital flight and outward investment from China and other emerging economies—partly in response to weak institutions and lack of accountability—is another form of secession of the wealthy.

In the United States, the secession of the rich includes 'white flight' to suburbs and gated communities. On a larger canvas, it refers to movements for secession by more prosperous and advanced regions, such as Lega Nord in Northern Italy and Slovenia in former Yugoslavia. Slovenia opting for closer cooperation with the EU, followed by Croatia, started the breakup of Yugoslavia. (If, however, such movements cross classes and include broad lower strata—such as in Catalonia, Flanders, Scotland, Brittany—this categorization doesn't apply.)

In developing countries, gated compounds of extended families go way back in time. Recent developments are modern high-rises on land from which poor communities have been displaced, gated communities with faux Mediterranean or British names, and idealization of Singapore as a middle-class utopia.[28] Thailand is a country of 64 million with a large rural hinterland. What countries such as Thailand face is the classic problem of modernity: how to integrate the peasant majority into modernity (Chapter 4.3). Singapore is a utopia for Asia's middle class precisely because it is a city state that lacks a peasant hinterland and the pesky problem of the poor majority.

Fascism in Italy, Germany, and Spain and Soviet communism were alternative modernization routes. If democracy threatens to bring socialism or communism, as in 1930s Europe, a significant segment of the middle class may opt for fascism or Nazism, witness the role of the Catholic Church and Catholic parties in Germany and Austria. Hence the adage of socialists from the late 19th century onward, 'socialism or barbarism'. When the middle class must choose sides, it may opt for a strong state. The problem is as old as Marx's *Eighteenth Brumaire of Louis Bonaparte* (1869).

Macpherson's discussion of 'possessive individualism' in liberal democracy suggests that from the outset democracy has been a way to safeguard property, rights, and privilege against arbitrary government intrusion.[29] For a segment of the middle class, upholding privilege can override democracy. If there are other, shorter ways of upholding privilege, they can be preferred. This doesn't just refer to material privilege; it may refer to ideological leanings (forebodings of political change), to cultural preferences (such as secularism in Egypt), or to women's rights. Hence democracy is contingent—it is the preferred option, other things being equal. But other things rarely are equal.

Another strand may be fear of the majority—as in the stereotype of the 'irrational crowd' in Lebon's mass psychology and Ortega y Gasset's 'rebellion of the masses'. Or, the majority may be viewed as too different or too heterogeneous—culturally, ethnically, ideologically, in terms of class or religion. The preference for democracy, then, is *conditional*. Democracy is fine if we agree with the outcome of elections. (Note in a different context, when Gaza elected Hamas, the US and Israel disavowed the outcome.)

The definition of the middle class in EM used in business forecasting, development economics, and political science is essentially numerical: (a) income bracket statistics provide the data, (b) economic and political history (European and American) provide the screenplay, (c) the characteristics of the middle class are derived and attributed, rather than observed. Missing from these accounts is *sociology* of the middle class; short of sociology and anthropology, the numerical accounts are abstract and may well be normative ideology passing for social science. Business and development economics speaks of 'the middle class', while sociology typically yields the plural, middle classes.

Sociology of the middle class offers markedly different accounts: (a) the middle class is differentiated and segmented in generation and age cohorts, old and new middle class, life-style milieus of ethnicity, regional origin, religion, etc., (b) the role of middle classes is contextual and contingent, (c) the middle class is plural, middle classes. The old middle class may oppose the claims and incursions of a new middle class (red shirts rallying in Bangkok included the new rural middle class from the Northeast while Bangkok's old middle class sided with the monarchy and military for the sake of stability). Sérgio Costa applies Norbert Elias's distinction between the established and the outsiders to identify frictions in Brazil between insiders (with access to exclusive social spaces) and new middle classes.[30] Eileen Yuk-Ha Tsang describes how in China the old-generation middle class that grew up during Mao's era has quite different, more modest consumption habits than the young, new middle class.[31] Abdul Rahman Embong describes marked differences in ethnic identity, religion, and relations to state institutions in Malaysia's middle class, with the Malay Muslim middle classes as major beneficiaries of the ruling party's pro-Malay economic policies.[32] Kenya's urban middle classes display wide differences in life styles, cultural milieus, and political leanings.[33] Among new emerging elites in EM are affluent, globally oriented segments of middle classes who compete for status distinction and position in the global education market, represent growing internal division in middle classes, and may be part, as Hagen Koo examines, of a global middle class.[34]

Given these divisions among and within middle classes, Laclau and Mouffe's *articulation* perspective according to which classes and social movements don't possess 'intrinsic' characteristics, is relevant.[35] The scripts that attribute general characteristics to the middle class—such as Weber's Protestant ethic and rationalization, Marx's polarization of bourgeoisie and proletariat, and various Enlightenment scenarios—have been largely based on programmatic readings of a narrow set of cases, mostly 19th-century European history. Subsequent developments such as the two World Wars, fascism, and Nazism have dramatically belied several of them. These perspectives sidelined the role of chauvinism, popular imperialism, gender, racism, and religion, treating them as aberrations and deviations from the 'real' character of the middle class, while in fact they show that what shapes the actual role of middle classes is their articulation with other social forces and institutions.

Class boundaries are blurry. Empirical research in developing countries shows there are no clear-cut dichotomies, such as middle class and peasants, industry and agriculture, urban and rural, formal and informal sectors, and these are not homogeneous categories. Intermediary classes crosscut general categories.[36] The urban-rural distinction (and assumptions such as urban/

progressive, rural/backward) ignores class differences.[37] Categories such as middle class and peasants (and assumptions such as middle class/progressive, peasants/traditional) overlook internal class differentiation (such as the lower middle class and rich peasants). These categories are fuzzy and liquid and their actual role depends on how they interact with other social dynamics.

Moral and political discourses may supersede or inflect categorical scripts. In India, while the middle class in Baroda, Gujarat shares a moral discourse on consumption that describes consumer culture as debased materialism, it also views it as central to middle-class social life.[38] Middle-class activists may articulate the goals and strategies of lower-class movements such as peasant and worker movements in rural Maharashtra,[39] or may join chauvinist Hindutva, as in Mumbai and Gujarat. Middle classes may join millenarian projects such as radical Islamism in the Middle East (the leadership of Al Qaeda, ISIL, and other militant movements usually belongs to the educated middle class). In Brazil, many flock to candomble and other forms of popular syncretism.[40] The growth of evangelical Christianity and charismatic Catholicism in the US, Europe, and developing countries points in the same direction.[41]

While the urban middle class is expected to display superior educational discipline, rural students in China often study harder and perform better in exams than their urban counterparts; in rural Shandong the educational discipline of 'peasants' runs counter to social scripts.[42]

A Pew study on the global middle class found that 'most are supportive of democratic ideas like free speech and competitive elections', yet are 'willing to compromise on those ideals when they seem to threaten prosperity'. 'In China, rural people who still see little benefit from their nation's economic growth are more likely to support democracy than the urban middle classes who now make up three fourths of Communist Party cadres'.[43]

Then, as now, general scripts for the middle class interact with economic, cultural, and political vortices, which often produce ambivalent or contradictory social outcomes. Scripts based on class (Marx) or rationality (Comte, Weber) were typically blindsided by nationalism, ethnicity, religion, and gender. This is again the case in contemporary scenarios. Easterly's 'middle-class consensus' can possibly be an *outcome* of development processes but is unrealistic as a description of initial conditions. 'Ethnic homogeneity' is a rare social condition, which eliminates most societies from the equation. Hence Easterly's approach is an exercise in teleological thinking which offers problem denial as problem solution. Besides, it doesn't hold empirically; ethnically diverse countries such as Taiwan have been able to achieve development.

Unbundling the middle class reveals several problems: homogenization, generalization, and essentialism. First, *homogenizing* the middle class: while most accounts differentiate between upper, middle, and lower-middle class, such distinctions are lost in grand middle-class narratives. Many accounts refer to 'the middle class' as a broad category, which includes many who are just a step above poverty and would not be able or willing to carry the burden of social reforms. Second, *generalization*: the actual purchasing power of the majority middle class belies the enthusiastic claims of new middle-class consumption in business reports and forecasts. Thus in China, most of the addition to the middle class occurred at the lower end ($2–4) in rural areas and in the mid-range ($4–10) in urban areas. The various scripts attributed to 'the' middle class are generalizations; they refer at most to a segment of the middle class.

The call for 'middle-class friendly policies' begs the question: friendly to *which* middle class? A 'middle-class consensus' is unrealistic given steep differences within middle classes. In effect, Birdsall's recommendation implies what is good for the *upper-middle class* is good for society, which is a much harder sell than what is good for the middle class. Third, *essentialism* is presenting the middle class as a category that is both abstracted from history (in view of its generic attributes and values) *and* is given a historical mission and capacity to intervene in history, which puts the cart before the horse.

There are, then, no valid general scenarios of how middle classes in EM respond to growing prosperity. While the classic script of modernity is disembedding from social institutions,[44] this is not what is generally indicated. Cultures of stratification—race in Brazil and South Africa, ethnicity in Latin America and Southeast Asia, caste and religion in South Asia, intersecting with patriarchy and authoritarianism—display a pathos of inequality that may *intensify* rather than weaken with economic growth. For instance, in recent years, prohibition of cross-caste marriage in India has been on the increase.[45] Whether growing prosperity will produce increasing middle-class conservatism or inclusive social horizons depends on factors that are not inherent in middle classes but depend on cultural narratives, government policies, economic trends, social movements, international influences, etc. Now let us turn to the next middle-class mission, democracy.

2 Democracy is coming, or just left

In the 1990s, democracy was the dominant imaginary of politics. A global trend towards democracy was celebrated, heralded at world summits, prominent in the discourse of transition in Eastern Europe, and institutionalized as part of international development policy where good governance became a condition of foreign aid. The worldwide scope of democracy was widely heralded. 'No doubt, the defining concept of the 1990s is democracy. Like *Coca-Cola*, *democracy* needs no translation to be understood virtually everywhere' (emphasis in original).[46]

Democracy was a keynote during the Cold War years: the free market and democracy go together, in stark contrast to communism and totalitarianism. Huntington's 'third wave of democracy' was an expression of this diagnosis. Fukuyama's 'end of history' followed suit. With fascism and communism defeated, liberal democracy is the one ideology that remains standing.

The high tide of democracy was a post-Cold War discourse. Democracy had been tied in with anti-communism and the 'Free World', and its rise coincided with the comeback of American hegemony (recovering from the

Vietnam War) and the rise of neoliberalism in the 1980s. It was part of the Washington consensus: liberalize markets, economies will grow and in time, democracy will follow (a subtext rather than a loud part because the IMF and World Bank are not supposed to meddle in politics).

The idea that democracy is coming has long been a leitmotiv in Western thinking. Grand narratives of the 'American century' rework 19th-century French and European ideas of progress and have been a driving force in American foreign policy from Woodrow Wilson's support for self-determination to postwar American support for decolonization. It was followed by policies to bring prosperity and democracy to various parts of the world—to Europe in the Marshall Plan; to Latin America and the Caribbean in the Alliance for Progress; to former East bloc societies through the National Endowment for Democracy and support for the 'color revolutions' in Eastern Europe and the Caucasus; and to 'bring democracy' to the Middle East and Central Asia by ending dictatorships and supporting moderate political forces and human rights (as in Afghanistan, Iraq, Libya).

These efforts have not been successful. In the early 2000s, a convergence took place between neoconservative objectives of American expansion and regime change and the American mission of bringing democracy, with Paul Wolfowitz as president of the World Bank. In hindsight, what has come instead of democracy is Balkanization, ethnonationalism, and ISIL. Battered by setbacks, this view continues to inform American foreign policy, for instance in support for Internet and social media connectivity in the Middle East, Iran, and North Korea.[47]

A large literature criticizes the contradictions in hegemonic narratives—such as double standards for allies or with a view to geostrategic interests. Nevertheless, in the late 20th century, democracy generated a working consensus across a wide political spectrum, from Fukuyama to the left. As the model of armed struggle and social revolution withered, leftwing parties began to contest in multiparty elections in El Salvador, Guatemala, Nicaragua, Honduras, Bolivia, Peru, Uruguay, Thailand, the Philippines, etc.

On a world scale, however, liberal democracy was not the only model that remained standing after the collapse of socialism. There were at least two rival models—Islamic theocracy and the EADS. A third alternative, social democracy is discussed later. Islamic theocracy did not have a fortunate career. Iran ceased to inspire; a counterpoint is the 'Green Revolution'. Saudi Arabia and Wahhabi influence, the FIS in Algeria, the Taliban in Afghanistan and Pakistan, the Muslim Brotherhood in Egypt, Al Qaeda, ISIL in Syria, Iraq, and Libya, likewise fail to inspire.

The EADS are a different case. The economic success of the Asian Tiger economies has stood out amid often dismal decades of development. The way it has been achieved runs completely counter to neoliberal tenets. The notion of the developmental state goes back to Chalmers Johnson's account of Japan's economic success and has been taken up by many scholars, also in the aftermath of the Asian crisis.[48] It foregrounds the role of the state in development and is the diametrical opposite of the neoliberal tenet of growth led by market forces.

Middle-income countries in Southeast Asia—Malaysia, Thailand, Indonesia, and the Philippines—sought to replicate the success of the Northeast Asian Newly Industrialized Countries (NICs). In Malaysia, the 'Look East' policy looked to the example of Japan and the Tiger economies. Mark Thompson noted:

> Malaysian Prime Minister Dr Mahathir Mohammad has recently attacked Western democracy as a 'religion' irrelevant to his country . . . accusing the West of 'ramming an arbitrary version of democracy down the throats of developed countries'. His focus on trade barriers against Third World imports despite professions of free trade by wealthy nations and his parry of criticisms of pollution in developing countries by pointing out that most environmental destruction occurs in the industrialized states led him to be hailed 'the Hero of the South' in Malaysia. . . . The Asian model of development dictatorship may become a kind of alternative political model to Western democracy. After the original Newly Industrialized Countries (NICs), ASEAN is second and China as well as Vietnam third generation in this tradition.[49]

Two arguments run side by side in this perspective, the role of the state and the question of democracy, a recurring theme in the 1990s. According to Adrian Leftwich:

> [n]o examples of good or sustained growth in the developing world have occurred under conditions of uncompromising economic liberalism, whether democratic or not. From Costa Rica to China and from Botswana to Thailand, the state has played an active role in influencing economic behaviour and has often had a significant material stake in the economy itself.[50]

This points to 'the primacy of politics, not simply governance, as a central determinant of development'.[51] Leftwich invokes Friedrich List and Marx in favor of the economic role of the state and refers to the examples of Bismarck Germany, Meiji Japan, Atatürk Turkey, the Soviet Union after 1917, China during the first quarter century after the revolution, and other instances.[52] Similar arguments we find in the work of Robert Wade, Ha-Joon Chang, and Joe Studwell.[53]

Democracy, in Leftwich's view, is a consensual politics of accommodation whereas 'non-consensual and non-democratic measures may often be essential in the early stages of developmental sequences in laying the foundations for growth—and also sustainable democracy in the long run'. Land reform is an example. 'Democratic politics is seldom the politics of radical economic change'.[54] Thus, democracy should come *after*, not before development. Development requires radical measures and these require state autonomy. In fact, postwar American modernization theory also stipulated growth, industrialization, and nation building as components of modernization, and for the same reasons did *not* include democracy.

According to Leftwich, development in its early stages and democracy are incompatible and the trend to make foreign aid conditional on good governance and democracy is erroneous. In his view, the current celebration of democracy is out of step with reality, the notion that democratization is a global trend is premature, and a series of democratic breakdowns is likely: 'In short, we are about to enter an era of democratic reversal, not democratic consolidation'.[55] In sum, this presents two theses: no early development without the state; and no early development with democracy. The first argument holds but the second poses problems.

The Asian crisis of 1997 highlighted problems of crony capitalism, which supported the new Washington priority of good governance and exposed wider problems. Why have the Southeast Asian tiger cubs not been able to follow the success of the Northeast Asian Tiger economies? We should look at democracy in Southeast Asia, and at a deeper level we should look at institutions.

In light of the experience of Northeast Asian countries, the first issue is not authoritarianism per se but whether authoritarianism is developmental or predatory and whether governance is capable or inept. Korea and Taiwan were authoritarian states when they achieved their major spurts of industrialization. China and Singapore achieved sustained growth with authoritarian political systems. Yet authoritarian governments in Myanmar, Laos, Cambodia, and, until recent years, Indonesia and Vietnam, did not achieve sustained growth. By many accounts, the failure of mid-tier Southeast Asian countries to follow the example of Northeast Asia is essentially the failure of institutions and a manifestation of elite capture.[56]

We need to unbundle the state—states may be capable and developmental, or weak and predatory; and unbundle democracy—what matters more than electoral democracy is institutions. Democracy is a wide heading, so wide and burdened that it can be distracting. Paul Collier refers to the West's fixation with elections as a mistake that largely stems from lingering Cold War habits. The Soviet dread of the ballot 'confused us into thinking that achieving a competitive election is in itself the key triumph. The reality is that rigging elections is not daunting: only the truly paranoid dictators avoid them'.[57] Still, electoral shortcomings don't mean we should give up on democracy altogether. It's the cheap imitation that should give us pause. 'Democracy is a force for good' as long as it is more than a façade.[58]

Democracy needs unbundling. If for democracy we read the principles of liberal democracy, it may be a distraction. Much of this ground has been covered in critiques such as the 'iron law of oligarchy' (Michels), possessive individualism (McPherson), the cultural particularity of liberal democracy (Parekh), the shift of decision making from parliaments to boardrooms and laboratories (Beck) and post-democracy (Crouch).[59] If, however, for democracy we read institutions and policies, the discussion is pertinent. We can have democracy but wrong institutions (such as in the US, gerrymandering, court appointments, campaign financing, corporate media, the electoral college). We can have good institutions but wrong policies (such as austerity in Europe). Or, we can have good policies and still only dent social inequality marginally (as in India's NREGA) because institutions and political culture don't support the policies. The actual conversation, then, is about institutions and regulatory frameworks that, arguably, can be established whether or not the overall political framework is democracy, which is taken up further in Section 4.

3 Waves of protest

Contemporary waves of protest have been occurring North and South. They are broadly synchronous, yet diverse; they are diverse, yet overlap. In the North, the emphasis is on neoliberal growth paths and immigration, and in the South on governance problems (inept policies, authoritarianism, corruption). Do the protests represent a momentum comparable to '1968'? Do they signal a historical episode, are they part of a conjuncture? Which protests are part of a conjuncture and which occur as part of separate configurations? In shorthand, according to the dominant issues, the following are major clusters of protest:

1   neoliberal capitalism and austerity;
2   governance crises in EM;
3   ethnonationalism.

Fluctuation in social movements is high. Issues and mobilizations change, at times rapidly. We hardly remember last year's protests. Each cluster has different temporalities or rhythms. Inequality is an undercurrent. Protests triggered by crisis, neoliberalism, and governance all involve inequality, and ethnic and regional unrest often concerns unequal development. The first two clusters are characteristic of 21st-century trends. The third cluster, ethnic and regional unrest, is of all times a constant process of repositioning (which may be co-determined by geopolitics and economic trends).

(1) The first cluster includes protests in the US and Europe and slow-down in EM. Occupy Wall Street focused on bailouts for banks and 'the 1% and the 99%'. Indignados in Europe protested against austerity, 'creeping liberalization', and precariousness.[60] In South Korea, trade unions mobilized against the growth of contract labor. Protests in China at Foxconn and Honda factories (2011) concerned labor conditions and wages, as part of high-exploitation capitalism. Their use of social media set an example for further actions such as the wild-cat strikes in Walmart stores across China against the company's new working hours system (2016).[61]

The Arab Spring followed the liberalization of economies and a drop in state investment that was not made up by private investment or FDI, with economic stagnation and growing unemployment across the region (except in the Gulf states). Liberalization, the *Infitah*, went together with authoritarian governments. American QE in 2009–10 triggered a sudden jump in staple food prices such as bread. The Jasmin revolution in Tunisia (2010) was a response to these conditions as was the Tahrir Square movement in Egypt shortly after, and other countries followed.

There are protests, then, because liberalization has brought no growth (MENA), there has been growth but no trickle-down, and growth is not inclusive (Brazil, Chile, China, Mexico, South Africa, US, UK, etc.), because austerity undermines social cohesion (EU), or because of flexibilization of the labor market (South Korea, Japan, EU), so the protests are all part of a general conjuncture, but in markedly different ways.

(2) The second cluster concerns governance crises in EMDC. Examples are many and diverse (protests in Brazil against spending on the World Cup and Olympic Games, rather than on public services such as adequate mass transit; in Russia, against authoritarianism, corruption, and inequality; in India, against corruption, bureaucratic centralism, and inequality; in China, against poor labor conditions, local government corruption, and land appropriations; in South Africa, against economic stagnation, poor public services, labor conditions in the mines, racial inequality, and the cost of higher education; in Turkey, against government authoritarianism and conservative Islamization; in Malaysia, against UMNO rule, etc.).

Protests in Ukraine targeted authoritarianism, corruption, and economic deterioration and led to a change of government. In several countries (Argentina, Brazil, Thailand) protests prefigured regime change and brought conservative or pro-business governments to power.

(3) Ethnonationalism and ethnic and regional strife carries several meanings—territorial and political turf battles, conflicts triggered by regional or geopolitical shifts, regional deprivation, or the 'secession of the rich'. The general theme is renegotiating the terms of cooperation (economic, political, or cultural) with the larger unit (the country). Examples are many (Uighurs in Xinjiang; hill peoples in Myanmar; the Muslim south in Thailand; the Shia majority in Bahrain; majority Sunnis in Syria; the Muslim North in Nigeria, etc.).[62]

More context specific are Russian expansion (in Crimea and eastern Ukraine) and Chinese expansion (in the South China Sea), and China's FTA with Taiwan, which triggered popular protests (in Taiwan, Vietnam, the Philippines).

Macro theories of 'global capitalism', 'global crisis', and neoliberalism are generalizing. 'Global capitalism' doesn't say much because capitalism is differentiated. 'Global crisis' doesn't apply because some EM only experienced slowdown (or were booming when commodity and energy prices were high). Neoliberalism as a general heading doesn't work because major EM (Northeast Asia, China, India) emerge outside neoliberalism. It also matters whether countries have been successful in achieving growth (such as Chile, Mexico, Turkey) or whether neoliberalism has brought economic stagnation (as in MENA).

Salient differences with the 1990s are (a) this is no longer the era of 'civil society' and NGOs, (b) the focus is no longer on the IMF and World Bank,

(c) American hegemony is no longer salient, (d) the 'clash of civilizations' has subsided as a theme because new frictions (such as ISIL, the Syrian crisis, and Syrian refugees) are viewed as context specific and no longer as 'civilizational'.

In advanced economies, the dynamics have shifted to populist movements. Populism refers to movements and parties that revolt against elites and claim to represent the will of the people or of the majority. Leftwing and rightwing populism now overlap in antagonism to trade pacts and how the way globalization is organized has left the majority behind. Leftwing populism targets elites and policies (as in Indignados, OWS, Black Lives Matter, the Sanders campaign, Syriza, Podemos, the Five Star movement) while rightwing populism blames 'foreigners', foreign countries (China), immigrants, and minorities (as in the Tea Party, the Trump campaign, UKIP, the National Front in France, Alternatives for Germany, the Freedom Party in Austria). According to Jan-Werner Müller, 'populists are often protest parties which can potentially play a constructive role in existing political systems' and 'genuine political choice serves as the best antidote to populism'.[63] In LME, however, genuine political choice is barely available; that markets and corporations come first is a bipartisan principle.

Does the upsurge of protest signal a social breakthrough? Does it signal a 'convergence of radicalisms'? The gap between leftwing and rightwing populism indicates divergence, not convergence and in several instances rightwing populism overtakes leftwing populism.

Besides opposition to neoliberalism, is there a unifying ideology? What are the alternatives? The Beijing consensus, Brasilia consensus, Delhi consensus, or Seoul consensus? The protests show there is no consensus in Brazil, India, China, or South Korea. Protest waves and the 'globalization of defiance' from Brazil to Turkey and developed countries, show a groundswell of discontent. But in several countries, after a change in government, there are cuts in public and social spending (Argentina, Brazil, Peru). Policies and institutions change to the detriment of the majority.

4 Governance gaps

> If my effective tax rate would be 0.05 per cent, falling to 0.005, I would have felt that maybe I should have a second look at my tax bill.
> Margrethe Vestager, EU Competition Commissioner, August 2016

The challenge for AE is how to manage industrial decline. This is far more difficult for LME than for CME. Because of their rule of markets and corporations first, (a) deindustrialization has been more drastic and caused more job losses than in CME, (b) the social safety nets that are necessary to buffer an economic course change have been eroded, (c) untrammeled financialization has cut investment in the real economy, (d) since media follow stock markets they give a distorted view of actual economic conditions. Since 2014, there were elections in 44 emerging markets and changes of government in several countries, but the largest course changes, Brexit, and the election of Trump, occurred in LME.

CME in advanced economies are in a stronger position to manage industrial decline—many industries are in better health; social and regulatory institutions though weakened remain robust; inequality isn't as steep; financialization hasn't done as much damage as in LME; less buffeted by 'quarterly capitalism', their time horizon is longer. What policies they adopt depends also, of course, on other than economic variables.

Elites patiently point out that trade, globalization, and openness benefit societies so the populist protests, right and left, are misplaced. Yet economists observe that 'after years of unusually sluggish and strikingly non-inclusive growth, the consensus is breaking down'.[64] Social movements point to billions for banks, economists complain about 'toxic politics' and in the G20 government leaders are 'urged to "civilise capitalism" to counter populists': 'Australian prime minister Malcom Turnbull, a former Goldman Sachs banker, warned his peers of the need to "civilise capitalism"' to 'placate public discontent'.[65] 'How to save capitalism from capitalists' has become a mournful chorus.[66] But what policies follow?

In August 2016, the EU Competition Commissioner presented Apple with a €13 billion bill in back taxes due to the Irish government. In response, the US government voiced a strong protest, Apple CEO Tim Cook called it 'total political crap' and 185 CEOs of corporate America rallied to Apple's side.[67] Apple's aggressive tax avoidance is egregious. EU scrutiny of possible anti-trust violations of Google and Amazon is underway. The hiatus between Washington and Brussels, between what is considered normal in LME and in CME rises to the surface. In the words of Margrethe Vestager, the daughter of Lutheran pastors in Jutland, 'For all the economic theories and the business models, it all comes down to greed'.[68] Rhetoric aside, the LME world is for corporations. Episodes such as these indicate that a course correction in LME is unlikely.

In the nineties, the Forum on Globalization, a US-based NGO, took an anti-globalization stance, but over time it changed its position, as did many NGOs and social movements. They were not against globalization but against neoliberal globalization. This was the theme of protests against the WTO in Gothenburg, Genoa, Seattle. Protests today by and large are not against trade, globalization, and openness per se but against the terms and conditions, T&C of trade and globalization that overwhelmingly benefit major corporations, particularly in LME. Governments and political leaders pontificate about the general benefits of globalization, meanwhile lawyers and lobbies see to the T&C, the fine print.

For developing countries, continuing industrial export-led growth has become difficult because industry has become more competitive with tight margins and increased supply of manufactured goods (with higher productivity and new entrants in industrial exports). With industry as part of global production networks and global value chains, remaining competitive means keeping wages low. Thus, the electronics industry in Malaysia, which is mostly a contract industry for MNCs and a regional supplier of parts and components, imports low-wage workers from Indonesia, Myanmar, etc. This keeps domestic wages low, which clashes with the objective of developing a service sector large enough to employ surplus labor from industry. Since most services are nontradable, they rely on domestic demand.

Robert Brenner observes that the profitability of industry has been declining worldwide.[69] Profit margins have tightened because the sector is increasingly dynamic and competitive, productivity is rising and NICs crowd the field, particularly China. Because of labor-saving technologies and the inflow of labor from developing countries and the former East bloc (3 billion since 1990), demand for labor is soft and there is pressure on wages.[70] The labor question becomes the social question.

This puts pressure on entire sectors. Honhai Precision Industries of Taiwan, the owner of Foxconn, the major maker of Apple products in China, is moving out of electronics assembly altogether because profits are low and is revamping itself as a company focusing on software.[71] But 'industry' is a wide category. The squeeze applies to basic industries, rather than to advanced and niche industries. China has announced major new investments in Latin America, no longer in resources, but in advanced and sophisticated manufacturing.[72]

Such challenges are part of the middle-income trap (MIT), a notion coined in 2007 by World Bank economists Gill and Kharas to denote middle-income countries that remain below the level of per capita income of $10,000, the threshold of high-income status, for longer than 14 years.[73] This has sparked extensive discussion—how many countries belong, by what criteria, what blocks further growth, what explains the trap, is it about industrialization, is it actually a trap?[74] Marc Saxer calls it a 'transformation trap' on the argument that the challenges are essentially political, rather than economic.[75] This makes sense, in line with the principle 'enter politics, exit economism' (Chapter 9.4). The emphasis shifts then from economics to politics and governance, where it belongs; yet even so economic nuts and bolts remain on the table.

A general principle is the more progressive a government's intentions, the more important is policy competence (as in Cuba, Venezuela, the ANC in South Africa). The additional challenge is not just competent policies but also capable institutions. Several concerns come to a head in *governance gaps* that developing and developed countries face:

Democracy and inequality—democracy, elections, and human rights don't settle questions of institutions and deregulation. The procedural emphasis on the mechanics of electoral democracy distracts from the role of institutions.

New technologies and regulation—how to develop institutions to manage new tech (ICT, artificial intelligence, global value chains, fracking, biotech, GMO, fintech)? A case in point are 'the monopolies of unfettered techno markets'.[76] The Apple episode signals that to regulate Silicon Valley, look to Brussels. 'Europe rewrites the rules for Silicon Valley', not Washington.[77] American corporations dismiss government decisions they don't agree with as just 'political'. Regulating the financial sector, again, is a problem particularly in LME (Chapter 6.2). Climate change is the most pressing challenge world-wide, and again LME and the United States are the major bottleneck.

Regionalism and democratic deficits—this is an era of growing regionalism, but actual regional and transnational governance is thin or slim. Regionalism continues onward, particularly in East Asia. Expectations for regional cooperation are high, but the actual regional institutions are meager, limited in authority, legitimacy, and regulatory rules and capacity. In addition, they are crosscut by transnational arrangements that are biased towards MNCs and incumbent powers, as in the WTO and many FTAs. The stillborn TPP and TTIP are cases in point. The negotiations were conducted in secret over many years and as participating governments were signing the TPP agreement, teams of lawyers were still working on the actual text of the agreement, which was not released until much later. The BRICS institutions, NDB and CRA change the horizon, but so far their effect is limited.

Globalization and global public goods—with high-density connectivity comes a greater need for transnational governance. Reforms are primarily national because that is where decision-making power resides, while dynamics such as global value networks, tax evasion, tax havens, transfer pricing are transnational in scope. Special Economic Zones and FTZs create 'zones of exception' sited outside the reach of sovereignty. FTAs often include foreign investment rules that extend zones of exception. With accelerated globalization comes a growing gap between the institutional nationalism of mainstream politics and the economic transnationalism of global political economy. A major conundrum of a hundred years of accelerated globalization is transnational institutional reform.[78] Examples are climate change, MNCs, international finance, and tax evasion. Yet in view of the varieties of capitalism, substantial concerted action is unlikely. An international financial transactions tax has long been under discussion in Europe, endorsed by France, Germany, and the EU Parliament (and held up by the UK), but is entirely outside the range and even the earshot of American politics.

Joseph Stiglitz opens an article on democracy by referring to Thomas Piketty's book, *Capital in the Twenty-First Century* and closes by saying 'The main issue confronting us today is not really about capital in the twenty-first century. It is about democracy in the twenty-first century'.[79]

The themes of inequality and democracy have become intertwined for some time, yet it isn't obvious *how* the two should be combined. Consider three points. First, during past decades, inequality has been growing virtually everywhere, democracy or not. It has been growing in India, a democracy, just as in China, not a democracy. Second, while democracy has been important since the 19th-century 'age of the democratic revolution', the age of emancipation movements and social struggles and the 20th-century age of decolonization, '1968', and waves of protest, it has stalled. In many countries, as Colin Crouch observes, it has become post-democracy, a ritualized spectacle of media and elections with prefab candidates. As a bundle of institutions, democracy carries a patina of routinization and lags behind the dynamics of globalization. According to Timothy Shenk:

> With public power increasingly concentrated in agencies outside imme-diate democratic oversight, and with national governments professing themselves unable to defy global markets, the value of a vote has decreased. The technocratic bargain was attractive during an earlier era of peace and prosperity, but it has become more suspect after the experts have proved incapable of holding up their side of it.[80]

Third, when it comes to addressing inequality, social democracy is relevant, rather than liberal democracy, but the international conversation—influenced by the US and UK—is almost exclusively about liberal democracy.

Does multiparty electoral democracy bring EM onto the terrain of incum-bents, a terrain of human rights discourse (and emphasis on individual rather than social rights) and democracy promotion by agencies such as the American National Endowment for Democracy? If neoliberal globalization is about weakening the state, some forms of democracy promotion also weaken the state. From liberal democracy, combined with free trade agreements, it may be a small step to *neoliberal democracy*. Liberal democracies in the US and UK brought us neoliberalism, deregulation, and institutions that privilege MNCs and banks and a steep increase in inequality, which undermines democracy.

We could argue that to address inequality, democracy is a necessary but not a sufficient condition; necessary because it establishes minimum conditions for accountability, not sufficient because the quality of institutions intervenes. Yet, even this cautious formulation may not hold universally.

In China, the world's oldest continuing state, the conversation is not about democracy (which many view as a Western kind of thing) but about rebal-ancing the economy, shifting the development model, addressing uneven development between coast and inland, East and West, uplifting the majority in the countryside, improving the lot of migrant workers and undoing the Hukou system of urban residence rights.[81] Political reform is on the agenda but in the background. In India, the conversation is not about democracy (the trappings are there) but about democratization, making the institutions of democracy work and deepening them.

In the United States, a one-time model of democracy, democracy has come to mean political polarization to the point of paralysis of governance. Gerrymandering in the states ensures that conservative politicians can outflank popular majority votes and may do so well into the future. At times it is consid-ered an achievement if Washington can keep government open at all. Median wages have barely risen since the 1970s while productivity has increased mani-fold. Terms in the air are a congress of millionaires, rich man's democracy, and plutocracy (Chapter 5.3). Besides ordinary state failure there is the case of 'sophisticated state failure', which is defined as having 'a functioning state in which nothing gets done'.[82]

Options in combining democracy and inequality are: (a) to address inequality, democracy is necessary—which Stiglitz's view implies; (b) to address inequality democracy needs reworking—which ongoing trends show and which brings us back to the distinction between liberal and social democracy; and (c) to implement structural reforms and address inequality democracy is not per se necessary—which past experience suggests (in South Korea, Taiwan, and Singapore), but this is part of a conjuncture that is no more.

Gini indices in North European social democracies are between .25 (Norway) and .30 (Germany) while those in liberal democracies are far higher, particularly in the US (.46 and .42 after taxes and transfers, 2013) and .36 in the UK (after taxes and transfers, 2013).[83] Social democracy (and Christian democracy) is appropriate to CME while liberal democracy syncs with LME. Liberal democracy assumes individualism and a society held together by contracts (rather than by deeper forms of social cohesion), which matches market oriented approaches. Since developing countries are mostly CME (and many are SME), much of the conversation about liberal democracy is beside the point. A report on democracy in Southeast Asia notes, 'social democratic values are hardly known and understood after the long period of US influenced liberal policy and dictatorships'.[84]

A book by Sandbrook and colleagues on *Social Democracy in the Global Periphery* compares Costa Rica, Kerala, Mauritius, and Chile as diverse 'experiments in equitable and democratic development' that have preserved or even improved their social achievements since neoliberalism emerged hegemonic in the 1980s. They find 'that even initially poor, heterogeneous, and agrarian-based former colonies can achieve rapid social progress' under left leadership of 'pragmatic and proactive social-democratic movements', which offers an antidote to the 'despairing tone of much contemporary scholarship' in the global North. 'Social-democratic policies and practices—guided by a democratic developmental state—can enhance a national economy's global competitiveness'.[85] The cases are meaningful, with reservations. They are middle-income states except Chile, and including Chile is questionable in view of its high inequality (Chapter 5.3). Kerala is a well-known example but is also a problem (in investment and employment). A limitation of these cases is that they lack scale.

As counterpoints and in relation to contemporary governance gaps we would look at high-income societies with a low Gini index (Chapter 5.3) and at societies that represent scale. Two major counterpoints to the trends discussed earlier are the developmental state in Northeast Asia and social democracy in Nordic Europe. The EADS has been a success in Northeast Asia and a failure in Southeast Asia essentially because of institutions and policies; whether or not the heading is democracy is a secondary question. The democracy discussion is essentially about accountability, institutions, and regulation, rather than multiparty elections. The conversation on the EADS has moved on from the authoritarian developmental state to democratic, agile developmental states. South Korea transformed from a developmental to a post-developmental state (from SME to CME) and IMF intervention in the Asian crisis (1998) set in motion a neoliberal turn.[86]

Social democracy in Europe has been sidetracked by EU and Eurozone processes—based on a compromise because the EU is a collage of capitalisms. The Third Way of New Labour (Blair, Schröder, and the SDP in Germany) moved towards LME and New Democrats (Clinton) chimed in. In relation to governance gaps, LME are typically missing in action because the gaps have been their own making (inequality, financialization, trade pacts) or the institutional capacity and political will to address them is lacking (climate change, technology, transnational governance). Their brand is deregulation, not regulation. In Nordic Europe and Northeast Asia, the political spectrum ranges far wider than in LME. Even so in relation to several governance gaps, governments and parties have missed the boat, have failed to rein in finance and address labor and social questions. In conclusion, whether democracy is coming or going does matter, but the larger issue is *which* democracy is coming and with what institutions.

Notes

1 Stiglitz 2006.
2 Mazzucato 2013.
3 Rodrik *et al.* 2004.
4 This paragraph and the next follows Ezrow *et al.* 2016, chapter 4.
5 E.g., B. Stocking, Male-dominated workplace culture alienates talented women, *Financial Times* 8/25/2016: 9.
6 Nederveen Pieterse 2015b.
7 G. Brown, How the west can reverse a decade of decline, *Financial Times* 12/9/2010: 13; Brown 2010.
8 Piper 2015: 12.
9 Landes 1998.
10 Morazé 1957 (trans. 1966).
11 ADB 2010: 4.
12 Birdsall 2010: 1–2.
13 Birdsall 2010; ADB 2010: 3.
14 Easterly 2001: 318.
15 Quoted in ADB 2010: 3
16 ADB 2010: 3.
17 ADB 2010: 4, 5
18 ADB 2010: 5
19 Birdsall 2010: 4–5.
20 ADB 2010: 5.
21 ADB 2010: 6
22 ADB 2010: 4.
23 See e.g., Sally 2016.
24 Rueschemeyer *et al.* 1992; Diamond 1999.
25 J. Hookway, Thai Junta takes populist tack in vein of deposed government, *Wall Street Journal* 6/19/2014: A10.
26 See Chen 2013.
27 AFP, Half of China's rich plan to emigrate, *Shanghai Daily* 6/16/2014: 9.

28 King 2004.
29 Macpherson 1962.
30 Costa 2016.
31 Tsang 2013.
32 Embong 2002, 2004.
33 Neubert and Stoll 2016.
34 Koo 2016.
35 Laclau and Mouffe 1985.
36 Breman 2001; Kannan and Rutten 2004.
37 Kay 2009.
38 Van Wessel 2004; cf. Kapur 2005.
39 Desai 1996.
40 Harding 2000; Dawson 2013.
41 Nederveen Pieterse 1992b.
42 Kipnis 2007 (though this may refer to rich peasants).
43 Foroohar and Margolis 2010: 42–43.
44 Giddens 1990.
45 J. Sangwan, Khap panchayat: signs of desperation? *The Hindu* 5/7/2010.
46 Norton 1993: 208.
47 Nederveen Pieterse 2012b.
48 Johnson 1982; Wade 1990; Leftwich 1996; Weiss 1998; Chang 2003; Studwell 2013; Henderson 2012.
49 Thompson 1993: 475, 481, 482.
50 Thompson 1993: 613.
51 Thompson 1993: 614.
52 Leftwich 1994: 373; 1993: 620.
53 Wade 1990; Chang 2003; Studwell 2007, 2013.
54 Leftwich 1993: 616.
55 Leftwich 1993: 605–606.
56 See Studwell 2007, 2013; Nederveen Pieterse 2015b.
57 Collier 2009: 48.
58 Collier 2009: 11.
59 Michels 1915; Parekh 2007; Beck 1992; Crouch 2004.
60 Standing 2011; Streeck 2011.
61 Y. Yang, Walmart staff organise strikes across China, *Financial Times* 7/8/2016: 6.
62 Examples, typology and discussion is in Nederveen Pieterse 2007.
63 J.-W. Muller, Genuine political choice serves as the best antidote to populism, *Financial Times* 10/4/2016.
64 M. A. El-Erian, Toxic politics versus better economics, *Project Syndicate* 10/15/2016.
65 G20 urged to 'civilise capitalism' to counter populists, *Financial Times* 9/6/2016: 3.
66 P. Stephens, *Financial Times* 9/16/2016: 11.
67 B. Jopson, Corporate America rallies for Apple: 185 CEOs attack €13bn Brussels tax bill, *Financial Times* 9/17/2016: 1. Also *Financial Times* 8/30/2016.
68 In R. Toplensky, A career that inspired 'Borgen', *Financial Times* 12/10–11/2016: 17.
69 Brenner 2002.
70 Chhachhi 2014; Felipe *et al.* 2012; Mehta 2014.
71 G. Guilford, Foxconn's new mantra: More software, less Apple. If only it were that easy, Quartz.com 11/13/2013. http://qz.com/146867/foxconns-new-mantra-more-software-less-apple-if-only-it-were-that-easy/.
72 L. Hornby, J. Leahy, China investors target Brazil in growth push, *Financial Times* 12/5/2016: 4.
73 Gill and Kharas 2007.

74 Griffith 2011; Kharas and Kohli 2011; Eichengreen *et al.* 2013; Bulman *et al.* 2014; Gill and Kharas 2015. With thanks to Marc Saxer for references.

75 Saxer 2014.

76 I. Kaminska, Inequality and the monopolies of unfettered techno markets, *Financial Times* 5/25/2016: 9.

77 P. Stephens, Europe rewrites the rules for Silicon Valley, *Financial Times* 11/4/2016: 11.

78 Nederveen Pieterse 2000.

79 J. E. Stiglitz, Distorted democracy only benefits the rich, *Shanghai Daily* 9/16/2014: 7.

80 Shenk 2016: 32.

81 Nederveen Pieterse 2015b.

82 J. Techau, Sophisticated states are failing, so politicians need to take risks, *Financial Times* 4/20/2016.

83 World Bank 2012.

84 Hofmann 2009: 26.

85 Sandbrook *et al.* 2007: 7, 12, ix.

86 Lim and Jang 2006.

9   Debugging theory

> We should not be dismayed that the global economic crisis and our
> uncertain exit from it has shaken up received wisdoms. The west has been
> acting for too long like a deaf prophet, so convinced of its own truths that
> it does not need to listen. Coming to grips with complexity—with, say,
> the numerous conceptions around the world of how markets function, or
> of political legitimacy—can only be a good thing; they are often the fruits
> of insights and experiences we can learn from.
> Mark Mazower[1]

The 21st century brings new rising forces and new configurations. To make
sense of the new emerging field requires a reflection on analytics, or else
making sense of many diverse developments becomes a jumble. The data are
many, contradictory, complex, in flux. They are many—at issue are global and
national dynamics; they are contradictory—with diverse and opposite trends;
they are complex—patterns crisscross; and in flux—as in market volatility,
political instability, and institutional changes.

What is emerging—markets, states, societies? What is the time frame of
analysis? Are 'Southern theories' such as postcolonial studies relevant in the
contemporary multipolar world, or are they late-dependency approaches that
remain wedded to North-South polarity in an increasingly East-South world?
Is transformation analysis a relevant tool?

A preliminary question is, do the data lead or does the paradigm lead? What
cognitive framework selects, produces, and processes data? Are assessments
inductive or deductive? How are representations arrived at and how are they
framed? Paradigm awareness matters. What is now unraveling is a hegemonic
constellation that has lasted for 200 years, 1800 to 2000. In sociology, Connell

asked 'why is classical theory classical?'[2] It is classical because it is wedded to a structural matrix; the leading macro theories have been embedded in colonial and hegemonic patterns, and now that the matrix is crumbling, different horizons emerge and the macro theories are no longer adequate guides. Although it no longer dominates, the matrix still casts its shadow forward. In later work, Connell refers to the new horizon as *Southern theory*,[3] which is part of a wider sensibility that is discussed later in this chapter.

Arguing continuity is easier than arguing trend breaks. Claiming trend breaks invites the autopilot response, you exaggerate, changes aren't nearly as large as you claim. New data may not be readily shared, don't fit familiar boxes, and once a new door opens there is no playbook, so resistance is considerable. In complex settings, ideological posturing and conceptual shortcuts are tempting. Part of hegemonic transition is ordinary white noise as well as black noise such as reporting that is biased or misleading (Chapter 7). It's not just a matter of kicking others when they're down but also when they're getting up. According to Ian Bremmer, with emerging economies comes the rise of state capitalism (or 'authoritarian capitalism'), which threatens the free market system (and American corporations).[4] Risk consultancies such as the Eurasia Group assist corporations to navigate political risk in emerging economies, to minimize corporate risk, and in effect to buffer the frictions among capitalisms.[5] According to Ikenberry, the rise of state capitalism may threaten the Western liberal order.[6] Print media (such as the *Financial Times*, *The Economist*, *Wall Street Journal*) offer recurrent assessments according to which globalization is reversing, which liberal capitalism is in trouble, etc. Part of the truthiness of a waning order is a sense of the unraveling of major markers.

Economics, the dominant social science through the 20th century, has been narrow and Westcentric all along. Since the 2008 crisis, economics is increasingly viewed as 'part of the problem' and is undergoing paradigm shifts, ranging from behavioral economics to neuro finance. Paradigm consciousness includes being wary of economism. In romantic love, Lee Siegel observes a change in perspectives:

> We are now living through one of those radical shifts in culture when people start looking at reality in a different way than they did just a half-generation ago. Nowadays the harsh disenchantments of high art have become the stuff of popular culture. No one is in love forever after one night or wondering how high the moon or declaring what kind of fool he is. In love as in the culture generally, transparency and full disclosure carry the day.[7]

So it is in development studies, too; the heady days of jumbo theories and large one-size-fits-all programs are over. Development is catching up—for 19th-century latecomers to industrialization; it is modernization—in postwar American theory with Big Push and nation building; it is overcoming dependency—in the polemics of dependency thinking; it is indigenous knowledge, grassroots movements, and NGOs—in the romance of alternative development; it is letting market forces rip—in the neoliberal utopia of the Washington consensus.[8] Nowadays, however, development studies is more about difficult trade-offs and institutional development, some of which emerges from historical patterns. Yet in assessing new trends, old cognitive habits sneak back in under new headings.

With emerging economies comes a new demand for knowledge and understanding, but most available analytical frameworks represent 20th-century concerns and perspectives. Can we understand emerging economies in terms of postcolonial studies? Can we grasp contemporary multipolarity in terms of existing international relations theory? Can we come to terms with the return of the East and the rise of Asia with mainstream development economics? Can we understand developmental states in terms of free market capitalism? Is liberal democracy the yardstick for democracy? Is world-system theory an adequate guide? Should we accept 'neoliberalism everywhere' as lodestar? Can we understand institutions such as the Chiang Mai Initiative, the New Development Bank, and the Asian Infrastructure Investment Bank in terms of the model of the Bretton Woods institutions? Should we look East because most new international institutions emerge in Asia? Can we understand new regionalism such as One Belt, One Road in terms of the model of the Marshall Plan or the European Union?

Table 9.1 outlines the demand for knowledge of EM, the available supply of major theories and frameworks, and in the third column, what existing theories lack and how they could be tweaked, points that are elaborated further later in the chapter.

1 Debugging

In the setting of multipolarity, classical social theory needs software updates. First, since this era is more globalized, social theory no longer applies to 'societies' in

Table 9.1 Demand and supply of knowledge of emerging economies

Demand	Supply	Lack
Return of East, rise of Asia	Development economics	History, oriental globalization
Multipolarity	International relations theory	Global political economy
Emerging economies	Postcolonial studies, dependency	East-South dimension
	Transformation analysis	Specification
CME, SME	Capitalism singular	Comparative capitalisms
New institutions NDB, CRA, AIIB	Bretton Woods institutions	Look East
New regionalism, OBOR	Economic integration, security	Moving complementarities
Stagnation of AE	Tech plateau, secular stagnation	Analysis of financialization

the 19th-century sense, but rather becomes a form of global theory. Second, multipolarity refers to a world in which different centers and zones of influence matter. Third, since these zones and regions are themselves stratified, we need an analysis in terms of multiple levels. Fourth, not only are there different zones but they also interact across the spectrum from complementarity to competition.

This means that theories and concepts become *plural* in a fundamental sense. The singular (as in capitalism, modernity) is appropriate to an era of universalism, an era in which a single center or zone of influence dominates as lodestar. During 1800–2000, this was the British Empire and then the USA, with a long period of hegemonic rivalry (1870–1945) in between. Classical social science was embedded in hegemony. With the British Empire came Victorian anthropology and the 'white man's burden'; French colonialism came with Orientalism and 'mission civilisatrice', and so forth. Common features of colonial horizons were notions of Enlightenment and progress. With American hegemony came modernization theory and the idea of the convergence of industrial societies. As the sun set on the Cold War, the Washington consensus and Fukuyama's end of history ushered in an epoch of American hyperpower. In foreign policy, neoconservatives believed that 'American values are universal values'. According to Paul Wolfowitz, liberating Iraq from dictatorship would be a cakewalk. Mishaps followed. Since 1990, Western wars have killed 4 million Muslims. The blowback from these interventions may be with us for decades to come. ISIL is part of the blowback.

An underlying pattern, following Foucault, is the tandem of power-knowledge. Power centers make truth claims and multiple power centers make multiple truth claims. This is the era of the Beijing consensus, Seoul consensus, Brasilia consensus, Delhi consensus, etc., each of which is contentious within and in the region. Knowledge from the viewpoint of a center of power is ethnocentric, no matter whether power centers are old or new.

Key problems facing contemporary social theory are North-South thinking, rather than East-South; thinking in the singular, rather than the plural; scale inflation, or assuming that one level of analysis pertains across all levels; methodological nationalism; and the heterogeneity of capitalisms.

Nation states remain the units of regulatory decision making and as such central, but global value chains and supply chains crosscut sovereignty and intertwine different capitalisms and business models. Nation states are outdated as units of analysis in the era of global production networks and network societies; consider notions such as 'Chindia', 'Chamerica', 'Chime' (China, India, Middle East), CRI (China, Russia, India), and IBSA (India, Brazil, South Africa). Processes of nationalization and denationalization, 'bordering' and 'debordering' occur simultaneously. The BRICS are heterogeneous multinational states in which diverse interest groups, paradigms, and subcultures interact, so the issue is to assess trends that shape the politics of articulation in each case. With the comeback of state-led capitalism as part of 21st-century changes, the attention shifts to the variety and caliber of state institutions across the spectrum of developmental, coercive, and inefficient states (Chapter 8).

The point of debugging theory is to open up conceptual space, and thus political and policy space to make room for emerging economies and China, and to open up different problematics. Keynotes of retooling theory in the setting of multipolarity include the following.

Thinking multicentric is a shift away from Eurocentrism and Westcentrism. All along and now more than ever before, different zones matter, each with different traditions, classics, standards of evaluation, and horizons. Contemporary multipolarity is a multiverse. It is not multilateralism under a single umbrella of hegemony or ideology; it involves multiple and intersecting concentric circles of influence, each with its own criteria of evaluation. Multiple zones and centers do not exist in isolation and engage in shifting relations of complementarity and rivalry, which also involve domestic institutions. A broad heading for these relations is moving complementarities (Chapter 3.2).

An undercurrent in many approaches is postwar convergence theory, the general idea that variations and time lags notwithstanding, over time societies will converge on modernity, capitalism, and liberal democracy. A defining feature of convergence thinking is the use of the singular, i.e., one modernity, one capitalism, one kind of democracy, which in effect casts the hegemonic variant as the norm and the *sole* option.

Thinking plural applies to ways of organizing social life or modernities, and ways of coordinating economies or capitalisms. Critical realism, a contemporary approach in sociology, also advocates *methodological pluralism.*[9]

A related approach is layered analysis. In every plurality such as modernities and capitalisms, there are common elements. The variants imply an invariant component. Yet the meaning of the common element is contextual; thus while state-led, coordinated, and liberal market economies are all market economies, the way the market economy is understood differs in each setting. The invariant or common element among the variants is itself variable in meaning. A layered analysis means that convergence occurs at one level, divergence of institutions and practices at another level, and at yet another level, mixing occurs and new combinations emerge, all occurring simultaneously. Applying one theory or generalization across levels (which classical theories tend to do) is scale inflation. Marx's 'iron laws of social change' and Weber's rationalization apply, but not necessarily at all levels and across the board.

Layered analysis also refers to spatial differentiation. Conditions are different in Mumbai and in Delhi, are different in old Delhi and New Delhi, different in the Mumbai Four Seasons from Mumbai slums, and different again in Chennai, Bihar, Assam, not to mention Kashmir.

2 What is emerging?

Many approaches to contemporary dynamics are deductive, starting out from generalizing assumptions, rather than inductive, which is apparent in the headings that are commonly used:

- *Emerging markets* is the common heading in finance and business. The portfolio category is EM. The key variable is growth, the focus is on the growing middle class and consumption, the perspective is short term, with headwinds and tailwinds. What matters is growth, rather than the quality of growth. This is not a development perspective but a return-on-investment perspective, in which one year (the standard period of holding stocks) is a long time and five years is very long.
- *Emerging economies*, a term in economics, is a wider angle than EM and refers to a wider set of indicators (such as per capita income, industrialization, exports as share of GDP).[10]
- *New industrializing countries*, NICs, a 1990s term used in development studies and global political economy, focuses on an important dimension of development.
- *Emerging powers* is a term in political science, international relations, geopolitics, and security studies. International relations frameworks (such as balance of power, realism, constructivism) and various empirical and normative angles (such as military capability, regional influence) shape these perspectives.
- Are economies and states emerging or also societies? *Emerging societies* is a term that is used occasionally in sociology and development studies.[11] It aims to be more comprehensive than the previous ones by including social forces and civil agency, which is increasingly relevant in view of waves of protest (Chapter 8).
- The *BRICS*, originally an investment category coined by Goldman Sachs, is used in finance, media, and global political economy. Because the BRICS are not geographically contiguous or share a common history, the heading lands us in the setting of globalization and geoeconomics. N-11, MINT, MIST, CIVETS, and other acronyms function as investment portfolio guideposts. A difference with other asset categories is that the BRICS have organized themselves in summit meetings and with initiatives such as the New Development Bank and the Contingent Reserve Arrangement (Chapter 4.2).
- Growth markets—South Korea and Taiwan are no longer emerging markets; they have emerged already. Since they grow at a faster rate than advanced economies, they are growth markets.

The categories emerging markets, emerging powers, and emerging societies match the big three in social science—market, state, and society—as lenses through which to map the new forces. An overview is in Table 9.2. A neutral term that avoids some limitations is *emerging forces*, which indicates they are diverse assemblages, with configurations and coalitions shifting around multiple anchor points. Meanwhile the notion of emergence is already passé. South Korea, Taiwan, and Mexico have emerged already, are members of the OECD, and are rated investment grade in international finance. Emergence is a category that belongs to a particular time frame; a transitional perspective,

Table 9.2 Perspectives on emergence

Units	Fields	Keynotes
Emerging markets	Finance, business	Growth, middle class
Emerging economies	Economics, development studies	Growth, trade, Asian drivers, East-South relations
Emerging powers	Political science, IR	Geopolitics, security
Emerging societies	Sociology	Social forces, social movements, cultural changes, protest
New industrializing countries	Development studies, international political economy	Industrial upgrading, innovation, productivity
BRICS, N-11, MINT, CIVETS, IBSA	Finance, business, global political economy	Investment, globalization, geoeconomics
Growth markets	Finance, business, global political economy	Growth

just as 'developing countries' is a provisional category and the 'Third World' is no longer relevant.

Deductive approaches are paradigm-based; theory comes first, evidence second. Inductive approaches are data-led, from the ground up. However, since data are large, unruly, heterogeneous, subject to multiple interpretations, findings become a jumble. Information becomes noise, another current amid crosscurrents; it becomes snap impressionism and journalistic reporting; or data are compartmentalized under narrow headings. The friction between deductive and inductive approaches, between nomothetic and idiographic approaches, between general principles ('laws') and concrete particulars is inherent to social science. Nomothetic and idiographic accounts are interdependent: without particulars, no regularities; without milk, no yogurt. Description implies selection and thus implies generalities, and vice versa. Extremes on this continuum are, at one end, vacuous theory (predictable reiterations of paradigms) and, at the opposite end, irrelevant descriptions (empirical details without a point). Data are theory-dependent and without pattern recognition, we are lost. Let us consider general options:

1   A theory applies but because the flux is great, we don't know which. In time, matters will settle and then we will know (which might take 20 years). This is wait and see, or patient theory.

2   Theories apply and developments are in part theory-driven. Behavior is ideological (the attitudes of American neoconservatives in the Iraq war are an example). Arenas of interests are ideologically constructed. By being attentive to reflexivities, we can deduce which theories and ideologies dominate specific arenas. There is flux and it matters to identify patterns. Here theory refers to *meta-theory*, a combination of regional theories and a theory of theories, which implies sociology of knowledge.

3   A theory applies and by articulating it, we can influence developments. Description is prescription. Neutrality is impossible; social science influences, mobilizes, and shapes agendas, which is part of its role. Here theory is a function of advocacy, including policy advocacy.

Perceived threats to American hegemony are often framed by selecting a fault line and declaring it *the* global fault line—such as Huntington's clash of civilizations, Bremmer's state capitalism (illiberal capitalism), Robert Kaplan's security threats. These approaches all involve scale inflation.

4   Retrieve old theory, brush up and relocate the dots in up-to-date places and then reconnect them. This is return on intellectual investment in theory that comes up in neo-Marxist as well as Weberian thinking, such as revisiting Pierre Bourdieu.[12]

5   A theory applies and it is chaos theory, the study of nonlinear effects.[13] Effects are nonlinear because of diverse initial conditions, and at each crossroads, different turns can be taken. To Douglas North's path dependence, we should add path disobedience. As we go up the level of reflexivity, there is greater room for agency and choice; hence, outcomes are contingent. That changes are not predictable is their inherent character. This approach is influential in many assessments, often unacknowledged:

- bricolage—for instance in Mittelman's assessment of the BRICS as global bricolage;
- heterogeneity and unevenness—as in 'variegated neoliberalization';
- hybridity—as an open-ended perspective.[14]

We can identify several variants of the chaos theory approach:

- total heterogeneity, no pattern whatsoever. In effect, this matches journalism, which often follows an implicit, hidden theory. Because theory is implicit, it is not reflected on and is usually uncritical;
- combinations of a general pattern and heterogeneity. An example is uneven neoliberalization, i.e., neoliberalization is the general pattern and unevenness is in the specific instances;[15]
- unbundle the overall theory in specific hypotheses, subject each to empirical testing, and thus arrive at a new piecemeal assessment.

6   The changes that are taking place are deep changes, so theories unravel and are due not just for maintenance and repair but for overhaul. We must wait and new theory will take shape, which brings us back to option 1 above.

After all, everything hinges on pattern recognition. Arguably, to assess the new forces we need mid-level rather than grand theory. Matters are unstable, multi-interpretable, and headed in different directions. Grand theories are sweeping and carry too many in-built assumptions and past legacies that are taken as givens. If they apply, they apply in limited spheres. Grand theories readily come to mind and it doesn't take great imagination or explicit discussion to be aware of their limitations—such as Fukuyama, the end of history; Huntington, the clash of civilizations; Ben Barber, Jihad v McWorld. Other examples are dependency theory, world-system analysis, and the transnational capitalist class perspective. Each of these implies a strong framework and there are plenty of examples of this being applied to emerging economies.

Macro theories tend towards circular reasoning (the label generates the analysis) and confirmation bias (ignore that which falls outside). Because they adopt a deductive approach in which a general theory leads, their assessments are often predictable. Regional, national, or local literatures[16] that take an inductive approach, empirical and from the ground up, are often more insightful than those that rehearse macro theories. At the other extreme is empiricism, driven by data and metrics. Of course, an 'evidence-based' approach implies a theory because it takes theory to identify what counts as evidence and which data matter, but it isn't necessarily self-reflexive theory.

Mid-range theory is not empiricist in the sense of theory-agnostic, but is not sweeping either. Dancers should not be 'too far ahead of the music' lest their dance be taken as foolishness. A further nuance, reflexive mid-range theory, involves being critical of assumptions, labels, and categories.

Grand assessments of the BRICS and 21st-century dynamics abound (Chapter 4.3). Assessments of an in-between character are Mittelman's repositioning and the notion of global rebalancing.[17] Repositioning is neutral, descriptive, open-ended, but it doesn't tell us much. Global rebalancing is dynamic and refers to ever-changing balance, domestic and international. However, it is also an ideological terminology that has been used in G20 platforms (Chapter 6.2). A forward perspective is Mohanty's global restructuring (Chapters 6 and 10).

3 Southern theories

Since ongoing changes could be described as a South-South turn, is 'Southern theory', as in the work of Connell and the Comaroffs, the way forward?[18] Genealogically the main strands of Southern theory are (a) dependency theory, also in its African and Asian variants, (b) variations on the theme of Orientalism and a continuation of critiques of Eurocentrism, and (c) reinterpretations of colonialism, such as Subaltern Studies and postcolonial studies. Contemporary dynamics have now mostly overtaken these trends and they need retooling.

Dependency theory in a broad sense is the political economy of decolonization and neocolonialism. Dependency theory rejects dependent accumulation and pursues national accumulation instead (and some strands question whether it is possible to achieve national accumulation at all). Even so, if it is achieved, different dynamics set in, which are captured under headings such as emerging economies and NICs. One strand of dependency thinking opts for delinking or dissociation from transnational capitalism, and, in Samir Amin's version, rejects capitalism.[19] However, if we reject capitalism then what are we for? For socialism, with Cuba, Venezuela, and North Korea as guideposts? This no longer makes sense. The divide between capitalism and socialism goes back to the Cold War and has made place for a different arena since the waning of the Cold War, an arena of capitalism versus capitalism.

Orientalism belongs to the epoch of occidentalism, the hegemony of the West. This has not vanished from the stage but has become much less dominant in the era of the comeback of oriental globalization. With Asian drivers as major forces in the world economy and developing countries, casting 'the Orient' as backward is absurd (rather, the recent target is 'Islam', which does not make sense either). Revisiting Orientalism, then, is looking at contemporary dynamics through the rearview mirror. A different approach is needed, a multicentric approach.

The main point of postcolonial studies is reinterpreting colonialism, which usually turns on a critique of precolonial, colonial, and postcolonial elites and power structures with a view to wider emancipatory sensibilities, as in Subaltern Studies and Walter Mignolo's 'epistemic disobedience'.[20] These perspectives remain relevant because EM rework structures of class, status, and power. Yet examining this through the lens of European colonialism puts us on the wrong track, because colonialism holds different meanings in different settings.

Many postcolonial studies refer to Africa (such as Mudimbe, Mbembe, Comaroff, Cooper, Ferguson). However, is the matrix of European colonialism relevant to the vortices generated by Asian drivers and other EM, or is it anachronistic and too crude an analytic? In Latin America, colonial legacies remain relevant, such as the hierarchy between those of European and indigenous descent. In East Asia and China, Japan's colonial imprint is relevant. In South and Southeast Asia, colonial and Cold War legacies are relevant but are no longer in the forefront of ongoing changes.

Analytics are often primarily search tools, research agendas, but are taken as 'theories'; that which is intended as a query is taken as an outcome. Ten years later the authors of the idea of the middle-income trap describe its origin as 'the absence of a satisfactory growth theory', 'a device to spark a discussion of policy choices in middle-income countries'. 'It was not a statement that middle-income countries are more likely to be trapped than other countries'.[21] The search and radar function is the most important function of theory.

Another function of theory is consciousness raising, advocacy, and mobilization. Vandana Shiva's monoculture is a tool of conscientization, mobilization, and agenda setting,[22] but its contribution as analytical tool is more limited. Some theories work as alerts but are too blunt or generalizing to work as analytical instrument. The language of postcolonial studies as genre—such as erasure, violation, governmentality, coloniality—is 'expressive rather than persuasive' but may succeed in articulating postcolonial stress disorder. If the 'rage against the machine' equates the Washington consensus and the Beijing consensus, it ceases to be analytically productive.

What some theories don't make clear is the boundaries of their claims, or the *degree* or domain of validity they claim, often because theorists themselves don't know yet because the search is still on. Transnational capitalist class alerts us to transnational collusion among 'the 1 percent', which no doubt matters, but does it fall within, so to speak, a 20 to 30 percent range of validity or a 70 to 80 percent range? Here what matters is the principle of falsification. Theories that aim at mobilization and conscientization generally do not seek falsification of their claims while theories that emphasize their search function are as keen on finding contrary data and negative cases as on finding confirmation.

Southern theories are a subset of North-South relations. Once this hegemony frays, its counterpoint, Southern theories, is decentered as well. The world of the Asian drivers is structurally different. Instead of the global North-South, we face different problematics:

- relations between emerging economies and advanced economies, as in the G20;
- relations *within* emerging economies such as in China, India, Brazil, Russia, South Africa;
- relations among emerging economies and other developing countries (such as relations between China, India, and Latin America; Africa and the Middle East; Chapter 3.5);
- regional problematics, such as the ramifications of OBOR;
- diverse distributions of and interactions between capitalisms.

The brave new world of EM is multicentric in terms of capitalisms and emancipations. Thus, capitalism in Northeast Asia is markedly different from Southeast Asia.[23] In terms of emancipation, Dalits in India have much in common with indigenes in Latin America, but the differences matter at least as much. A general theory of the emancipation of the dispossessed, the marginalized, and minorities is possible, but regional theories (and policies) are more relevant (Chapter 5.4).

Previous hegemonic scenarios of progress and modernization excluded or silenced perspectives from the point of view of minorities and indigenous peoples. In scripts emerging from new regional centers—Beijing, New Delhi, Sao Paulo, Jakarta, Ankara, Abuja, etc.—they may be silenced anew, or co-opted as part new scenarios of regional or national 'modernizations'. Urbanization and 'townization' in China, land appropriations for Special Economic Zones in India, deforestation of the Amazon to make room for soybeans, and dam building and hydroelectricity in many countries are examples of ongoing 'new modernizations'. EM (such as Saudi Arabia, Brazil, China, South Korea, and Japan) leasing land (or 'land grabbing') in African countries and Pakistan introduce new asymmetries (Chapter 4).

Southern theories play a part in retooling theory in the multipolar world but need reworking.

1   Dependency thinking can contribute to analyzing asymmetric relations between, say, China and Africa or China and Southeast Asian countries, but the old core-periphery matrix centered on the West no longer applies;

instead we need more flexible and grounded analyses of regional and inter-regional asymmetries. For instance, in institutionally dense settings where norms are strong China follows rules, but where rules are weak or absent, it follows its own interests. China both follows rules and establishes new rules, as in 'globalization with Chinese characteristics'.[24]

2   Orientalism should be opened up with a view to different centrisms such as Sinocentrism (and Han hegemony in Yunnan, Xinjiang, and Tibet), Indocentrism (as in Kashmir, Assam), Java-centrism in the Indonesian archipelago of 1,700 islands, and so forth.

3   Perspectives from the point of view of minorities and indigenous peoples need updating to reflect the role of new actors and circuits of influence. Spectrums have become wider and more varied. Brazilian tropicalism, Shariati's Islamic Marxism, and Subaltern Studies address different problematics and what common ground they share is as meaningful as the differences among them.

4 Capitalisms, layered analysis

Both critics and advocates of ongoing changes often refer to capitalism in the singular, as in 'global capitalism' and the capitalist world-system. Some accounts cast the 'Davos class' as a de facto world ruling class and, deviations notwithstanding, everything is falling or will fall under its sway. That it is only a matter of time for global capitalist convergence to take hold is a view that is shared by many advocates as well as critics of capitalist expansion.

This kind of capitalist teleology short-circuits the question of where the emerging forces are on the spectrum of institutions that coordinate economies. The rise of emerging economies could be understood in terms of the 'rise and decline of nations within the world-system',[25] or as a reshuffling within the bounds of Western capitalism. Yet, whether or not they unfold within the sphere of Western capitalism is not a given but part of the problem to be examined.

The 2008 crisis highlights the variation in capitalisms. While the impact of crisis is global, it is not uniform. Societies across the world are affected, but are affected in markedly different ways. Crisis is a threat for some and an opportunity for others. Some institutions are crisis-prone and others are crisis-resistant (note the difference between Wall Street and Canadian banks in the crisis). Thus, a key dimension of assessing current trends is whether they are viewed through the lens of capitalism or capitalisms.

During the 1997 Asian crisis, Anglo-American capitalism was upheld as the sole viable model. The 2008 crash shattered the headquarters of the erstwhile exemplar. Several after-crisis assessments reclaim the paradigm of a single standard-bearing capitalism—in relation to which also Europe is an outlier. However, the 2008 crisis exposed the frailties of Anglo-American capitalism on all levels—as ideology (laissez-faire), as paradigm (efficient market theory), as economics (shareholder short-termism, financialization), as policy (deregulation, liberalization), as institutions (accounting, rating agencies, regulators, market analysts), as methodology (financial mathematics, quantitative investments), and as culture (bonus culture, predatory CEOs). The 2008 crisis is part of a series from the American Savings & Loan crises of the early nineties, the bailout of LTCM, the collapse of Enron and other corporations to the subprime mortgage crisis, and the Goldman Sachs and Libor episodes.[26] The shareholder approach fosters short-termism (boost quarterly earnings to ensure high stock ratings, which raise CEO stock options), and financialization fosters a growing disconnect between finance and the economy of goods (Chapter 6.4). The 2016 trend break (Brexit and election of Trump) marks another watershed.

Yet most perspectives, explicitly or implicitly, treat capitalism in the aggregate. This holds for mainstream views in media and economics as well as for neo-Marxist views such as world-system analysis and transnational capitalist class. Crisis, then, becomes a crisis of capitalism tout court, not of a particular type or modality of capitalism.

The main variation this view acknowledges is historical, between stages of accumulation and phases of capitalism, between early and latecomers to industrialization and modernity. In treating capitalism in the singular, unilinear theories of capitalism from Marx to world-system analysis view variation mainly as variation over time (with 'dependent capitalism' as a major outlier). This perspective is unsuited to examining regional variation because, like postwar modernization theory, it assimilates regional variation into historical patterns (such as 'lagging behind' or 'catching up'). While much post-crisis discussion focuses on 'the future of capitalism', a more productive question would be 'futures of capitalisms'. Capitalism survives thanks to the diversity of capitalisms: 'the flexibility of capitalism derives from *capitalisms* and regional variation'.[27] Diversity is not disappearing but the terms of diversity are changing and capitalisms are realigning.

For decades, the Washington consensus lorded over the developing world; in the 21st century, lecturing changed direction and emerging economies talked back. From China to Europe, critical comments about American capitalism have come not just from backrooms but also from official podiums. The tables have turned and a different refrain is in the air: the West must learn from the Asian crisis and must learn economic prudence from Asia (Chapter 3.1).

Indexes such as the 'economic freedom' and 'competitiveness index' typically assume a single model of capitalism. However, the question the 2008 crash poses anew is the absence of a general growth model or standard for the relations between state, capital, and civil society (Chapter 8.4). This variation is central to rebalancing. Institutions matter as part of economic imbalances and as part of rebalancing. Some institutions are crisis-prone and others crisis-resistant. Since institutions are political and social formations, analyzing this involves, besides institutional economics, politics and ideology. Is there a general benchmark by which to gauge institutional change?

The idea that Anglo-American capitalism will incorporate emerging economies underestimates their different ways of organizing capitalism amid the political and social pressures they face. With the lead model imploding under corporate scandals, toxic finance, feeble institutions, inept governance, outdated infrastructure, aging populations, mammoth debt, and government eviscerated by deregulation and tax cuts, the CME and developmental state capitalisms in the East and South emerge as more dynamic—depending on the caliber of states and institutions (Chapter 8). Whether they are also more sustainable is a different question. The Asian crisis was attributed to crony capitalism; in 2008, permissive capitalism in the US turned out to be a much greater weakness. The public sector in EM is a source of strength if it is accompanied by robust institutions of accountability and competent policies. This is not a matter of state or market; what matters is what *kind* of state. In the US, the concentration of wealth and power combined with free market ideology has contributed to an 'anti-state state',[28] which makes a comeback in the Trump administration.

Methodological nationalism means taking nations as the units of analysis. We speak of 'China' and 'the United States' because that is how economic data pile up, but what matters as much are classes and regions within and across these units. This is a two-way street: because tech, business, and communication interweaving is growing, national units are of limited purchase; yet nations are units of political decision making, legal frameworks, institutions that coordinate economic conduct and forums of public reflexivity. There is a continuously shifting balance between multiple factions in each country. In China, the New Right (entrepreneurial, neoliberal), the New Left (social and green), the old left (neo-Maoist), and the old right (nationalist, neo-communist) vie for influence, each with different shades of nationalism.[29]

Varieties of capitalism, LME, CME, and SME don't neatly line up with nations; this was the limitation of the original varieties of capitalism approach.[30] They also represent factions within each country, as in fractions of capital analysis, and crosscut national boundaries.

Multilevel approaches are standard fare in fields such as multilevel governance in European Union decision making. In social geography, multi-scalar approaches address the spatial scales at which processes unfold, such as processes of globalization at global, national, regional, and local scales.[31] The World Bank and UNDP gather data and analyze processes at multiple scales—global, regional, national, and often micro-regional and urban as well. New regionalism combines regional, national, and local levels to understand production networks and clustering.[32]

A parallel perspective in cultural studies is that while many expect globalization to produce cultural standardization and 'McDonaldization' (CNN-ization, Disneyfication, etc.), this happens, but only in some spheres and to some extent. Regional, national, and local variations continue with dynamics of their own, interspersed with transnational cultural assemblages and confetti, and generate hybrids and new patchworks of difference, which has been described as 'global multiculture'.[33]

Methodological globalism is taking the global as unit of analysis—as in global capitalism, global culture, global modernity, global crisis, global inequality, global exclusion, global policing, etc. Does paying attention to national variation and dynamics mean we must therefore ignore or sideline the transnational dimension? Does paying attention to transnational dynamics mean we have to gloss over national and local processes? Do we have to choose between one or the other? The smarter option is layered analysis in which multiple levels of analysis are relevant. Thus, not just nations are valid units but also firms, combinations of firms, global production networks, international supply chains, technologies, and so forth. Totalizing theories commit the fallacy of generalizing and privileging one scale of analysis and produce scale inflation. A précis of layered analysis is in Table 9.3.

Different theories privilege different units and scales of analysis. The varieties of capitalism approach tends to be statecentric and underplay transnational forces (global value chains, transnational corporations, international institutions, etc.). The transnational capitalist class approach and world-system analysis emphasize the transnational level and often downplay national differences. Some approaches seek to bridge these levels of analysis.[34]

A multilevel approach means using a wide bandwidth and moving across wavelengths, and shuttling between wide-angle, panoramic vision, and zooming in on micro detail, from wide synthesis (global studies, comparative studies) to on-the-ground footprint (which I have called the elevator approach to theory).[35]

Also when it comes to the bulky question of convergence or divergence, a more sophisticated approach is layered analysis that unbundles nation states and takes into account that *convergence* is taking place at one level (such as in technology, logistics, ISO, Special Economic Zones, the WTO), *divergence* at

Table 9.3 Layered analysis

Layers	Dynamics	Analytics
Transnational	Global value chains, MNCs, banks, international institutions, international covenants, ISO, technology, hegemony	World-system analysis, transnational capitalist class, international organizations
	Indices, consultancies, accounting, law firms, risk analysis	Regional, national differences
Regional	Civilizations, regional cooperation, regional development banks, diasporas	New regionalism
National	Institutions, legal frameworks, corporate governance, labor relations, trade and innovation policies, interest rates, currencies	Comparative capitalisms
Local	Institutional densities, clustering, learning environments, firms	Economic geography, business studies, anthropology

another level (institutions of economic coordination, corporate governance, labor market, law), and *mixing* in yet other spheres (marketing, product mixes, consumption, media).[36] Technology unifies the world, but how it is applied is widely diverse. California, the world's seventh largest economy, only has a single-track train (passenger and cargo) between north and south, like much of the US, which is unthinkable anywhere else at this level of economic development. Layered processes produce layered outcomes—with diverse, combined, and uneven patterns of transnational, regional, national, and local cooperation (an overview is in Table 9.3). Regional entities such as the EU, the Gulf Cooperation Council, and ASEAN follow agendas of their own. Besides, there is local variation, such as between China's Pearl River Delta and Harbin in the north, and between Urumqi, Chongqing, and Changchun. Hence, capitalist convergence and divergence occur at the same time. Elites and business classes in different countries and regions cooperate *and* follow their own ways, which brings us back to the classic theme of combined and uneven development (Table 9.4).

There are several layers of complexity. General trends affect different political economies differently (Chapter 5). Making non-ideological, 'clinical' assessments is increasingly difficult; crisscrossing variables are many and metrics no longer deliver, neither do simple theories. Changes unfold at macro (international institutions, world economy), meso (governments), and micro levels (firms). Analysis involves unbundling categories; recognizing factionalism within countries; the diverse effects of trends and policies; disentangling general trends from diverse effects in different political economies.

This book combines variables wide apart in the vein of global studies, examines their interaction from the viewpoint of development studies and global political economy, sets forth scenarios and discusses their probabilities. While the variables in these probabilities may be fairly straightforward, their interaction is unstable and many outcomes depend to a large extent on political processes. After all, almost everything is a matter of political struggle. It is a fiction that economic models can script societal change. As Polanyi observed, markets are embedded; they are embedded in institutions and political formations, so markets are ultimately political. In contrast to the principle 'enter economism, exit politics',[37] what is at issue is enter politics, exit economism, in

Table 9.4 Uneven and combined development

Tendencies	Dynamics	Scales
Convergence	Technology, ISO, communication, production systems, logistics, consumption	Transnational, firms, international organizations
Divergence	National, regional and local cultures; corporate governance; law; consumption	National, regional, local
Mixing	New combinations	Across scales

other words, take economism out of economics and put politics back in. While there are overall patterns and trends, changing political tides alters equations. It is impossible to take politics out of the equation and with politics *in* the equation, outcomes are contingent and unpredictable.

In Asia, as elsewhere, extreme positions are to embrace American-style capitalism or to reject capitalism tout court. Neoliberals in Asia advocate similar forms of privatization, liberalization, deregulation as in the US and UK.[38] Singapore has long advocated liberalization policies, but has combined this with a strong and overall capable state.[39] Both the right and the left in Asia and Latin America tend to think of capitalism in the singular, which tends to work to the advantage of the right because it implies convergence: if we are converging on a liberal model, we might as well adopt policies that anticipate the inevitable. On the left, this perspective plays a bogeyman role: accept more transnational capitalism and we risk losing our sovereignty, autonomy, identity, and more.

A recent book by an editor of Foreign Affairs deals with 'immigration reform, economic stagnation, political gridlock, corruption, and Islamic extremism'. The title is *How Nations Survive in a World in Decline*.[40] The casual implication is that what applies to the United States applies to the world, which fails to recognize the possibility that as one region declines, another rises. This kind of provincialism is not innocent. Extrapolating categories and theories that are of a regional nature to a global level is also scale inflation. Another 2016 book is titled *The Global Rise of Populism*.[41] Again the scope is 'global'. In Latin America, however, populism carries a different meaning (in view of the legacy of Peronism) than in the US and Europe. Again, provincialism yields scale inflation.

Let's be wary of totalizing scripts, whether they come from the World Economic Forum or the World Social Forum. There is no single model. Universalism belongs to the era of hegemony. Ideological and political battles are fought as if they are about principles, such as state or market; but often the issues are about identifying the mean, in Aristotle's sense, or the optimal mix of government and market—which depends on circumstances and context. All economies are mixed economies—which combination of government, market, and social forces is best under which circumstances (Chapter 8.4)?

5 There is no master key

Let me briefly tease out some implications for research methods. Assessing the *degree* of change is often crucial. The usual recourse is to metrics. If you cannot count it, does it count? However, metrics follow paradigms. In Hazel Henderson's words, people measure what they treasure.[42] Data are theory-dependent; hence the problem of indicators. Indicators such as GDP measure economic activity on the basis of limited assumptions.[43]

Metrics matter but because measurements reflect limited assumptions, quantitative data are usually qualitative assessments in disguise. When it concerns system change, assessing the degree of transformation is difficult because the *criteria* of assessment are contingent and are different when viewed from within or outside the box.

Methods must follow theory—lest they themselves pass for theory, which may be the case in methods-driven research. The gap between qualitative and quantitative approaches in social science is largely fictional. Empiricists in American political science, sociology, economics, and international political economy view quantitative approaches as 'more rigorous'.[44] However, data and metrics, no matter how copious and meticulous, are never better than the theory that guides and informs them.

Many data sources, secondary and primary, are of limited use because they use aggregate categories (such as rural and urban, middle class and poor) without unpacking them. Many government statistics need further breakdown. The Pew World Values Survey is relevant but its use must be qualified; at times, it reflects the limited or ideological character of public discourse.

Data selection implies biases of its own. Benjamin Page finds that studying millionaires is quite different from studying billionaires—billionaires are not reachable, don't respond to questionnaires, refrain from public statements (besides a select fringe), and typically operate by means of 'stealth politics', such as membership of boards of foundations and think tanks, so they require different research tools. In Jane Mayer's term, 'dark money' drives the radical right in the US.[45]

Research and data require both contextualizing and decontextualizing. Context supplements general, wide-angle approaches with regional and local understanding.[46] Anthropology, thick business studies, social geography, and multi-sited ethnography get past macroeconomics and ground understandings in everyday experience and reflexivity in diverse settings.[47] This enters the social tissue of transformation more deeply by looking at different panels of global coexistence, comparing societies and strata placed differently on the spectrum of global imbalance, not just in metrics and generalizing judgments but also in experiential and ideological terms. Decontextualizing and 'distant understanding' also matter, so comparative studies are an important research tool. Decontextualize from a particular setting or region and see whether the general argument still holds. Negative cases (anticipated outcomes do not materialize) are as illuminating as positive ones. All the same, methodological finesse will not deliver without theoretical finesse. Theoretical finesse begins with the awareness that there is no master key. Theories are essentially search tools, and using them requires, most of all, exercising judgment.

Notes

1 M. Mazower, The world no longer listens to the deaf prophets of the west, *Financial Times* 4/14/2015: 7.
2 Connell 1997.
3 Connell 2007.
4 Bremmer 2011.

5 Zorub 2014.
6 Ikenberry 2008.
7 L. Siegel, The truth about romantic love, *Wall Street Journal* 2/14-15/2015: C1-2.
8 Nederveen Pieterse 2010a.
9 Danermark *et al.* 2005.
10 Kose and Prasad 2010.
11 An example is the Routledge series Emerging Societies (which I edit).
12 Rehbein 2015.
13 Eve *et al.* 1997.
14 Mittelman 2013; Brenner *et al.* 2010; Nederveen Pieterse 2015b.
15 Brenner *et al.* 2010; Peck and Theodore 2007.
16 E.g., Achcar 2013; Tsang 2013; Kapdan 2013; Costa 2016.
17 Mittelman 2013; Nederveen Pieterse Chapter 6.2 this volume.
18 Connell 2007; Comaroff and Comaroff 2011; Mbembe 2001.
19 A critique of delinking is Nederveen Pieterse 2010a.
20 Mignolo 2009.
21 Gill and Kharas 2015: 4.
22 Shiva 1993.
23 Nederveen Pieterse 2015b.
24 Henderson 2008; Henderson *et al.* 2013.
25 Friedman 1982.
26 Nederveen Pieterse 2004, 2008.
27 Nederveen Pieterse 2004: 146.
28 MacLennan 1997.
29 E.g., Leonard 2012; Pettis 2013.
30 Hall and Soskice 2001.
31 E.g., Dicken 2007.
32 Yeung 2013.
33 Nederveen Pieterse 2007, 2015a.
34 Soederberg *et al.* 2005.
35 Nederveen Pieterse 2014c.
36 Discussed in Nederveen Pieterse 2007.
37 Teivanen 2002.
38 E.g., D. Feith, Interview with Xia Yeliang: The China Americans don't see, *Wall Street Journal* 10/26-27/2013: A11; Bhagwati and Panagariya 2013.
39 Fukuyama 2005.
40 Tepperman 2016.
41 Moffit 2016.
42 Henderson 1996.
43 Stiglitz *et al.* 2010.
44 See Cohen 2014: chapter 1.
45 Page 2009; Mayer 2016.
46 See Nederveen Pieterse 2015b.
47 E.g., Marcus 1995; Burawoy 2000; Tsing 2005; Redding and Witt 2010.

10 Conclusion

Global restructuring?

In the 1970s developed countries moved basic industries to developing countries (which were then called the 'Third World'). Washington institutions promoted trade liberalization and industrialization for export. Developing countries had borrowed extensively in the 1970s when the world was awash in oil dollars, then interest rates rose and when the debt crisis came, the IMF stepped in with loans and conditionalities and the World Bank with structural adjustment programs, SAP ('Suck African People', according to Fela Kuti). During this period, the Asian Tigers rose along with China and India—not affected by the Washington institutions because they had hardly been exposed to foreign borrowing. In the late nineties and the noughties, relations between Asia and Africa and Latin America took off with demand for commodities, as inputs for Asian industrialization and urbanization, a surge of growth in developing countries, loans, investments, and cheap manufactured goods from Asia, especially from China. High-growth developing countries were renamed emerging markets and emerging economies. This period also spawned the BRICS.

Asian countries recovered rapidly from the 1997 Asian crisis. In the annals of the World Bank, the *East Asian Miracle* (1993) was followed by the *East Asian Renaissance* (2007) that showed the fast recovery from the Asian crisis. The renaissance applied to Northeast Asia, China, and India (which had not been affected by the Asian crisis anyway, only South Korea was). It did not apply to Southeast Asia, where the 'middle-income trap' applied.

The combination of financialization and economic stagnation in advanced economies, especially the US with quantitative easing and low interest rates, and overall additional liquidity in the order of $25 trillion (Chapter 6.4), saw funds flowing into emerging economies' equities, in loans and asset inflation. With the 2008 Wall Street crisis spreading to Europe, growth in China and Asia slowed down. With the ensuing drop in commodities prices and energy prices, slowing demand in Asia and advanced economies, many emerging economies slipped back to being developing countries, with debt popping, knocking on the door of the IMF, which provided loans with conditionalities, much as before.

Reform of international institutions, the WTO, IMF, and World Bank, was slow, same old, and new institutions emerged, the BRICS NDB, CRA, China's AIIB, and financial buffer funds such as the Asian Bond Fund. China initiated a major new Silk Roads program, OBOR, 'bringing half the world together' and a new round of investments in developing countries, no longer focused on resources but on manufacturing.

Advanced liberal market economies facing income polarization, economic stagnation, and political impasse, imploded in populist protests, which led to Brexit and the election of Trump. What ensued was the rejection of trade pacts which the US had been sponsoring for ten years, TPP and TTIP. In Europe it led to the rejection of reform in Italy and rightwing populism overtaking incumbent parties in several countries.

Twenty-first-century globalization comes with pattern changes and trend breaks, the story continues and of course there is no 'conclusion' in any conventional sense. Bullet points of what has and has not changed in 21st-century globalization are as follows:

What has changed in 21st-century globalization?

- Goldilocks globalization has switched from advanced economies to EM;
- emerging economies drive the world economy;
- Asian middle-class consumption takes over from American middle-class consumption;
- growing East-South trade, investment, and loans;
- the rise of sovereign wealth funds of emerging economies;
- new international and regional institutions;
- China embarks on major global surplus recycling, OBOR (Chapter 6.4).

What has not changed?

- the weak position of labor in relation to capital (Chapter 8.4);
- growing social inequality (with few exceptions, Chapter 5.3);
- financialization and hegemony of finance in LME (Chapter 6.4);
- the deterioration of institutions in liberal market economies;
- migration as a flashpoint of transnational inequality and conflict;
- after crisis, the IMF steps in with conditionalities for developing countries;
- the decline of American hegemony;
- the rise of China and EM;
- the sustainability turn.

These changes and continuities need sorting. We must disentangle changes that are structural in the sense of long term and will be important 20 years from now, and changes that are temporary. Structural is the rise of Asia, China, and emerging economies. Fluctuating is the repositioning of AE. There are two types of fluctuation—oscillations within a trend and fluctuations that may come with trend breaks.

The rise of emerging economies has shaped 21st-century globalization with Northeast Asia in the lead, then China and the BRICS. Since 2011, EM have been on a rollercoaster of being (a) the darling and safe haven of financial markets, (b) a risky bet that is best avoided, and (c) a fallback when the US economy slides. A sample of headlines illustrates the fluctuations:

> Hopes rise for emerging markets growth: An uptick in commodity prices and a rebound in EM equities and currencies have revived optimism (J. Wheatley, *Financial Times* 7/12/2016)
> Emerging market bonds lure investors seeking yield (J. Wheatley, *Financial Times* 8/2/2016)
> EM investing: Why it is back in fashion: Switch into emerging markets is less about potential growth and more to do with stagnation at home (*Financial Times* 8/7/2016)
> The rally in emerging markets masks frailties (Editorial, *FT* 8/27–28/2016)
> Emerging economies at risk from developed world's central banks (H. Sender, *FT* 8/31/2016)
> Fund managers find summer rewards in EM (S. Foley, *FT* 9/7/2016)
> Emerging markets risk sparking new global financial crisis (*FT* 9/21/2016)
> Dollar's rapid gain triggers Angst in emerging markets (*Wall Street Journal* 11/19–20/2016)

Variables in play include stagnation and monetary policies; protectionism and a shift to fiscal policies in AE; China's growth; an uptick in commodity prices; and economic health reports of specific countries. Because of loose monetary policies and economic stagnation in AE, investors look to EM for yield. Upon indications of higher yield in AE (higher interest rates), funds flow out of EM. These moving parts are predictable and are the subject of weekly or daily reporting. Yet, these are fluctuations within a general upward trend. According to economist Michael Spence, we are in the midst of a 'century-long journey in the global economy. The end point is likely to be a world in which perhaps 75 percent or more of the world's people live in advanced countries'.[1] According to Gideon Rachman:

> The rise of non-western economies is a deeply rooted historic shift that can survive any number of economic and political shocks. It would be a big mistake to confuse a temporary crisis with a change to this powerful trend. . . . today's turmoil will not change the fact that emerging markets will grow faster than the developed world for decades to come. . . . The rise of emerging economies during the past forty years has been propelled by lower labor costs, rising productivity, huge improvements in

the communications and transport that connect them to global markets, a rising middle class, a boom in world trade as tariffs have fallen and the spread of best practice in everything from management techniques to macroeconomic policy.[2]

The idea of EM decoupling from AE, or the East-South turn replacing North-South relations, is off the table. EM depend on trade and are concerned about protectionism in AE. According to Singapore's deputy prime minister, failure to ratify the TPP trade deal would be 'a major setback for the standing of the US in Asia'. He criticizes the populism of the right and the left as well and the failure of the US to make 'aggressive enough efforts to help those left behind by global competition':

> No one can blame technology, it's just not fashionable, so you blame globalization because it's about another country or about the global elite. And it takes attention away from where the light should really be shone— which is on your domestic politics.[3]

Brexit and the election of Trump are part of the political crisis that has followed the 2008 economic crisis (a delayed reaction in case policies would change, which did not happen). Populism follows economic crisis, as it did in 1873 and the 1930s. 'The revenge of globalisation's losers' is a common interpretation.[4] Fukuyama interprets the turnaround as democratic forces protesting against liberal market forces,[5] in other words, an implosion *within* liberal market economies. The implosion occurs in the two countries that have led the way to neoliberalism, societies where inequality is highest, financialization most advanced, and social protection most eroded. In LME, growing inequality is built in, which undercuts demand, hampers recovery, erodes hope, and fuels populism and division. Financialization is politically embedded, out of control, and crisis prone. Because of structures and institutions built over decades, major course changes in LME are not likely. The spread of options is narrow.

A likely scenario of the Trump administration is back to the old normal of supply-side economics and trickle-down. What institutional buffers there are to rein in banks, shadow banks, and corporations will shrink further. American corporations are hoarding cash and corporate tax cuts adding more, also from overseas, will boost stock buy-backs and CEO stock options, but investment? The American middle class is now proportionally smaller than in most developed countries (smaller than in Poland, Russia, and Uruguay),[6] malls are closing, retailers are folding.

Advanced economies and emerging economies have come to a fork in the road; popular sentiment and social movements in AE increasingly reject trade and globalization while EMDC welcome trade and globalization (Chapter 7.2). AE and EM have traveled accelerated globalization together since the 1970s with industries relocating in developing countries, in the WTO, with China and Russia joining, in global production networks, global value chains, and Walmart capitalism, but now they begin to part company with protectionism and tariffs in AE.

The Trump administration represents a major trend break and 'a bonfire of certainties'. The rejection of TPP would have happened anyway. The 'pivot to Asia', a position adopted in 2011 with the declaration that the South China Sea is in the vital national security interests of the United States, had two components, a trade agreement and military. Now only the military component remains, at a time when alliances are unraveling, with the Philippines and Muslim countries, Indonesia and Malaysia stepping back. Emerging economies have been sternly criticized for disrupting the liberal international order, but now an American government changes the rules by sliding to transactional deal making. If the old problem was double standards, the new problem is no standards. The Trump cabinet of billionaires is a return to the Gilded Age with generals for muscle. It is an entrepreneurial state, not in an ordinary sense but the entrepreneurialism of plutocracy, the state apparatus placed in the service of capitalism with a big C. A no-pretense version of the anti-government ethos adopted since the Reagan administration (get government off our backs), anti-government government, gloves off. Those who advocate dismantling government agencies are appointed to head the agencies (such as labor, education, energy, environment, housing) so as to better implement deregulation from the inside.

This is part of a slow deterioration of institutions that has been in motion since the Reagan era. A cover headline of *The Economist* is 'The debasing of American politics',[7] but it is the debasing of institutions that matters more. If market incentives lead and everything is for profit—healthcare, education, utilities, prisons, media, warfare—institutions gradually decline, such is the logic of LME bereft of countervailing powers. Corporate media are a major factor in the decline of the public sphere. Part of the profile of EMDC is rickety institutions. Investigations and trials for corruption in several countries indicate that norms and standards have been rising during recent years, while in the United States the reverse is happening and the country may be slipping to emerging economy status.[8] Big Boss behavior is no longer tolerated in several emerging economies, while in the US it has become the new normal.

Following the implosion in leading LME, the momentum shifts to other spheres of influence, in particular Europe and Northeast Asia, both typically CME and zones where inequality is relatively low. There is greater room for institutional and policy change in CME than in LME, but it has hardly been used. Europe has been engrossed in the architecture problems of the EU and the Eurozone, austerity, and Germany's economic narcissism. Governments and progressive parties have failed to rein in finance and corporate globalization. Elites have had a 'Marie Antoinette moment'.[9] No wonder populism has taken hold. Yet differences between LME and CME persist in the quality of institutions, in the public sphere, and social institutions. Pressure by Brussels on American companies seeking tax shelters in Ireland (Apple) and Luxembourg (McDonalds, Starbucks) and on tech monopolies (Google, Amazon) has been increasing (Chapter 8.4). Frictions between CME and LME may be widening, even as they are papered over by thinking in terms of 'the West' and global capitalism that hides from view the core problem—LME and neoliberalism.

Northeast Asia is increasingly tethered to China, the largest trade partner of Japan, South Korea, and Taiwan (and also Germany). Now the mantle of global trade leadership falls to China. The demise of TPP leaves room for China's Regional Comprehensive Trade Partnership, which is acknowledged right away (within days after the election of Trump on 11/8/2016):

> Xi seizes chance to resurrect rival trade push as US vote seals TPP's fate (*Financial Times* 11/11/2016)
> China readies to take trade mantle (*Wall Street Journal* 11/12–13/2016)
> US change of guard offers Beijing whip hand on trade (*Financial Times* 11/18/2016)
> China's influence grows in ashes of the Trans-Pacific Trade Pact (*New York Times* 11/20/2016)

China is already the de facto leader of global trade. With the US stepping back ('America First') China's role comes to the fore. China has long anticipated protectionism and stagnation in the West and factored it in in changing its development model.[10] Hence, the shift to investment and domestic-demand-led growth and hence the regional turn, of which OBOR is the flagship (Chapter 6.5). The US stepping back and withdrawal from trade pacts leaves room for OBOR and the AIIB and gives China greater access in Asia and Latin America. ASEAN has opted for closer association with China. ASEAN plus Six may be on the table. China has extended an invitation to Latin America to join OBOR. Kevin Rudd outlines several postures in China for dealing with the Trump situation.[11]

China is the leading driver of emerging markets and developing countries, the driver of Asia, and much depends on the fortunes of OBOR. Commodities prices fluctuate according to China's health reports. This opens the large and sprawling China files, which is not for this occasion.[12]

Global restructuring is on the cards. Scenarios of the late 20th century (the Washington consensus) no longer function. The reorganization of globalization has been in motion since the turn of the millennium. The parting of the ways of advanced economies and emerging economies means that the reorganization of globalization becomes manifest, whether or not it is ready for prime time.

Notes

1 Spence 2011.
2 G. Rachman, The future still belongs to the emerging markets, *Financial Times* 2/4/2014.
3 J. Vasagar and J. Anderlini, Singapore warns on US trade retreat, *Financial Times* 10/24/2016: 5.
4 W. Muenchau, The revenge of globalisation's losers, *Financial Times* 4/25/2016: 9.
5 F. Fukuyama, US against the world, *Financial Times* 11/12–13/2016: 1–17.
6 E. Porter, Richer but not better off, *New York Times* 10/30/2016: 4.
7 The debasing of American politics, *The Economist* 10/15–21/2016.
8 J. Authers, Ugly new world risks bringing even US back to emerging status, *Financial Times* 11/19–20/2016: 18.
9 W. Muenchau, The liberal elite's Marie Antoinette moment, *Financial Times* 11/28/2016: 11.
10 Chi 2010.
11 K. Rudd, Beijing's brutally pragmatic response to a shifting world order, *Financial Times* 12/2/2016: 11.
12 Pettis 2013; Pei 2016; Nederveen Pieterse 2017; Guo *et al.* 2017.

Glossary

Agency	Influence of social movements, organizations, individuals
AIIB	Asian Infrastructure Investment Bank, China 2015
Asian Tigers	South Korea, Taiwan, Hong Kong, Singapore
Astronauts	International commute families
Asymmetric information	Market actors do not typically have equal information
Austerity	Policy that prioritizes government deficit reduction
Balance of payments	All transactions between domestic residents and foreigners
Basel III	Bank of International Settlements' regulations for international banks
Beijing Consensus	A strategic, gradual, autonomous approach to globalization
Black swan	Unexpected occurrence that throws averages, models; Nicholas Taleb
Bolsa Família	Cash transfer to poor families who enroll children in school, Brazil
Bonus culture	End of year bonus on top of salary in financial sector
Bretton Woods system	Financial system based on the parity of US dollar and gold, 1945–71
BRICS	Brazil, Russia, India, China, South Africa
Bricolage	Improvised combination of diverse elements (as in flea market)
Bubble	Overinvestment
Business cycle	5 to 10-year economic cycle
Capital controls	Policies that restrict the flow of foreign capital
Casino capitalism	Speculative finance dominates (Susan Strange)

Center-periphery relations	The metropolitan center dominates the periphery
Centrism	History viewed from a center of power or civilization
Chaebol	South Korean conglomerates (Samsung, Hyundai, SK, LG, Hanwha)
Chaos theory	Study of nonlinear effects because of differences in initial conditions
Chicago school	Resumes neoclassical economics; incentives, rational choice
'Chime'	China, India, Middle East
CIVETS	Colombia, Indonesia, Vietnam, Egypt, Turkey, South Africa, 2009 (diverse, dynamic economy, young population)
Clash of civilizations	Samuel Huntington 1993 article on tensions between West and Islam
Class analysis	Examine the role of class interests in social change
Commercial bank	Deposit bank for private customers
Comparative advantage	Sectors in which countries can profitably specialize
Conditional cash transfer	CCT, programs that provide cash to the poor on conditions
Conditionalities	Terms on which the IMF provides loans
Confucian ethic hypothesis	Explains the success (or stagnation) of East Asian countries
Conglomerate	Large holding company of diverse products or services
Constructivism	Social institutions exist because and as long as people believe in them
Convergence theory	Industrializing countries will converge on similar structural features
Corporate governance	Principles and rules according to which firms are run
CRA	Contingency Reserve Arrangement, financial pool (BRICS, 2015)
CSR	Corporate social responsibility, voluntary adoption of social norms
Credit rating agencies (CRAs)	Rank countries and firms' creditworthiness; private, US based

Crisis	Turning point in economic cycle
Culturalism	Explanations based on cultural factors (cf. psychologism, biologism)
Currency war	Manipulate currencies to influence trade balance
Current account	A country's external debt
Dalits	'Children of God', outcastes, untouchables in India
Deglobalization	Reversal or deceleration of globalization trends
Demand management	Keynesian policy of government spending to counteract slowdown
Dependency theory	Metropolitan economies & MNCs dominate dependent economies
Developmental state	A state dedicated to furthering national development
Discourse analysis	Examine how ideas are expressed; close reading of texts
Dodd-Frank Bill	US bill that re-regulates banking, 2014
Dutch disease	Resource wealth that triggers currency appreciation, inflation
Economism	Placing exclusive emphasis on economic explanations and variables
Efficient Market Theory (EMT)	Markets function best when left alone
EM	Emerging markets (aka emerging economies), asset class
EMDC	Emerging markets and developing countries
'End of history'	Francis Fukuyama 1993 article on the US winning the ideological war
Endogenous development	Development from within (in contrast to exogenous)
Ethnonationalism	Ethnically driven nationalism
Eurocentrism	European or Westcentric approach to history
Export-led growth	Export-oriented industrialization, EOI
Externalities	The side-effects or conditions of economic activities
FDI	Foreign direct investment (in contrast to portfolio investment)
Federal Reserve	Central bank of the United States
Financialization	The growing share of finance in corporate profits
FIRE	Finance, insurance, real estate as leading urban sectors

Fiscal debt	The gap between government revenue and spending
Flexible accumulation	Small batch production; lean corporation, Toyotism
Flexibilization	Casualization of labor, temporary employment
Fordism	Standardized mass production and distributive regulation
Foreign aid	International development cooperation
'Fragile five'	India, Indonesia, Brazil, South Africa, Turkey, 2013
FTA	Free trade agreement
FTZ	Free trade zone
Futures	Contracts on future commodity price; options, swaps, derivatives
FX	Foreign exchange
G3	US, EU, Japan (dollar, euro, yen, leading currencies)
G20	Group of leading economies, 2009; previously G7, G8 with Russia
GDP	Gross domestic product
Gini coefficient	Measure of inequality (0 is complete equality; 1 is maximum inequality)
Glass-Steagall Act, 1933	Split commercial and investment banks, dismantled 1999
Globalization	Trend of growing worldwide interconnectedness and awareness
Global civil society	Transnational networks of civic groups and organizations
Global South	Developing countries; previously 'Third World'
Global value chains, networks	Splice production and spread to where relative cost is low
GNI	Gross national income (per capita, factors in population size)
Governance	Non-market coordination of economic activity
Gramscian approach	Emphasizes civil society and culture in social transformation
GSRM	Global surplus recycling mechanism
Guanxi	Social connections, China
Hadrahmi	Migrants from Hadramaut valley, Yemen
Happiness economics	Focus on wellbeing (rather than growth)

Hayek, Friedrich	Austrian economist opposed to government economic planning
Hedge fund	Private investment partnership of wealthy investors ($2.4tr 2013)
Hegemony	Leadership
HIPC	Heavily indebted poor countries
Historical materialism	Marxist approach to history
Hot money	Short-term crossborder money flows
HTF	High-frequency trading (especially in currency market, $4tr per day)
Human development	Views human skills as the main tool and goal of development
Human Development Index	HDI, combined measure of income, education, longevity
Human Development Report	Published annually by UNDP, largest UN agency
Hybridization	Mixing diverse elements gives rise to new forms
IBSA	Economic cooperation of India, Brazil, South Africa
ICT	Information communication technology
IFIs	International financial institutions (IMF, World Bank)
IHDI	Inequality-adjusted Human Development Index
ILO	International Labor Organization, Geneva
Industrial policy	Government subsidies, loans, contracts for select industries
Industrial upgrading	Moving from low- to high-value activities
Industries, heavy	Steel, chemicals, machine goods
Industries, light	Apparel, footwear, toys, canned food, consumer electronics
Insider trading	Trading stock on the basis of company inside information
Institutional investors	Pension funds, insurance companies, endowments
Interactive decision making	Government consulting citizens
International Criminal Court	ICC, The Hague

International Court of Justice	UN institution, The Hague
International division of labor	IDL, crossborder economic specialization and cooperation
Investment bank	Bank that provides financial services for corporations
Investment grade	Threshold rating at which institutional investors may invest
'Invisible hand'	Price fluctuations move markets
Initial public offering, IPO	First sale of company stock
ISIL	Islamic State (aka IS, ISIS, Daesh)
ISDS	Investor-state dispute settlement (in TPP, TTIP)
ISI	Import-substitution industrialization
Keynes, John Maynard	Leading British economist, devised anti-Depression policies
Keynesianism	Government intervention to mitigate business cycles
Keynesianism, military	Military spending as economic multiplier; 'war economy'
Kleptocracy	Rule by thieves
Knowledge economy	The growing knowledge intensity of production
Kondratiev wave	50-year cycle of upturn (A phase) and downturn (B phase); long wave
LDCs	Least Developed Countries (24 in 1971, 49 in 2013)
Long 16th century	1450–1620, birth of the 'modern world-system'
Longue durée	Long-term structural social transformation (Fernand Braudel)
Look East policy	Follow developments in Northeast Asia (Mahathir, PM of Malaysia)
Macroeconomic policies	Fiscal and monetary policies
Managerialism	Managers, rather than owners driving corporate policy
McDonaldization	Fast-food management model of efficiency, rationalization, predictability (G Ritzer, 1993)
McJihad	American oil money funds extremist Islam (Timothy Mitchell)
MDG	UN Millennium Development Goals

Mercantilism	Strengthen national economy by limiting imports, promoting exports
Methodological nationalism	Taking the nation state as the unit of analysis
Methodological globalism	Assuming the world as unit of analysis
MINT	Mexico, Indonesia, Nigeria, Turkcy
MIST	Mexico, Indonesia, South Korea, Turkey
Mode of production	Overall constellation of forces and relations of production
Modernization theory	Leading American development theory 1960–70; stages of growth
Monetarism	The money supply as crucial economic variable (Milton Friedman)
Monoculture	Economic reliance on one product or resource
MSR	Maritime Silk Road
MST	Movimiento de Sem Terra, Movement of the Landless, Brazil
Multicurrency world	The US dollar becoming less dominant as world trading currency
Multilateralism	The cooperation of multiple governments
Multinational corporations (MNCs)	Corporations with large overseas operations
Multipolarity	Multiple poles of influence in international affairs
NDB	New Development Bank, Beijing (BRICS bank, 2015)
Neoclassical economics	Supply and demand tend towards equilibrium, late-19th century
Neoliberalism	Ideology according to which markets are self-regulating
Neoliberal capitalism	Low taxes, low wages, low regulation, low services, no unions
New silk roads	Economic cooperation of Asia and the Middle East
Newly industrialized country	NIC, NIE
Next Eleven	N-11, developing countries with major economic promise

NGOs	Non-governmental organizations (non-profits, voluntary)
NIDL	New international division of labor, 1970s: relocate in low-cost zones
Non-Aligned Movement	1955 Bandung conference, neutrality of global South in the Cold War
North-South relations	Pattern of global relations dominant from 1800
NREGA	Rural livelihood scheme of 100 days of work per year, India
OBM production	Original brand manufacturing (Samsung, Acer, Asus, etc.)
OBOR	One Belt, One Road, Chinese regional infrastructure projects, 2013
Occidentalism	Westcentric approach
OECD	Organization for Economic Cooperation and Development, 1961, now 34 wealthy countries
OEM production	Original equipment manufacturing; 'full package' production
Offshoring	Locating production overseas (crossborder)
Oil-dollar system	OPEC agreement with US to sell oil in USD, 1975
O'Neill, Jim	Coined BRIC, N-11, Growth markets, GES; Goldman Sachs
OPEC	Organization of Petroleum Exporting Countries, 1973
Opportunidades	Mexico's program of conditional cash transfers to the poor
Orientalism	Western view according to which the Orient is backward
Oriental globalization	Globalization led from Middle East (6C) and Asia (10–18C)
Outsourcing	Subcontracting production or services overseas or crossborder
OWS	The Occupy Wall Street movement
Path dependency	The course taken in economic development determines further steps
Precariat	Insecure labor force (flexible, part-time, temp, interns)

Predatory state	The use of state power to plunder market and society
Privatization	Selling-off public assets to private sector
Protectionism	Limiting imports to protect domestic production
Public sector	Government sector
Purchasing power parity	PPP, adjustment to make prices comparable internationally over time
Quantitative easing (QE)	Central bank buying financial assets, injecting liquidity
Quantitative investment	Investment according to mathematical models, algorithms; quants
Race to the bottom	Competition to lower production cost by cutting wages, benefits
Recession	Two consecutive quarters of contracting economic growth
R&D	Research and development
Reflexive development	Viewing development as a collective learning process
Regionalism	Trend towards regional cooperation (customs union, free trade, etc.)
Regulation	Rules governing economies; mode or regime of regulation
Remittances	Moneys sent home by migrants
Renminbi	RMB, yuan, China's currency
Rent	Revenue from nonproductive sources
Resource curse	Resource wealth hampers diversification, correlates with currency appreciation, weak governance and ecological damage
Reshoring	Return of manufacturing to the country of origin
Retarding lead	Early investments hamper further innovation
Salafis	Ultraconservative Muslims; literal interpretation of Koran
Shar'ia	Islamic law
Schumpeter, Joseph	Schumpeterian approach emphasizes the role of entrepreneurs
SDR	Special Drawing Rights, IMF issue of credit from common pool

Semiperiphery	In-between core (export manufactures) and periphery (export raw materials)
Seoul consensus	G20 meeting in 2011, agreed on shared growth as standard
Shareholder capitalism	Organized according to the interests of shareholders
Silk roads	Ancient trade routes linking Asia and the Mediterranean
Sinic civilization	Civilizational area influenced by Chinese culture
'Slicing up the value chain'	Breaking production process into geographically separate steps
Smart power	Power exercised not over but with others, through cooperation
SOEs	State-owned enterprises, China
Soft power	Ideological influence and cultural appeal
Social dumping	Competing to attract foreign investment by cutting social benefits
South-South cooperation	Cooperation among developing countries
Sovereign wealth fund	SWF, government-owned investment corporation
Special economic zone	SEZ, free of restrictive regulations
Spice routes	From Southeast Asia to Europe (pepper, nutmeg, cloves, etc.)
Stakeholder capitalism	Organized according to the interests of stakeholders (owners, managers, workers, community, consumers, government)
Strategic groups	Interest groups that seek to capture state power
Structural adjustment	World Bank programs of lending conditions, SAPs
Structural functionalism	Leading approach in postwar American sociology; Talcott Parsons
Structuralism	Emphasizes the influence of large-scale constellations and forces
Subaltern studies	Examines the role of lower strata in social transformation, India
Super cycle	A decade or longer of high prices (e.g., commodities)

Supply-side economics	Lowering barriers, taxes and deregulation stimulate growth
Sustainable development	Meet present needs while safeguarding needs of future generations
Sustainability turn	Growing emphasis on efficiency in energy and resource use
T&C	Terms and conditions (contracts, debt)
Transnational corporation	TNC (the company HQ is no longer national but dispersed)
Trickle-down	Idea that wealth accumulating at the top benefits bottom of society
UNCTAD	UN Conference on Trade and Development
UN Development Program	UNDP, annual Human Development Reports 1990, largest UN agency
UNESCO	UN Educational, Scientific and Cultural Organization, Paris, 1945
Uneven and combined development	Advanced countries influence developing countries; Leon Trotsky
Unequal exchange	Unequal terms of trade between manufactures and raw materials
Unipolarity	One pole (center of power) rules
Varieties of capitalism	Differences between liberal, coordinated and state-led market economies
Vendor financing	Seller lends the money that enables the buyer to buy
Washington consensus	Economists' consensus about requirements for economic growth, 1980–2000, implemented by IFIs
Westphalian state system	Territorial sovereignty, est. modern state; 1648 Treaty of Munster
World Economic Forum, WEF	Annual meeting of MNCs, banks in Davos, end January
World Social Forum, WSF	Annual meeting of social movements, NGOs, unions; Porto Alegre
World-system theory	According to I Wallerstein, modern world-system of global capitalism took shape in 16C NW Europe, incorporated peripheral areas
WTO	World Trade Organization, Geneva, 1995

Regional formations

AFTA	ASEAN Free Trade Area
APEC	Asia Pacific Economic Cooperation
ASEAN	Association of Southeast Asian Nations, 1967, ten nations, Jakarta
ASEAN plus Three	Plus Japan, South Korea, China, 1997
ASEAN plus Six	With India, Australia, New Zealand (prospective)
CAFTA	Central American Free Trade Agreement
Chiang Mai Initiative	East Asian monetary fund
East Asia Economic Caucus	Established 1995
EU	European Union (previously European Community)
Gulf Cooperation Council	GCC (Gulf Emirates, Saudi Arabia, Oman)
LAFTA	Latin America Free Trade Association
Maastricht Treaty	Established EU monetary union, eurozone, 1992
MENA	Middle East and North Africa
Mercosur	Agreement of Argentina, Brazil, Paraguay, Uruguay, Venezuela, 1991
NAFTA	North American Free Trade Agreement, 1994
Pacific Alliance	Mexico, Colombia, Peru, Chile, 2012
RCEP	Regional Comprehensive Economic Partnership, China initiative 2012
Regional development banks	Asian, African, Inter American, European Development Bank
RTA	Regional trade agreements (3 in 1961, 524 in 2013)
SCO	Shanghai Cooperation Organization; China, Russia, Central Asia
TPP	Trans-Pacific Partnership
TTIP	Trans-Atlantic Trade and Investment Partnership

References

Abdel-Malek, A. (1981). *Civilizations and social theory*. 2 Vols. London, Macmillan.
—— (1994). Historical initiative: the new 'Silk Road', *Review* 17, 4: 451–99.
Abrahamanian, Ervand (2003). The US media, Huntington and September 11, *Third World Quarterly* 24, 3: 529–44.
Abramsky, S. (2013). *The American way of poverty*. New York, Nation Books.
Abu-Lughod, Janet L. (2000). Review of A. G. Frank, *ReOrient, Journal of World History*, spring: 111–14.
Acemoglu, Daron and James A. Robinson (2012). *Why nations fail: the origins of power, prosperity and poverty*. New York, Crown.
Acharya, Amitav (2014). *The end of American world order*. Cambridge, Polity Press.
Achcar, Gilbert (2013). *The people want: a radical exploration of the Arab uprising*. Berkeley, University of California Press.
Ademola, Oyejide T., Abiodun S. Bankole and Adeolu O. Adewuyi (2009). China–Africa trade relations: insights from AERC Scoping Studies, *European Journal of Development Research* 21: 485–505.
Agtmael, Antoine van (2007). *The emerging markets century*. New York, Free Press.
Akram-Lodhi, A. H. and C. Kay, eds. (2009). *Peasants and globalisation: political economy, rural transformation and the agrarian question*. London, Routledge.
Alatas, S. F. (2013). *Ibn Khaldun*. London, Routledge.
Alden, Chris (2007). *China in Africa*. London, Zed Books.
Altman, Roger C. (2009). The great crash, 2008: a geopolitical setback for the West, *Foreign Affairs* 88, 1: 2–14.
Alvaredo, Facundo and Thomas Piketty (2014). *Measuring top incomes and inequality in the Middle East: data limitations and illustration with the case of Egypt*. Paris, Paris School of Economics.
Amable, Bruno (2003). *The diversity of modern capitalism*. Oxford, Oxford University Press.
Amin, Samir (1989). *Eurocentrism*. London, Zed Books.
—— (1997). *Capitalism in the age of globalization*. London, Zed Books.
Amsden, Alice H. (2003). *The rise of 'the rest': challenges to the West from late-industrializing economies*. New York, Oxford University Press.
Anan, Kofi (2013). Africa Progress Report 2012, *Africa Progress Panel*, presented in Cape Town, World Economic Forum on Africa.
Armijo, Leslie Elliott (2007). The BRICs countries (Brazil, Russia, India, and China) as analytical category: mirage or insight? *Asian Perspective* 31, 4: 7–42.

Armijo, L. E. and S. W. Burges (2010). Brazil, the entrepreneurial and democratic BRIC, *Polity* 42, 1: 14–37.

Arrighi, G. (2007). *Adam Smith in Beijing*. London, Verso.

Arrighi, G., T. Hamashita and M. Selden, eds. (2003). *The resurgence of East Asia: 500, 150 and 50 year perspectives*. New York, Routledge.

Asian Development Bank (2010). *Key indicators for Asia and the Pacific 2010*. Part I, The rise of Asia's middle class. Manila, ADB, 3–57.

Bagnai, A. (2009). The role of China in global external imbalances: some further evidence, *China Economic Review* 20, 3: 508–26.

Baker, Dean (2009). *Plunder and blunder: the rise and fall of the bubble economy*. Sausalito, CA, PoliPoint.

Barma, N., E. Ratner and S. Weber (2007). A world without the West, *The National Interest* 90, July–August.

Beck, U. (1992). *Risk society: towards a new modernity*. London, Sage.

Bello, Walden (1992). *People and power in the Pacific*. London, Pluto.

Berger, Guy (2008). What is there in media for poor women and men? The case of South Africa, in L. Rudebeck and M. Melin, eds. *Whose voices? Media and pluralism in the context of democratisation*. Uppsala, University of Uppsala, 87–98.

Berman, Paul (2003). *Terror and liberalism*. New York, Norton.

Bernstein, Henry (2004). Changing before our very eyes: agrarian questions and the politics of land in capitalism today, *Journal of Agrarian Change* 4, 1/2: 190–225.

Beteille, André, ed. (1969). *Social inequality*. Harmondsworth, Penguin.

Bhagwati, J. and A. Panagariya (2013). *Why growth matters: how economic growth in India reduced poverty and the lessons for other developing countries*. New York, Public Affairs.

Biao, Lin (1965). *Long live the victory of people's war!* Beijing, Foreign Languages Press.

Bijlert, Martine van (2009). Imaginary institutions: state building in Afghanistan, in P. van Lieshout, M. Kremer, R. Went, eds. *Doing good or doing better: development policies in a globalising world*. Amsterdam, Scientific Council for Government Policy, Amsterdam University Press, 157–75.

Birdsall, Nancy (2010). The (indispensable) middle class in developing countries; or, the rich and the rest, not the poor and the rest. Washington, DC, Center for Global Development Working Paper 207.

Blyth, Mark (2013). *Austerity: the history of a dangerous idea*. New York, Oxford University Press.

Bond, Patrick, ed. (2013). *BRICS in Africa: anti-imperialist, sub-imperialist or in between?* Durban, South Africa, University of KwaZulu-Natal Centre for Civil Society.

Booth, Anne (2002). Rethinking the East Asian Development Model, *ASEAN Economic Bulletin* 19, 1: 40–51.

Bramall, Chris (1993). *In praise of Maoist economic planning: living standards and economic development in Sichuan since 1931*. Oxford, Clarendon Press.

Braudel, F. (1980). *On history*. London, Weidenfeld and Nicolson, orig. edn. 1969.

—— (1984). *The perspective of the world: civilization and capitalism, 15th–18th century*, Vol 3. New York, Harper and Row.

Breman, J. C. (2001). *Op weg naar een slechter bestaan*. Amsterdam, Vossiuspers UvA.

Bremmer, Ian (2011). *The end of the free market: who wins the war between states and corporations?* New York, Portfolio Trade.

Brennan, B., E. Heijmans and P. Vervest, eds. (1997). *ASEM trading new Silk Routes: beyond geopolitics and geo-economics—towards a new relationship between Asia and Europe*. Amsterdam, Transnational Institute and Bangkok, Focus on the Global South.

Brenner, N., J. Peck and N. Theodore (2010). Variegated neoliberalization: geographies, modalities, pathways, *Global Networks* 10, 2: 182–222.

Brenner, Robert (2002). *The boom and the bubble: the US in the world economy*. London, Verso.

Breslin, Shaun (2006). Serving the market or serving the party: neo-liberalism in China, in Robison, ed., 114–34.

—— (2009). *China and the global political economy*. London, Palgrave Macmillan.

Broadman, Harry G. (2007). *Africa's Silk Road: China and India's new economic frontier*. Washington, DC, World Bank.

Broeze, Frank ed. (1989). *Brides of the sea: port cities of Asia from the 16th–20th centuries*. Honolulu, University of Hawaii Press.

Brown, Gordon (2010). *Overcoming the first crisis of globalization*. New York, Simon & Schuster.

Bryceson, D., C. Kay and J. Mooij, eds. (2000). *Disappearing peasantries? Rural labour in Africa, Asia and Latin America*. London, Practical Action Publishing.

Brzezinksi, Zbigniew (1997). *The grand chess game: American primacy and its geostrategic imperatives*. New York, Basic Books.

Bulman, D., M. Eden, N. Maya, H. Nguyen (2014). *Transitioning from low-income growth to high-income growth: is there a middle income trap?* World Bank, Policy Research Working Paper Series 7104.

Burawoy, M. *et al.* (2000). *Global ethnography*. Berkeley, University of California Press.

Burgis, Tom (2016). *The looting machine: war lords, oligarchs, corporations, smugglers, and the theft of Africa's wealth*. New York, Public Affairs.

Burity, Joanildo A. (2009). Inequality, culture and globalization in emerging societies: the Brazilian case, in Nederveen Pieterse and Rehbein, eds., 161–81.

Buruma, Ian (2003). Asia world, *New York Review of Books*, June 12: 54–7.

Camarate, P., P. Hoijtink and M. Puttergill (2016). A new map for business in Africa, *Strategy + Business* 83: 9–11.

Central Intelligence Agency. (2010). *The world factbook*. Retrieved from: www.cia.gov/library/publications/the-world-factbook/index.html.

Chamarik, Saneh and S. Goonatilake, eds. (1993). *Technological independence: the Asian experience*. Tokyo, UN University Press.

Chan, A. (2001). *China's workers under assault: the exploitation of labor in a globalizing economy*. Armonk, NY, M. E. Sharpe.

Chan, A. and Siu, K. (2010). Analysing exploitation: the mechanisms underpinning low wages and excessive overtime in Chinese export factories, *Critical Asian Studies* 42, 2: 167–190.

Chang, Ha-Joon (2002). *Kicking away the ladder*. London, Anthem.

Chang, Ha-Joon (2003). *Globalisation, economic development and the role of the state*. London, Zed Books.

Chang, Kyung-Sup (2010). *South Korea under compressed modernity: familial political economy in transition*. London, Routledge.

Chen, Jiagui and Zhang, Xiaojing (2010). Despite shared rapid economic growth, BRICs have different development modes, *China Economist* 24, January–February: 45–55.

Chen, Jie (2013). *A middle class without democracy: economic growth and the prospects for democratization in China*. Oxford, Oxford University Press.

Chen, Long and Yang, Ping (2012). China model in globalization process, *Journal of Globalization Studies* 3, 1: 67–78.

Chen, Xiangming (2005). *As borders bend: transnational spaces on the Pacific Rim.* Boulder, CO, Rowman & Littlefield.

Cheru, Fantu and Cyril Obi, eds. (2010). *The rise of China and India in Africa.* London, Zed Books.

Chhachhi, Amrita (2014). The labour question in contemporary capitalism: introduction, *Development and Change* 45, 5: 895–919.

Chi, Fulin, ed. (2010). *Change of China's development models at the crossroads.* Beijing, China Intercontinental Press.

Chung, Jae Ho (2015). Views from Northeast Asia: a Chinese-style pivot or a mega-opportunity? *Global Asia* 10, 3: 22–26.

Ciochetto, Lynne (2011). *Globalization and advertising in emerging economies.* New York, Routledge.

Cipolla, C. M. (1980). *Before the industrial revolution: European society and economy, 1000–1700.* New York, Norton.

Cohen, Benjamin J. (2014). *Advanced introduction to international political economy.* London, Edward Elgar.

Cohen, Warren I. (2000). *East Asia at the center: four thousand years of engagement with the world.* New York, Columbia University Press.

Collier, Paul (2009). *Wars, guns, and votes: democracy in dangerous places.* New York, HarperCollins.

Comaroff, Jean and John Comaroff (2011). *Theory from the south: or, how Euro-America is evolving toward Africa.* Boulder, CO, Paradigm Press.

Conard, Edward (2012). *Unintended consequences: why everything you've been told about the economy is wrong.* New York, Penguin.

Connell, R. W. (1997). Why is classical theory classical? *American Journal of Sociology* 106, 6: 1511–57.

—— (2007). *Southern theory: social science and the global dynamics of knowledge.* Cambridge, Polity.

Costa, Sérgio (2016). Millionaires, the established, the outsiders and the precariat. Social Structure and Political Crisis in Brazil. Berlin, Working Paper desiguALdades.net 99. Retrieved from www.desigualdades.net/Working_Papers/index.html.

Cowen, Tyler (2011). *The great stagnation.* New York, Dutton.

Crouch, Colin (2004). *Post-democracy.* Cambridge, Polity.

Cuadros, Alex (2016). *Brazillionaires.* Berlin, Spiegel & Grau.

Cullather, Nick (2006). 'The target is the people': representations of the village in modernization and US national security doctrine, *Cultural Politics* 2, 1: 29–48.

Cumings, Bruce (2010). *The Korean war.* New York, Modern Library Chronicles.

Cummine, Angela (2016). *Citizens' wealth: why (and how) sovereign funds should be managed by the people for the people.* New Haven, CT, Yale University Press.

Curran, James and Myung-Jin Park, eds. (2000). *De-westernizing media studies.* London, Routledge.

Danermark, B., M. Ekström, L. Jakobsen and J. Ch. Karlsson (2005). *Explaining society: critical realism in the social sciences.* London, Routledge.

Davidson, Basil (1978). *Let freedom come: Africa in modern history.* Boston, MA, Little Brown.

Davis, Mike (2006). *Planet of slums.* London, Verso.

Dawson, Andrew (2013). *Santo Daime: a new world religion.* London, Bloomsbury.

Derber, Charles (2007). *The wilding of America.* New York, Worth, 4th edn.

Desai, Manisha (1996). Informal organizations as agents of change: notes from the contemporary women's movement in India, *Mobilization: An International Quarterly* 1, 2: 159–73.

Desai, Radhika (2007). Dreaming in technicolour? India as a BRIC economy, *International Journal* 62, 4: 781–804.

Diamond, Larry (1999). *Developing democracy: toward consolidation.* Baltimore, MD, Johns Hopkins University Press.

Dicken, Peter (2007). *Global shift: mapping the changing contours of the world economy.* New York: Guilford, 5th edn.

—— (2011). *Global shift: mapping the changing contours of the world economy.* New York, Guilford, 6th edn.

Dirlik, A. (2000). Reversals, ironies, hegemonies: Notes on the contemporary historiography of modern China, in A. Dirlik, V. Bahl and P. Gran, eds. *History after the three worlds: post Eurocentric historiographies.* Boulder, CO, Rowman and Littlefield, 125–56.

Dirlik, A. (2006). Beijing Consensus: Beijing 'Gongshi'. Who recognizes whom and to what end? *Globalization and Autonomy Online Compendium.* Retrieved from www.globalautonomy.ca/global1/article.jsp?index=PP_Dirlik_BeijingConsensus.xml.

Dobbin, C. (1996). *Asian entrepreneurial minorities: conjoint communities in the making of the world-economy, 1570–1940.* Richmond, Curzon Press.

Donaldson, John A. (2008). Growth is good for whom, when, how? Economic growth and poverty reduction in exceptional cases, *World Development* 36, 11: 2127–43.

Draper, Peter, Tsidiso Disenyana and Philip Alves (2010). Chinese investment in African network industries, in Cheru and Obi, eds.

Duménil, G. and D. Lévy (2001). Costs and benefits of neoliberalism: a class analysis, *Review of International Political Economy* 8, 4: 578–607.

Dussel Peters, Enrique (2012). Qualitative and quantitative socioeconomic challenges of China for Latin America. University of Oregon Asia conference paper, May.

Easterbrook, Gregg (2009). *Sonic boom: globalization at mach speed.* New York, Random House.

Easterly, William (2001). The middle class consensus and economic development, *Journal of Economic Growth* 6, 4: 317–35.

Edwards, Chris (2001). Poverty reduction strategies: reality or rhetoric? Paper presented at The Hague, Institute of Social Studies.

Ehrenreich, Barbara (1990). *Fear of falling: the inner life of the middle class.* New York, Harper Perennial.

Eichengreen Barry, Park, Donghyun, and Shin, Kwanho. (2013). Growth slowdowns redux: new evidence on the middle-income trap, NBER Working Paper No. 18673. Retrieved from www.nber.org/papers/w18673.pdf.

Ekecrantz, Jan (2007). Media and communication studies going global, *Nordicom Review,* Jubilee issue: 169–81.

El-Erian, Mohamed A. (2008). *When markets collide: investment strategies for the age of global economic change.* New York, McGraw-Hill Professional.

—— (2016). *The only game in town: central banks, instability, and avoiding the next collapse.* New York, Random House.

Elverskog, Johan (2010). *Buddhism and Islam on the Silk Road.* Philadelphia, University of Pennsylvania Press.

Embong, Abdul Rahman (2002). *State-led modernization and the new middle class in Malaysia.* London, Palgrave Macmillan.

—— ed. (2004). *Globalization, culture and inequalities.* Selangor, Malaysia, Penerbit Universiti Kebangsaan Malaysia.

Engdahl, William (2016). *One Belt, One Road: China and the new Eurasian century.* Beijing, China Publishing Group (Chinese edn.).

Etzioni, Amitai (2016). The Asian Infrastructure Investment Bank: a case study of multifaceted containment, *Asian Perspective* 40: 173–96.

Eve, R. A., S. Horsfall and M. E. Lee, eds. (1997). *Chaos, complexity and sociology.* London, SAGE.

Ezrow, Natasha, Erica Frantz and Andrea Kendall-Taylor (2016). *Development and the state in the 21st century.* London, Palgrave Macmillan.

Fanon, Frantz (1967). *The wretched of the earth.* Harmondsworth, Penguin.

Feldman, Noah (2015). *Cool war: the United States, China, and the future of global competition.* New York, Random House.

Feldstein, Martin (2008). The U.S. trade deficit: resolving the global imbalance: the dollar and the U.S. saving rate, *Journal of Economic Perspectives* 22, 3: 13–25.

Felipe, J., A. Abdon and U. Kumar (2012). Tracking the middle-income trap: what is it, who is in it, and why? Levy Economics Institute, Working Paper 715. Retrieved from http://ssrn.com/abstract=2049330.

Ferguson, James (1999). *Expectations of modernity.* Berkeley, University of California Press.

Fernández Jilberto, Alex E. and Barbara Hogenboom, eds. (2012a). *Latin America facing China: South-South relations beyond the Washington consensus.* Oxford, Berghahn.

—— (2012b). Latin America and China: South-South relations in new era, in Fernández Jilberto and Hogenboom, eds., 2012a, 1–32.

Fleury, Sonia (2014). Building democracy in an emerging society: challenges of the welfare state in Brazil, in J. Nederveen Pieterse and A. Cardoso, eds. *Brazil emerging: Inequality and emancipation.* New York, Routledge, 11–31.

Florida, Richard (2008). *Who's your city?* New York, Basic Books.

Foroohar, R. and M. Margolis (2010). The other middle class, *Newsweek* 3/15: 42–3.

Frank, A. G. (1992). The centrality of Central Asia, *Bulletin of Concerned Asian Scholars* 24, 2: 50–74.

—— (1996). The underdevelopment of development, in S. Chew and R. Denemark, eds. *The underdevelopment of development.* London, SAGE, 17–55.

—— (1998). *ReOrient: global economy in the Asian age.* Berkeley, University of California Press.

—— (1999). *Luxury fever: why money fails to satisfy in an era of excess.* New York, Free Press.

—— (2006). *Richistan: a journey through the American wealth boom and the lives of the new rich.* New York, Crown.

—— (2007). *Falling behind: how rising inequality harms the middle class.* Berkeley, University of California Press.

Fraser, Nancy (2013). A triple movement? Parsing the politics of crisis after Polanyi, *New Left Review* 81.

Fraser, Steve (2015). *The age of acquiescence: the life and death of American resistance to organized wealth and power.* New York, Little Brown.

Freeland, Chrystia (2012). *Plutocrats: the rise of the new global superrich.* London, Allen Lane.

Friedman, E., ed. (1982). *Ascent and decline in the world-system*. London, SAGE.

—— (2014). Alienated politics: labour insurgency and the paternalistic state in China, *Development and Change* 45, 5: 1001–18.

Friedman, Thomas L. (2005). *The world is flat*. New York, Farrar Straus and Giroux.

—— (2006). The first law of petropolitics, *Foreign Policy*, May-June: 28–36.

Fukuyama, Francis (2005). *State-building*. London, Profile Books.

G20-Pittsburgh Meeting (2009). London, Newsdesk Publications.

Galbraith, James K. (2012). *The end of normal*. New York, Simon and Schuster.

Gamble, Andrew (2014). *Crisis without end? The unraveling of Western prosperity*. London, Palgrave.

Gat, Azar (2007). The return of authoritarian Great Powers, *Foreign Affairs* 86, 4.

Geda, A. and A. G. Meskel (2010). China and India's growth surge: the case of manufactured exports, in Cheru and Obi, eds.

Giddens, A. (1990). *The consequences of modernity*. Stanford, Stanford University Press.

Gill, Indermit and Homi Kharas (2007). *An East Asian renaissance: ideas for economic growth*. Washington, DC, World Bank.

—— (2015). *The middle income trap turns ten*. Pacific Trade and Development Working Paper Series YF37–09.

Goetzmann, William N. (2016). *Money changes everything*. Princeton, NJ, Princeton University Press.

Gong, Min (2012). Global specialization and the China-US economic imbalance, in J. Nederveen Pieterse and J. Kim, eds., 271–94.

Goodman, R., G. White and Huck-ju Kwon eds. (1998). *The East Asian welfare model*. London, Routledge.

Goody, Jack (2010). *Renaissances: the one or the many?* Cambridge, Cambridge University Press.

Gordon, Robert J. (2016). *The rise and fall of American growth*. Princeton, NJ, Princeton University Press.

Gore, M. S. (1993). *The social context of an ideology: Ambedkar's political and social thought*. London and Delhi, SAGE.

Gosh, Parthya S. (2006). Beyond the rhetoric, *Frontline* 10/6: 7–9.

Gosset, David (2012). The wisdom in China's Tao of centrality, *China Daily-European Weekly*, June 29-July: 5, 10.

Greig, Alastair, David Hulme and Mark Turner (2007). *Challenging global inequality: development theory and practice in the twenty-first century*. London, Palgrave.

Griffith, B. (2011). The middle income trap, in Y. Shahid, B. Griffith, R. Bhattacharya, eds. *Frontiers in development policy: a primer on emerging issues*. Washington, DC, World Bank.

Guevara, Che (1967). Message to the tricontinental. Retrieved from www.marxsite. com/guevara.htm.

Guo, Changgang, Debin Liu and Jan Nederveen Pieterse, eds. (2017). *China's contingencies and globalization*. London, Routledge.

Guthrie, Doug (2006). *China and globalization: the social, economic and political transformation of Chinese society*. New York, Routledge.

Hacker, Jacob and Paul Pierson (2010). *Winner-take-all politics: how Washington made the rich richer—and turned its back on the middle class*. New York, Simon and Schuster.

Hall, Peter A. and David Soskice, eds. (2001). *Varieties of capitalism: the institutional foundations of comparative advantage*. Oxford, Oxford University Press.

Harbaugh, Daniel (2013). *The vanity wars*. Raleigh, NC, LuLu Press.

Harding, Rachel E. (2000). *A refuge in thunder: Candomble and alternative spaces of Blackness*. Bloomington, IN, Indiana University Press.

Harris, Dan and Brad Luo (2008). The impact of China's labor contract law, *China Law Blog*, posted 9/15/2008.

Hart-Landsberg, Martin (1993). *The rush to development: economic change and political struggle in South Korea*. New York, Monthly Review Press.

Harvey, David (2004). *The new imperialism*. New York, Oxford University Press.

—— (2005). *A brief history of neoliberalism*. New York, Oxford University Press.

Haspelmath, M., M. S. Dryer, D. Gil, and B. Comrie, eds. (2005). *The world atlas of language structures (WALS)*. Oxford, Oxford University Press.

Helleiner, E., S. Pagliari, H. Zimmermann, eds. (2010). *Global finance in crisis*. New York, Routledge.

Henderson, Hazel (1996). Fighting economism, *Futures* 28, 6–7: 580–3.

Henderson, J., R. Appelbaum and S. Y. Ho (2013). Globalization with Chinese characteristics: externalization, dynamics and transformation, *Development and Change* 44, 6: 1221–53.

Henderson, Jeffrey (2008). China and global development: towards a global-Asian era? *Contemporary Politics* 14, 4: 375–92.

Henderson, Jeffrey (2012). *East Asian transformation*. London, Routledge.

Hertie School of Governance (2013). *The Governance Report 2013*. Oxford, Oxford University Press.

Hobson, John M. (2004). *The Eastern origins of Western civilisation*. Cambridge, Cambridge University Press.

Hoerder, Dirk (2002). *Cultures in contact: world migrations in the second millennium*. Durham, NC, Duke University Press.

Hofmann, Norbert von (2009). *Social democratic parties in Southeast Asia: chances and limits*. Jakarta, Indonesia, Friedrich Ebert Stiftung.

Hogenboom, Barbara (2012). Mexico and China: the troublesome politics of competition, in A. E. Fernández Jilberto and B. Hogenboom, eds., 55–76.

Hossain, Naomi and Mick Moore (2005). So near and yet so far: elites and imagined poverty in Bangladesh, in Reis and Moore, eds., 91–126.

Huntington, S. P. (1993). The clash of civilizations, *Foreign Affairs* 72, 3: 22–49.

Hwang, Suk-Man and Hyun-Chin Lim (2016). *Legacy of developmental state: globalization, income polarization and welfare spending in Korea*. Society for the Advancement of Socio-Economics conference paper.

Ibrahim, Anwar (1996). *The Asian renaissance*. Singapore, Times Books.

Ikenberry, John G. (2008). The rise of China and the future of the West: can the liberal system survive? *Foreign Affairs* 87, 1: 23–37.

Im, Hyug Beg (2014). Social welfare, globalization and democracy in South Korea, in Lim, Schäfer, Hwang, eds., 125–46.

Jenkins, Rhys and E. Dussel Peters (2008). The impact of China on Latin America and the Caribbean, *World Development* 36, 2: 235–53.

Jeong, Seongjin and Richard Westra (2010). The chimera of prosperity in post-IMF South Korea and the alter-globalization movement, in Westra, ed., 192–203.

Johnson, C. (1982). *MITI and the Japanese miracle*. Stanford, Stanford University Press.

—— (1998). Economic crisis in East Asia: the clash of capitalisms, *Cambridge Journal of Economics* 22, 6: 653–61.

Johnson, Simon and James Kwak (2011). *13 Bankers: the Wall Street takeover and the next financial meltdown*. New York, Vintage.

Kalati, N. and J. Manor (2005). Elite perceptions of poverty and poor people in South Africa, in Reis and Moore, eds., 156–81.

Kannan, K. P. and M. Rutten (2004). The plurality of labour, capital and state in Asia: some reflections, *Indian Journal of Labour Economics* 47, 3: 463–76.

Kapdan, Onur (2013). Reflections on Turkey's Gezi Park Protests, *International Marxist-Humanist Webzine*. August. Retrieved from www.internationalmarxist humanist.org/.

Kaplinsky, R. (1994). *Easternisation: the spread of Japanese management techniques to developing countries*. London, Frank Cass.

Kaplinsky, R. and D. Messner (2008). Introduction: the impact of Asian drivers on the developing world, *World Development* 36, 2: 197–209.

Kapur, Devesh and John McHale (2005). *Give us your best and brightest*. Washington, DC, World Bank, Center for Global Development.

Katzenstein, Peter J., ed. (2012). *Sinicization and the rise of China*. New York, Routledge.

Kawai, M. (2015). *From the Chiang Mai Initiative to an Asian Monetary Fund*. Asian Development Bank Institute Working Paper No 525.

Kay, Cristóbal (2002). Why East Asia overtook Latin America: agrarian reform, industrialisation and development, *Third World Quarterly* 23, 6: 1073–102.

—— (2009). Development strategies and rural development: exploring synergies, eradicating poverty, *Journal of Peasant Studies* 36, 1: 103–37.

Keet, Dot (2010). South-South strategic bases for Africa to engage with China-in-Africa, in Cheru and Obi, eds.

Kennedy, Paul (2001). Maintaining American power: from injury to recovery, in S. Talbott and N. Chanda, eds. *The age of terror: America and the world after September 11*. New York, Basic Books, 53–80.

Kentikelenis, A. E., T. H. Stubbs and L. P. King (2016). IMF conditionality and development policy space, 1985–2014, *Review of International Political Economy* 23, 4: 543–82.

Khanna, Parag (2011). *How to run the world: charting a course to the next Renaissance*. New York, Random House.

Kharas, H. and H. Kohli (2011). What is the middle income trap, why do countries fall into it, and how can it be avoided? *Global Journal of Emerging Market Economies* 3, 3: 281–9.

Khondker, Habibul H. (2010). Wanted but not welcome: social dimensions of labor migration in the UAE, in Nederveen Pieterse and Khondker, eds., 205–34.

—— (2011). Globalization and social inequality in Asia, in Rehbein, ed., 31–49.

Kim, Hyoung Tae (2016). Does the Korean economy depend too much on Samsung? *On Korea* 9: 8–23.

Kim, Kyong-dong, ed. (2008). *Social change in Korea*. Paju, South Korea, Jimoondang.

Kim, Seung Kuk (2012). East Asian community as hybridization: a quest for East Asianism, in Nederveen Pieterse and Kim, eds., 179–210.

King, Anthony D. (2004). *Spaces of global cultures: architecture, urbanism, identity*. London, Routledge.

Kipnis, A. (2007). Neoliberalism reified: suzhi discourse and tropes of neoliberalism in the People's Republic of China, *Journal of the Royal Anthropological Institute* 13: 383–400.

Koo, Hagen (2016). The global middle class: How is it made, what does it represent? *Globalizations* 13, 4: 440–53.

Korea Herald, ed. (2008). *Korean Wave*. Paju, South Korea, Jimoondang.

Kose, M. Ayan and Eswar S. Prasad (2010). *Emerging markets: resilience and growth amid global turmoil*. Washington, DC, Brookings Institution Press.

Krishna, A. and J. Nederveen Pieterse (2008). Hierarchical integration: the dollar economy and the rupee economy, *Development and Change* 39, 2: 219–37.

Krugman, Paul (2003). *The great unraveling*. New York, Norton.

—— (2009). *The conscience of a liberal*. New York, Norton, 2nd edn.

Kumar, Arun (2013). *The Indian economy since independence: persisting colonial disruption*. New Delhi, Vision Books.

Kumar, Ravinder and Neera Chandhoke, eds. (2000). *Mapping histories: essays presented to Ravinder Kumar*. New Delhi, Tulika.

Laclau, E. and C. Mouffe (1985). *Hegemony and socialist strategy*. London, Verso.

Landes, David (1998). *The wealth and poverty of nations*. New York, Norton.

Lee, Byeong Cheon and Jun Ho Jeong (2011). Dynamics of dualization in Korea, Seoul, SNUAC International Conference, Global challenges in Asia.

Lee, Sungkyun (2012). Economic crisis, labor market flexibility, and wage inequality: the Korean case (unpublished).

Leftwich, A. (1993). Governance, democracy and development in the third world, *Third World Quarterly* 14, 3: 605–24.

—— (1994). Governance, the state and the politics of development, *Development and Change* 25, 2: 363–86.

—— (1996). On the primacy of politics in development, in A. Leftwich ed. *Democracy and development*. Cambridge, Polity, 3–24.

Leicht, Kevin T. and Scott T. Fitzgerald (2007). *Postindustrial peasants: the illusion of middle class prosperity*. New York, Worth.

Leonard, Mark, ed. (2012). *China 3.0: understanding the new China*. London, European Council on Foreign Relations.

Lewis, Michael (2010). *The big short: inside the doomsday machine*. London, Allen Lane.

Lewin, Moshe (1985). *The making of the Soviet system*. New York, Pantheon.

Li, Minqui (2010). Limits to China's capitalist development: economic crisis, class struggle, and peak energy, in Westra, ed., 88–98.

Li, Peilin (2012). China's new development stage after the crisis, in Nederveen Pieterse and Kim, eds.

Lieberman, Victor, ed. (1999). *Beyond binary histories: re-imagining Eurasia to c.1830*. Ann Arbor, University of Michigan Press.

—— (2003). *Strange parallels: Vol. 1: integration of the mainland—Southeast Asia in global context, c. 800–1830*. Cambridge, Cambridge University Press.

Lim, Hyun-Chin and Jin-Ho Jang (2006). Neoliberalism in post-crisis South Korea, *Journal of Contemporary Asia* 36, 4: 442–463.

Lim, Hyun-Chin, Wolf Schäfer and Suk-Man Hwang, eds. (2010). *New Asias: global futures of world regions*. Seoul, Seoul National University Press

Lipton, M. (1977). *Why poor people stay poor: a study of urban bias in world development.* London, Maurice Temple Smith.

Liu, Hong (1998). Old linkages, new networks: the globalization of overseas Chinese voluntary associations and its implications, *The China Quarterly* 155: 582–609.

Liu, Shih-Diing (2015). The new contentious sequence since Tiananmen, *Third World Quarterly* 36, 11: 2148–65.

Lo, Bobo (2008). *Axis of convenience: Moscow, Beijing and the new geopolitics.* New York, Brookings Institution Press.

Lowenstein, Roger (2007). The inequality conundrum, *New York Times Magazine*, June 10: 11–14.

MacLennan, Carol A. (1997). Democracy under the influence: cost-benefit analysis in the United States, in James G. Carrier, ed. *Meanings of the market: the free market in Western culture.* Oxford, Berg, 195–224.

Macpherson, C. B. (1962). *The political theory of possessive individualism: Hobbes to Locke.* Oxford, Oxford University Press.

Maddison, Angus (2007). *Contours of the world economy, 1–2030 AD: essays in macro-economic history.* Oxford, Oxford University Press.

—— (2010). *Statistics on world population, GDP and per capita GDP, 1–2008 AD.* Groningen, The Netherlands, Groningen Growth and Development Centre, University of Groningen.

Magnus, George (2010). *Uprising: will emerging markets shape or shake the world economy?* New York, Wiley.

Mahadevia, D. (2006). *Shanghaing Mumbai: visions, displacements and politics of a globalizing city.* Ahmedabad, Gujarat, India, Centre for Development Alternatives.

Mahbubani, K. (2009). *The new Asian hemisphere: the irresistible shift of global power to the east.* New York, Perseus.

Mallory, J. P. (1991). *In search of the Indo-Europeans: language, archaeology and myth.* London: Thames and Hudson.

Manji, Firoze and Stephen Marks, eds. (2007). *African perspectives on China in Africa.* Cape Town, South Africa, Fahamu.

Marber, Peter (1998). *From Third World to world class: the future of emerging markets in the global economy.* Reading, MA, Perseus.

Marcus, George (1995). Ethnography in/of the world system: the emergence of multi-sited ethnography, *Annual Review of Anthropology* 24: 95–117.

Margulis, M. E., N. McKeon and S. M. Borras, eds. (2013). Land grabbing and global governance, *Globalizations* special issue 10, 1: 1–209.

Mayer, Arno (1981). *The persistence of the old regime.* New York, Pantheon.

Mayer, Jane (2016). *Dark money: the hidden history of the billionaires behind the rise of the radical right.* New York, Doubleday.

Mazzucato, Mariana (2013). *The entrepreneurial state.* London, Anthem Press.

Mbembe, Achille (2001). *On the postcolony.* Berkeley, University of California Press.

McKinsey Quarterly, Chat Focus Newsletter: Chart Focus: Moving early to capture emerging-market consumers, September 2010.

Mearsheimer, John and Stephen Walt (2006). The Israel lobby, *London Review of Books*, March 23: 3–12.

Mehta, Aashish (2014). Five ways to lessen inequality as demand for labor decreases worldwide, *Development Economist* blog, December 5.

Meisner, M. (1977). The Maoist legacy and Chinese socialism, *Asian Survey* 17, 11: 1016–27.

Michels, Robert (1915). *Political parties: a sociological study of the oligarchical tendencies of modern democracy*. Trans. E. and C. Paul. Kitchener, ON: Batoche Books, 2001.

Mignolo, Walter D. (2009). Epistemic disobedience, independent thought and decolonial freedom, *Theory, Culture & Society* 26, 7–8: 1–23.

Milanovic, Branko (2005). *Worlds apart: measuring international and global inequality*. Princeton, NJ, Princeton University Press.

Mitchell, Timothy (2002). McJihad: Islam in the US global order, *Social Text* 20, 4: 1–18.

Mittelman, James H. (2013). Global bricolage: emerging market powers and polycentric governance, *Third World Quarterly* 34, 1: 23–37.

Moene, Karl Ove (2013). Scandinavian equality: a prime example of protection without protectionism, in J. Stiglitz and M. Kaldor, eds *The quest for security*. New York, Columbia University Press, 48–74.

Moffitt, Benjamin (2016). *The global rise of populism: performance, political style, and representation*. Stanford, Stanford University Press.

Mohanty, M. (2009). China and India: Competing hegemonies or civilisational forces of Swaraj and Jiefang, Siler Forum lecture, unpublished paper.

—— (2015). India, China and the emerging process of building a just world, in Mohanty et al., eds. *Building a just world: essays in honour of Muchkund Dubey*. Hyderabad, Andhra Pradesh, Orient Black Swan, 162–82.

Mohanty, M., R. Baum, R. Ma and G. Mathew, eds. (2007). *Grassroots democracy in India and China*. New Delhi, SAGE.

Moore, R. I. (2003). The eleventh century in Eurasian history: a comparative approach to the convergence and divergence of medieval civilizations, *Journal of Medieval and Early Modern Studies* 33, 1: 1–21.

Morazé, C. (1957). *Les bourgeois conquérants*. Paris, Leclerc. Trans. *The triumph of the middle classes*. London, 1966.

Morris, Charles R. (2008). *The two trillion-dollar meltdown*. New York, Public Affairs.

Morris, Mike, Raphael Kaplinsky and David Kaplan (2012). *One thing leads to another: promoting industrialisation by making the most of the commodity boom in Sub-Saharan Africa*. Milton Keynes, Open University Press.

Nanda, Meera (1999). Who needs post-development? Discourses of difference, the Green Revolution of agrarian populism in India, *Journal of Developing Societies* 151: 1–31.

Nederveen Pieterse, J. (1989). *Empire and emancipation: power and liberation on a world scale*. New York, Praeger.

—— ed. (2000). *Global futures: shaping globalization*. London, Zed Books.

—— (2001). Participatory democracy reconceived, *Futures* 33, 5: 407–22.

—— (2003). Social capital and migration: beyond ethnic economies, *Ethnicities* 3, 1: 5–34.

—— (2004). *Globalization or empire?* New York, Routledge.

—— (2005). Paradigm making while paradigm breaking: Andre Gunder Frank, *Review of International Political Economy* 12, 3: 383–6.

—— (2007). *Ethnicities and global multiculture: pants for an octopus*. Lanham, MD, Rowman & Littlefield.

—— (2008). *Is there hope for Uncle Sam? Beyond the American bubble.* London, Zed Books.

—— (2009). Multipolarity means thinking plural: modernities, *Protosociology* I, 26: 19–35.

—— (2010a) *Development theory: deconstructions/reconstructions.* London, SAGE, 2nd edn.

—— (2010b) Views from Dubai: oriental globalization revisited, *Encounters* 2: 15–38.

—— (2012a) Growth and social policies: towards inclusive development, in R. Traub-Merz, ed. *Redistribution for growth? Income inequality and economic recovery.* Shanghai, Friedrich-Ebert Stiftung, 12–22.

—— (2012b) Leaking superpower: WikiLeaks and the contradictions of democracy, *Third World Quarterly* 33, 10: 1909–24.

—— (2012c) Histories of globalization, *New Global Studies* 6, 2: 1–25.

—— (2014a) Protest begets progress, probably: the Human Development Report 2013—the rise of the South, *Development and Change* 45, 5: 1205–18.

—— (2014b) Rethinking modernity and capitalism: add context and stir, *Sociopedia Colloquium* (e-journal).

—— (2014c) Response to comments: the elevator approach to theory, *Sociopedia Colloquium* (e-journal).

—— (2015a) *Globalization and culture: global mélange.* Lanham, MD, Rowman & Littlefield, 3rd edn.

—— (2015b) What happened to the Miracle Eight? Looking East in the twenty-first century, *Canadian Journal of Development Studies* 63, 3: 263–82.

—— China's contingencies and globalization, in Guo *et al.*, eds., 1985–2001.

—— (2017 forthcoming). Economic stagnation or systemic fragility? *Journal of Post Keynesian Economics.*

Nederveen Pieterse, J. and B. Parekh, eds. (1995). *The decolonization of imagination.* London, Zed Books.

Nederveen Pieterse, J. and B. Rehbein, eds. (2009). *Globalization and emerging societies: development and inequality.* London, Palgrave Macmillan.

Nederveen Pieterse, J. and H. H. Khondker, eds. (2010). *Twenty-first century globalization: perspectives from the Gulf.* Abu Dhabi, Zayed University Press.

Nederveen Pieterse, J. and Jongtae Kim, eds. (2012). *Globalization and development in East Asia.* New York, Routledge.

Neubert, Dieter and Florian Stoll (2016). *Socio-cultural diversity of the African middle class: the case of urban Kenya.* Bayreuth University, Bayreuth African Studies Working Papers 14.

Niblock, Tim, Alejandra Galindo and Degang Sun, eds. (2016). *The Arab States of the Gulf and BRICS: new strategic partnerships in politics and economics.* Berlin, Gerlach Press.

Noah, Timothy (2012). *The great divergence: America's growing inequality crisis.* New York, Bloomsbury.

Norton, A. R. (1993). The future of civil society in the Middle East, *Middle East Journal* 47, 2: 205–16.

Okimoto, D. I. (2009). The financial crisis and America's capital dependency on Japan and China, *Asia-Pacific Review* 16, 1: 37–55.

Okun, A. (1975). *Equality and efficiency: the big trade-off.* Washington, DC, Brookings Institution.

Ong, Aihwa (2006). *Neoliberalism as exception: mutations in sovereignty and citizenship.* Durham, NC, Duke University Press.

Ostry, J. D., A. Berg, and C. G. Tsangarides (2011). Redistribution, inequality and growth. IMF Staff Discussion Note, SDN/14/02.

Ostry, J., P. Loungani and D. Furceri (2016). Neoliberalism: oversold? *Finance & Development* 53, 2: 38–41.

O'Toole, F. (2009). *Ship of fools: how stupidity and corruption sank the Celtic Tiger.* London, Faber and Faber.

Overholt, William H. (2015). Posture problems undermining One Belt, One Road and the US pivot, *Global Asia* 10, 3: 16–21.

Oversloot, Hans (2006). Neoliberalism in the Russian Federation, in Robison, ed., 58–78.

Oxfam International (2014). *Working for the few: political capture and economic inequality*, by Ricardo Fuentes-Nieva and Nick Galasso, Oxfam Briefing Paper 178.

Page, Benjamin (2009). *Class war? What Americans really think about economic inequality.* Chicago, University of Chicago Press.

Palan, Ronen, R. Murphy, C. Chavagneux (2010). *Tax havens: how globalization really works.* Ithaca, NY, Cornell University Press.

Palley, Thomas (2011). *The end of export-led growth: implications for emerging markets and the global economy.* Shanghai, Friedrich Ebert Stiftung Shanghai Briefing Paper 6.

Pantham, Thomas (1995). Proletarian pedagogy, Satyagraha and charisma: Gramsci and Gandhi, in R. Roy, ed. *Contemporary crisis and Gandhi.* New Delhi, Discovery, 165–89.

Parekh, Bhikhu (2007). The cultural particularity of liberal democracy, *Political Studies* 40, 1: 160–75.

Parekh, Bhikhu in conversation with Ramin Jahanbegloo (2011). *Talking politics.* New Delhi, Oxford University Press.

Partanen, Anu (2016). *The Nordic theory of everything.* New York, Harper.

Peck, Jamie and Adam Tickell (2002). Neoliberalizing space, *Antipode* 34, 3: 380–404.

Peck, Jamie and Nik Theodore (2007). Variegated capitalism, *Progress in Human Geography* 31: 731–72.

Pei, Minxin (2016). *China's crony capitalism: the dynamics of regime decay.* Cambridge, MA, Harvard University Press.

Pelfini, Alejandro (2011). Global and national political elites in Latin America, in Rehbein, ed., 194–210.

Petras, James (2006). *The power of Israel in the United States.* Atlanta, GA, Clarity Press.

—— (2009). *Global depression and regional wars.* Atlanta, GA, Clarity Press.

Pettis, Michael (2013). *Avoiding the fall: China's economic restructuring.* Washington, DC, Carnegie Endowment for International Peace.

Phillips, Kevin (2006). *American theocracy: the peril and politics of radical religion, oil, and borrowed money in the 21st century.* New York, Viking.

—— (2009). *Bad money: reckless finance, failed politics and the global crisis of American capitalism.* New York, Penguin, rev. edn.

Piketty, Thomas (2013). *Capital in the twenty-first century.* Cambridge, MA, Harvard University Press.

Piper, Laurence (2015). *The BRICS phenomenon: from regional economic leaders to global political players*. The Hague, BRICS Initiative for Critical Agrarian Studies (BICAS), Working Paper 3.

Pizzigati, Sam (2011). Why greater equality strengthens society, *The Nation*, December 26: 11–15.

Pomeranz, Kenneth (2000). *The great divergence: China, Europe and the making of the modern world economy*. Princeton, NJ, Princeton University Press.

Prahalad, C. K. (2004). *The fortune at the bottom of the pyramid: eradicating poverty through profits*. Philadelphia, University of Pennsylvania, Wharton School Press.

Prestowitz, Clyde (2005). *Three billion new capitalists: the great shift of wealth and power to the East*. New York, Basic Books.

Putnam, R. D. (1993). *Making democracy work: civic traditions in modern Italy*. Princeton, NJ, Princeton University Press.

Quigley, C. (1966). *Tragedy and hope: a history of the world in our time*. New York, Macmillan.

Rajan, Raghuram G. (2010). *Fault lines: how hidden fractures still threaten the world economy*. Princeton, NJ, Princeton University Press.

Rasmus, Jack (2016). *Systemic fragility in the global economy*. Atlanta, GA, Clarity Press.

Redding, G. and M. A. Witt (2010). *The future of Chinese capitalism: choices and chances*. Oxford, Oxford University Press.

Reed, Ananya M. (2010). Neoliberalism in India: how an elephant became a tiger and flew to the moon, in Westra, ed., 67–87.

Rehbein, B., ed. (2011). *Globalization and inequality in emerging societies*. London, Palgrave Macmillan

—— (2015). *Critical theory after the rise of the Global South*. London, Routledge.

Reich, Robert (2010). *Aftershock: the next economy and America's future*. New York, Knopf.

Reid, Anthony (1993). *Southeast Asia and the age of commerce*, Vol. 1. New Haven, CT, Yale University Press.

—— (1995). *Southeast Asia in the age of commerce, 1450–1680*, Vol. 2, New Haven, CT, Yale University Press.

—— ed. (1997). *The last stand of Asian autonomies*. Basingstoke, Macmillan.

—— (2000). *Charting the shape of early modern Southeast Asia*. Singapore, Institute of Southeast Asian Studies.

Reifer, T. E. (2005). Globalization, democratization, and global elite formation in hegemonic cycles: a geopolitical economy, in J. Friedman and C. Chase-Dunn, eds. *Hegemonic declines: past and present*. Boulder, CO, Paradigm, 183–203.

Reis, Elisa P. (2006). Inequality in Brazil: facts and perceptions, in G. Therborn, ed. *Inequalities of the world*. London, Verso, 193–219.

Reis, Elisa P. and M. Moore, eds. (2005). *Elite perceptions of poverty and inequality*. London, Zed Books.

Richey, Lisa Ann and Stefano Ponte (2008). Better Red™ than dead? Celebrities, consumption and international aid, *Third World Quarterly* 29, 4: 711–29.

Robison, Richard, ed. (2006). *The neo-liberal revolution: forging the market state*. London, Palgrave.

Rodrik, Dani (2001). Institutions for high-quality growth: what they are and how to acquire them, *Studies in Comparative International Development* 35, 3: 3–31.

—— (2005). Feasible globalizations, in M. M. Weinstein, ed. *Globalization, what's new?* New York, Columbia University Press, 196–203.

—— (2010). Making room for China in the world economy, *American Economic Review* 100, 2: 89–93.

—— (2015). *Premature deindustrialization*, NBER Working Paper 20935. Retrieved from www.nber.org/papers/w20935.pdf.

Rodrik, D., Subramanian, A. and F. Trebbi (2004). Institutions rule: the primacy of institutions over geography and integration in economic development, *Journal of Economic Growth* 9, 2: 131–65.

Rosenau, J. N. (1999). The future of politics, *Futures* 31, 9–10: 1005–16.

Rothkopf, David (2008). *Superclass: the global power elite and the world they are making*. New York, Farrar Strauss and Giroux.

Roubini, Nouriel (2006). The unsustainability of the U.S. twin deficits, *CATO Journal* 26, 2: 343–56.

Roubini, Nouriel and Stephen Mihm (2010). *Crisis economics: a crash course in the future of finance*. New York, Penguin.

Roy, Arundhati (2010). Walking with the comrades, *Outlook India*, March 29. Retrieved from www.outlookindia.com/article.aspx?264738–0.

Rueschemeyer, D., E. Stephens and J. Stephens (1992). *Capitalist development and democracy*. Cambridge, Polity.

Sainath, P. (1996). *Everybody loves a good drought*. New Delhi, Penguin.

Sakamoto, Y. (2000). An alternative to global marketization: East Asian regional coop- eration and the civic state, in Nederveen Pieterse, ed., 98–117.

Sally, Razeen (2016). *Economic liberalism in Asia*. Kuala Lumpur, Malaysia, Institute for Democracy and Economic Affairs.

Sandbrook, R., M. Edelman, P. Heller and J. Teichman (2007). *Social democracy in the global periphery: origins, challenges, prospects*. Cambridge, Cambridge University Press.

Saxer, Marc (2014). *Building the good society in Thailand*. Bangkok, Thailand, Friedrich Ebert Stiftung.

Schiller, Dan (1999). *Digital capitalism: networking the global market system*. Cambridge, MA, MIT Press.

Seagrave, S. (1996). *Lords of the Rim*. London, Corgi Books.

Seisdedos, Paul Cooney (2010). 'Late neoliberalism' in Brazil: social and economic impacts of trade and financial liberalization, in Westra, ed., 39–66.

Shaw, Timothy M. (2010). China, India and (South) Africa: what international relations/political economy in the second decade of the 21st century? In Cheru and Obi, eds.

Shenk, Timothy (2016). Democracy's revenge, *The Nation* 11/7: 27–32.

Shi, Kai 1 and Li Nie (2012). Adjusting the currency composition of China's foreign exchange reserve, *International Journal of Economics and Finance* 4, 10: 170–9.

Shiva, Vandana (1993). Monocultures of the mind, *Trumpeter* 10, 4. Retrieved from www.icaap.org/iuicode?6.10.4.11.

Shoukat, Ayesha (2016). *Power reconfigurations and enterprise development: elite contesta- tions and the rise of business groups in Pakistan*. Kuala Lumpur, Malaysia, University of Malaya doctoral thesis.

Simpfendorfer, Ben (2009). *The new Silk Road*. London, Palgrave Macmillan.

Sirkin, H. L., J. W. Hemerling, A. K. Bhattacharya (2008). *Globality: competing with everyone from everywhere for everything*. New York, Business Plus.

Sklair, L. (2001). *The transnational capitalist class*. Oxford, Blackwell.

Soborski, Rafal (2013). *Ideology in a global age: continuity and change.* London, Palgrave Macmillan.

Soederberg, S., G. Menz and P. G. Cerny (2005). *Internalizing globalization: the rise of neoliberalism and the decline of national varieties of capitalism.* London, Palgrave Macmillan.

Sohn, Joo (2007). *East Asia's counterweight strategy: Asian financial cooperation and evolving international monetary order.* UNCTAD, G-24 Discussion Paper No 44.

Sotero, P. and L. E. Armijo (2007). Brazil: To be or not to be a BRIC? *Asian Perspective* 31, 4: 43–70.

Spence Michael (2011). *The next convergence: the future of economic growth in a multispeed world.* New York, Farrar, Straus and Giroux.

Speth, J. G. (1996). Global inequality, *New Perspectives Quarterly* 13, 4: 32–3.

Standing, Guy (2011). *The precariat: the new dangerous class.* London, Bloomsbury.

Stavrianos, L. S. (1981). *Global rift: the Third World comes of age.* New York, Morrow.

—— (1998). *A global history: from prehistory to the 21st century.* New Jersey, Prentice Hall, 7th edn.

Stiglitz, Joseph E. (2006). *Making globalization work.* New York, Norton.

—— (2013). Inequality impedes recovery, *New York Times* 1/20: 1, 8.

Stiglitz, Joseph E. and A. Schiffrin (2004). The importance of critical thinking, in A. Schiffrin and A. Bisat, eds. *Covering globalization: a handbook for reporters.* New York, Columbia University Press, 1–14.

Stiglitz, Joseph E., A. Sen, J-P. Fitoussi (2010). *Mismeasuring our lives: why GDP doesn't add up.* New York, New Press.

Strange, Susan (1996). *The retreat of the state: the diffusion of power in the world economy.* Cambridge, Cambridge University Press.

Streeck, Wolfgang (2011). The crises of democratic capitalism, *New Left Review* 71: 5–29.

—— (2013). *Re-forming capitalism: institutional change in the German political economy.* Oxford, Oxford University Press.

Studwell, Joe (2007). *Asian Godfathers: money and power in Hong Kong and Southeast Asia.* London, Profile Books.

—— (2013). *How Asia works.* London, Profile.

Sugiyama, Jiro (1992). From Chang'an to Rome: transformation of Buddhist culture, in T. Umesao and T. Sugimura eds. *The significance of the Silk Roads in the history of human civilizations.* Osaka, National Museum of Ethnology, 55–60.

Swaan, Abram De, James Manor, Else Oyen and Elisa P. Reis (2000). Elite perceptions of the poor, *Current Sociology* 48, 1: 43–58.

Taibbi, Matt (2010). *Griftopia: bubble machines, vampire squids, and the long con that is breaking America.* New York, Random House.

Taleb, Nasseem Nicholas (2007). *The black swan: the impact of the highly improbable.* New York, Penguin.

Taylor, Ian (2006). *China and Africa: engagement and compromise.* London, Routledge.

—— (2009). *China's new role in Africa.* Boulder, CO, Lynne Rienner.

Teichman, Judith (2014). Struggling with the social challenges of globalization: Mexico, Chile and South Korea, in R. Sandbrook and A. B. Güven, eds. *Civilizing globalization: a survival guide.* Albany, NY, SUNY Press, 2nd ed., 63–75.

Teivanen, Teivo (2002). *Enter economism, exit politics: experts, economic policy and the damage to democracy.* London, Zed Books.

Tejpal, Tarun J. (2006). India's future, beyond dogma, *Tehelka, The People's Paper*, 11/25: 3.

Tepperman, Jonathan (2016). *The fix: how nations survive in a world in decline*. New York, Tim Duggan Books.

Teslik, Lee H. (2009). Sovereign wealth funds, *Council on Foreign Relations*. Retrieved from www.cfr.org/sovereign-wealth-funds/sovereign-wealth-funds/p15251.

Thapar, Bal Krishen (1992). India's place on ancient trade routes, in T. Umesao and T. Sugimura eds. *The significance of the Silk Roads in the history of human civilizations*. Osaka, National Museum of Ethnology, 117–26.

Thompson, Mark (1993). The limits of democratisation in ASEAN, *Third World Quarterly* 14, 3: 471–84.

—— (2010). The dialectic of 'good governance' and democracy in Southeast Asia, in Lim, Schäfer and Hwang, eds., 175–208.

Titarenko, Mikhail (2004). Russia, China and India: context for interaction, *World Affairs* 8, 4: 22–33.

Traub-Merz, R., ed. (2012). *Redistribution for growth? Income inequality and economic recovery*. Shanghai, Friedrich-Ebert-Stiftung, Shanghai Coordination Office for International Cooperation.

Tsang, Eileen Yuk-Ha (2013). *The new middle class in China: consumption, politics and the market economy*. London, Palgrave.

Tsing, Anna L. (2005). *Friction: an ethnography of global connection*. Princeton, NJ, Princeton University Press.

Tu Weiming (2000). Implications of the rise of 'Confucian' East Asia, *Daedalus* 129, 1: 195–218.

Tudor, Daniel (2012). *Korea: the impossible country*. New York, Tuttle.

UNDP (1994, 1996, 1997, 1998, 1999). *Human Development Report*. New York, Oxford University Press.

—— (2005). *Human Development Report*. New York, UNDP.

—— (2011). International Human Development Indicators. Retrieved from http://hdrstats.undp.org/en/tables/.

—— (2013). *Human Development Report 2013: the rise of the South*. New York, UNDP.

US Census Bureau (2010). *Data access tools*. Retrieved from www.census.gov/main/www/access.html.

Varoufakis, Yanis (2015). *The global minotaur: America, Europe and the future of the global economy*. London, Zed Books.

Vitalis, Robert (2006). *America's kingdom: mythmaking on the Saudi oil frontier*. Palo Alto, Stanford University Press.

Vukovich, Daniel (2010). China in theory: the orientalist production of knowledge in the global economy, *Cultural Critique* 76: 148–72.

Wade, R. (1996). Japan, the World Bank and the art of paradigm maintenance: the East Asian miracle in political perspective, *New Left Review* 217: 3–36.

—— (2004). Is globalization reducing poverty and inequality? *World Development* 32, 4: 567–89.

—— (2009). From global imbalances to global reorganisations, *Cambridge Journal of Economics* 33: 539–62.

Wade, Robert H. (1990). *Governing the market: economic theory and the role of government intervention in East Asian industrialization*. Princeton, NJ, Princeton University Press.

Wallerstein, I. M. (1984). *The politics of the world economy.* Cambridge, Cambridge University Press.

—— (2013). The itinerary of world-systems analysis; or, how to resist becoming a theory, in I. Wallerstein, C. Lemert and C. A. Rojas, eds. *Uncertain worlds: world-systems analysis in changing times.* Boulder, CO, Paradigm, 195–217.

Wang Hui (2005). An Asia that isn't the East, *Le Monde diplomatique*, February: 1–3.

Weiss, L. (1996). Sources of the East Asian advantage: an institutional analysis, in R. Robison, ed. *Pathways to Asia: the politics of engagement.* St Leonard's, NSW, Australia, Allen and Unwin, 171–201.

—— (1998). *The myth of the powerless state.* Ithaca, NY, Cornell University Press.

Wessel, Margit van (2004). Talking about consumption: how an Indian middle class dissociates from middle-class life, *Cultural Dynamics* 16, 1: 93–116.

Westra, Richard, ed. (2010). *Confronting global neoliberalism: third world resistance and development strategies.* Atlanta, GA, Clarity Press.

Whitfield, Susan (2003). The perils of dichotomous thinking: ebb and flow rather than East and West, in S. C. Akbari and A. Iannucci, eds. *Marco Polo and the encounter of East and West.* Toronto, ON, University of Toronto Press.

—— ed. (2004). *The Silk Road: trade, travel, war and faith.* Chicago, Serindia Publications.

Wild, Leni and David Mepham, eds. (2006). *The new Sinophere: China in Africa.* London, Institute for Public Policy Research.

Wilkinson, Richard and Kate Pickett (2009). *The spirit level: why more equal societies almost always do better.* London, Allen Lane.

Wing Thye Woo (2012). China meets the middle-income trap: the large potholes in the road to catching-up, *Journal of Chinese Economic and Business Studies* 10, 4: 313–36.

Winters, Jeffrey A. and Benjamin I. Page (2009). Oligarchy in the United States? *Perspectives on Politics* 7, 4: 731–51.

Wolf, Martin (2010). *Fixing global finance.* New Haven, CT, Yale University Press (updated edition).

Wood, Frances (2003). *The Silk Road: two thousand years in the heart of Asia.* Berkeley, University of California Press.

World Bank (1993). *The East Asian miracle: economic growth and public policy.* New York, Oxford University Press.

—— (2007). *Africa Development Indicators 2007.* Washington DC, World Bank.

—— (2008). *World Development Report 2008: agriculture for development.* New York, Oxford University Press.

—— (2010). *Rising global interest in farmland.* Washington, DC, World Bank.

—— (2012). *World development indicators.* Retrieved from http://databank.worldbank.org/ddp/home.do.

Yamashita, Shinji and J. S. Eades, eds. (2003). *Globalization in Southeast Asia: local, national, and transnational perspectives.* New York, Berghahn.

Yang, Bin (2004). Horses, silver and cowries: Yunnan in global perspective, *Journal of World History* 15, 3: 281–322.

Yeung, Henry Wai-chung, ed. (2013). *Globalizing regional development in East Asia: production networks, clusters, and entrepreneurship.* New York, Routledge.

Yoon, Sangwon (2012). Who really runs Korea? *Bloomberg Businessweek*, 11/26–12/2: 19–20.

Yunling, Zhang (2015). One Belt, One Road: a Chinese view, *Global Asia* 10, 3: 8–12.

Zafar, Ali (2007). The growing relationship between China and Sub-Saharan Africa: macroeconomic, trade, investment, and aid links, *World Bank Research Observer* 22, 1: 103–30.

Zakaria, Fareed (2008). *The post-American world*. New York, Norton.

Zhou, Xiaohong (2007). Rural political participation in the Maoist and post-Maoist periods, in Mohanty, Baum, Ma and Mathew, eds., 73–92.

Zingales, Luigi (2012). *A capitalism for the people: recapturing the lost genius of American prosperity*. New York, Basic Books.

Zoellick, Robert B. (2010). *The end of the third world? Modernizing multilateralism for a multipolar world*. Washington, DC, World Bank.

Zorub, Daniel (2014). Education and the tumult of globalization: considering risk management for international education. University of California Santa Barbara, Global studies MA Thesis.

Zwan, Natascha van der (2014). Making sense of financialization, *Socioeconomic Review* 12, 1: 99–129.

Index